Drag Racing Basics

Christmas Tree to Finish Line

Cindy Crawford

ISBN 0-929758-22-6

Published by Beeman Jorgensen, Inc.
7510 Allisonville Road, Suite 122, Indianapolis, IN 46250 U.S.A.

Printed and bound in the United States of America
Cover design by Llew Kinst, Cupertino, California
Cover photography by Steve Gruenwald, Jupiter, Florida

First Printing, May 2003

Foreword

I got my start in drag racing by going to the motorcross races with my dad and brother. I was raised on and around motorcycles so it was inevitable that I would end up racing them.

I have overcome many obstacles including my size, my gender and my appearance. People look at me and doubt my ability, my determination and my will to win, because I don't have the look that they think a female racer should have. I think the look on the outside has nothing to do with the heart and the iron will that a person may have on the inside!

This book is written to provide insights for females, males, as well as youngsters, to learn and enjoy the world of drag racing, as I have come to enjoy.

See you at the track!

Angelle Savoie

This book is dedicated to my son Bobby, who shares my wild and carefree racing spirit and his sweetheart Sarah and Kayla, my first granddaughter. And for my daughter Bambi, who likes Chevys better than Fords, Pablo and their precious new daughter, Chantel.

For my ex-husband, Roland who was always there for me and has helped me through the years to attain the goals that I have strived for and achieved.

For my mom, Jackie King, who has always stood by my side, will always be my best friend and loves racing just as much as I do. For my dad and step-mom, Sid & Eileen Candage, who instilled in me the free spirit and courage to race. For my step-dad, Ed King, who never did seem to understand why I drag race but still loves me. For my brother Bryan King who still "thinks" his Steeda is faster than mine. For his wife Jessica and my nephews Zackary and Nicholas. For my half-brother Craig, his wife Cathy and their family, for their long-distance support and humor through these years. For my numerous other family members, including Eddie King, Gloria Grigg, Sharon Warren, Charlene & and many others, for standing behind me in my endeavors.

For Randy Sphaler, my racing partner, who inspired me with his positive and fun-loving attitude and his unfaltering humor. For his son, Steve Sphaler who guided me up to the starting line again and again with a winning spirit.

For George Klass, Tech Director for Fun Ford Events for guidance in the technical aspects of this book. For Javier Gottardi and Richard Martin, owners of Super Street Racing in Miami, Florida, for their expertise, technical advice and mechanical fortitude helping my research.

For my current racing sponsors: Tree's Wings, Super Street Racing, Vortech Engineering, Inc., FAST (Fresh Air Systems Technologies, Inc.), Hoosier Tires, Jung Performance, Dr. Howard Busch, Dr. Gabor Bodnar, D.M.D., Chassis Engineering, Mothers Car Wax, Recaro North America, Inc., JDsPerformance.com, Team Simpson and Weldon Pump for their monetary help to keep up with my racing endeavor.

To hardcore racers Marty DeWinter, Jr., Steve Grebeck, Jerry Gannon and "Geech" who have recently lost their lives. And get well wishes to injured racers: John Lingenfelter, Gerald Cook, Harry Groessel, Tom Heatley, Jr., Jimmy Heavner, Bob Mendenhall, Sal Passarelli, Billy Williams, Thomas Lawrence, Jr., Dennis Mirante, John Cislak and Paul Zgoda.

Special thanks to Angelle Savoie, #1 NHRA Drag Bike racer, for her words of encouragement and her inspiration, which led me to write this book.

Finally, for my 11-year old Old English Mastiff, Sinbad, who lay by my side and comforted me while writing this book.

Cindy Crawford

One of the biggest influences in my life, my mom

Contents

Introduction

Some say the term *drag racing* was coined one day when a car lifted the front wheels (now called a wheelie) and they noticed that the back end dragged the pavement. Drag racing has been around for many years and spectators find that it is an extremely entertaining and thrilling sport to watch. What could be more breathtaking than watching the racers thrill the crowds with their smoky burn outs, their wheelstanding action and launch their cars at neck-breaking speeds.

Drivers are there to entertain the crowds with some fast action runs, showcase their driving abilities and show off the high performance of their car. They try to conduct good sportsmanship, demonstrate their professionalism as a racer, be consistent and ultimately, win the race.

Drag racers will be the first to admit that their love of drag racing is truly an addiction. From watching the burn outs, the nitrous purges, the supercharger whines, revs of the motors, the race fuel smells, wheelie action and the cheers of the spectators, some call it a *racer's high*. It is this adrenaline rush which most racers strive for.

Drag racing is a hobby for some, but can be serious business for others. Billions of dollars are invested into the sport each year. A rookie driver with little experience can move up to become a professional racer by learning the sport with hands on experience, asking questions, observing and reading materials. These learned skills allow a driver to win races and prove himself to fellow competitors, which will also help attract sponsors to help with the costs of racing.

Don't start into racing with thoughts of making money, as very few racers do. An old saying is, "whatever you win racing, you will eventually put back into it." Actually, drag racing can drain your bank account quite quickly leaving you penniless – all for the thrill and adrenaline rush of speed. Another old saying is, "the only way to make a small fortune in drag racing is to start out with a large one." It is an extremely expensive sport and can be very habit forming. Racers usually *breathe, eat, drink and sleep* drag racing. It is so much a part of their lives that it can be overwhelming.

However, most dedicated racers will tell you that racing at the track is worth almost any price. They love racing and will overcome any and all odds to continue racing as it is their passion and niche in life. Most drivers would love to quit their jobs and professionally race. This would be a racer's dream to actually get paid for having fun and doing what you enjoy most! For a racer to quit racing is like a death in the family. It is always in a racer's blood to compete and impossible to get rid of that feeling.

Racers are certainly a different breed of people. They love to thrill an audience, they dare to stand out from the crowd. Think of all the positive things you can do as a racer to help the community, fellow racers and spectators. You can make a difference in your life and in the lives of others. You have the abilities and powers deep inside you to give a positive outlook on life as a whole to others that view you.

Drag racing is fun for people of all ages, from ages 8 to 80 plus. I recently met a 74 year old gentleman by the name of Chris *The Golden Greek* Karamesines, driving a 7000 horsepower Top Fuel Dragster *(see photo previous page)*. He is the oldest driver ever to break the 300 mph barrier and the oldest licensed fuel dragster driver in the world. He is a native of Chicago, Illinois and has been racing for over 50 years. Back in 1959 he won his first National Title at the World Series of Drag Racing in Moline, Illinois. In 1960, he was the first to exceed 200 mph. He ran 4.73 seconds in the quarter mile at an NHRA (National Hot Rod Association) event. He has run 312 mph at The Strip in Las Vegas, Nevada and he is one of NHRA's Top 50 Drivers. If that does not give the inspiration to race, nothing will!!

Many families frequent the track and there are a lot of father/son or daughter teams and husband/wife teams. Tracks have incorporated a Junior Drag Racing class for youngsters age 8-17 to race and this is a great way for the whole family to participate and race together. My own family loves to participate in the drag racing events and are members of my team. They travel to most of the out of state races to cheer me on and help out as much as they can. Among my biggest fans are my parents!

When frequenting the tracks, it is apparent that people involved in racing are some of the friendliest and most helpful people around. It is not uncommon to see pit crew members of one team helping another team. There is a sense of camaraderie and a certain bond that is established between racers. This is one of the reasons why I was attracted to the drag racing circuit and continue to be a dedicated racer.

What is so great about racing is that anyone can compete. Whether you are young or old, male or female. All that is needed is a valid driver's license, NHRA or IHRA (International Hot Rod Association) competition license (if required) and their entrance fees. Your vehicle will have to pass the technical inspection and possess all the necessary safety items required. Also necessary are good reflexes, ability to focus and a *kick-ass attitude*.

This book is a guide on how to begin or brush up on drag racing and will provide some advice and guidance in the sport. It is full of information and tips for racing to give that special edge over other drivers. Enjoy Racing!!

My biggest fans, my dad and step-mom, Sid & Eileen Candage

Types of Drag Racing

A drag race is the pairing of two vehicles in a race with no turns from a designated starting point over a measured distance. These distances are usually either quarter-mile (1320 feet) or eighth-mile (660 feet).

The object of the drag race is to be the first person to reach the finish line. These races are controlled by a Christmas Tree, which is an electronic device visible from the starting line of the race track. The Christmas Tree features a countdown of lights, yellow and green, (similar to a traffic light) to which the racer reacts. When each car leaves the starting line it activates a timer. This timer will record the elapsed time (ET) for the race which will determine the winner and the loser. Winners generally progress to the next round of racing.

The two most common types of drag racing are *heads up* and *bracket racing*. There is also an exhibition class, which is for show vehicles only. Owners of these vehicles are generally paid by the track to show up and entertain the crowds.

Heads Up

Heads up racing is when two cars are directed by the lights on the Christmas Tree to leave the starting line simultaneously and compete against each other to see who will get to the finish line first. The class winner is the car that wins every round in which it competes. Others are eliminated from additional competiton following a single loss.

Most professional drag racing series use the heads up format. Money is always an issue in these classes, as it is necessary to constantly modify and update these fast-action vehicles to stay on top. These classes are not for a beginner.

Heads up cars are running remarkable times these days and are extremely competitive. Records continue to be broken as speeds keep increasing with new technology and knowledge. Heads up classes are exhilarating and most spectators visit the track solely to view these ground-shaking cars perform.

Bracket Racing

Bracket racing allows an even playing field and brings enjoyment to all racers, no matter what their income and the speed of their cars. This type of racing is much easier for newcomers and low budget racers. Here the driver's skill can win the race, not just how fast the car is.

It is very easy to start in bracket racing. First, the driver makes a few practice runs down the track and record the times. After reviewing these numbers, he predicts the time that he thinks he will be running. This process is called *dialing in.* The estimated ET is called the *dial-in number* and is written on the vehicle's front and rear windows with white shoe polish. The dial-in number on the vehicle is the key to bracket racing.

When two cars compete, the slower car (higher dial-in number) always gets a head start. The dial-in numbers are subtracted from each other, so the faster driver has to wait until the time difference elapses. Whoever reaches the finish line first wins; however, they cannot go faster than their dial-in time.

Going quicker than the dial-in time is called a *break out* and will result in disqualification. If both drivers break out, then a double break out occurs and whoever ran closest to their dial-in is declared the winner and progresses to the next round. The goal is to run the dial-in or as close as possible to it without going under.

One of the old tricks of bracket racing is called *sandbagging*, which is dialing in a time slower than the car is capable of running. The idea is to get a good reaction time at the light, catch the opponent and just barely pass him. Before reaching the traps at the end of the track, the driver applies the brakes.

This can make the other driver push his car, trying to get ahead and possibly cause him to break out.

Another trick, if the leading driver thinks he might be going too fast for the dial-in and could possibly break out, is to lightly jab on the brakes before the traps. This may prevent the break out and result in a win.

The best way to win in bracket racing is by being consistent. It does not matter how fast or slow the car is. It is always based on skill as a racer and reaction time to the Christmas Tree. It is important to learn the changes in dial-ins that are appropriate for the car in various weather conditions and altitudes on any given day or night. If you consistently pick a good dial-in number and get good reaction times, you are well on your way to being an excel-

Michelle Moore's view of the dragstrip

lent bracket racer.

Car Equipment

Modifications made to your car should be based on the rule book of the sanctioning body with which you are planning to compete. Many additional performance related modifications will be needed for your vehicle and there are numerous mail-order companies, as well as local speed shops, that supply parts. It is a good idea to ask local racers which companies have the best reputations.

Exhaust System

Free Flow Mufflers: Low restriction mufflers such as those made by Flowmaster help the exhaust system to breathe, allowing greater exhaust flow capacity with as little restriction as possible, reducing back pressure. They increase horsepower by approximately five to eight percent and cost under $200 per pair uninstalled.

Hi-Flow Cats/Test Pipes: Hi-flow cats are replacements for the standard catalytic converters. They give a modest horsepower increase for a little under $150 each. Test pipes are free flow pipes that are used to replace the catalytic converters. They are quite inexpensive, but are not legal for street use.

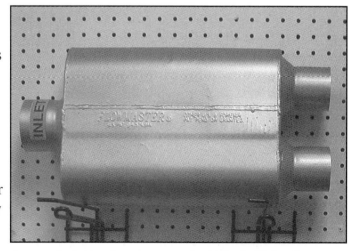

Inexpensive bolt-on horsepower can be obtained with free flow exhaust components, most of which are legal for street use

X & H-Pipes: These are connector pipes that fit between dual exhausts, so that both sides have equal pressure. They result in significant horsepower gains and are priced under $200.

Headers: Headers or free flow exhaust manifolds on a stock engine will not add much horsepower. For instance, shorty headers on an unmodified car will add a minimal horsepower increase. Long tube headers may raise this increase to well over 25 horsepower. However, on a heavily modified motor or one with a power adder, there will be huge gains in power. They are made by a number of companies and prices range from about $400 to over $1000.

Headers are often selected as an early perfomance addition for first time racers

Intake and Fuel Components

Air Silencer: Mustang owners should remove the air silencer, which is located before the air filter element in the air box housing. It is worth approximately 3 horsepower.

High Flow Air Filters: The very first and least expensive modification you can make to your vehicle is installing a low restriction air filter such as those made by K & N. They allow for maximum air flow, but still prevent foreign objects from getting into the intake system. They will also add considerable horsepower compared to the original filter elements. Also, the K & N filter is completely washable and has a million mile warranty, so it only has to be purchased once. Price is around $50.

Mass Air Meter: A larger mass air meter is an electronic device that improves the flow potential of the inlet system. It measures the air flow and tells the computer how much fuel is needed. If installed on a stock car, expect up to ten percent additional horsepower. It needs to be properly matched with the fuel injectors and the fuel system. Price is approximately $300 uninstalled.

Injectors: When buying a mass air meter, consider buying larger injectors, because if you are making more power, the engine will need more fuel. Injectors supply the engine with the correct amount of fuel. If they are acquired later, the mass air meter will need to be recalibrated or else the air/fuel mixture will be incorrect. It is also advised to run stainless steel-braided fuel lines and aftermarket billet fuel rails (located between the fuel lines and injectors) to allow adequate fuel flow.

High flow air filter is part of this cold air induction system

Fuel Pump: Do not get a fuel pump with capacity too high for your application. A fuel regulator and a fuel management unit (FMU) along with appropriately sized injectors will need to be calibrated with the pump to assure optimal performance.

Throttle Body: A throttle body is CNC-machined from aluminum alloy (some are plastic), and controls the airflow after the mass air sensor. It mounts on top of the intake manifold and increases horsepower by around ten percent. Price is approximately $200.

Other Engine

Underdrive Pulleys: Underdrive pulleys reduce the power lost to the engine used driving the water pump and alternator. They may not be appropriate for street usage, because after changing the pulley sizes, these accessories will not turn as fast. They are inexpensive, easy to install and, depending on engine type, can provide between 5 to 7 additional horsepower. Approximate price is $200.

Timing Adjuster: A timing adjuster allows the driver to advance the spark timing or retard timing in either direction in two-degree increments. It relocates the crank-trigger sensor to the outside of the engine. The timing can be adjusted either up or down by loosening the two set screws and removing the sensor bracket. The installation can be completed within a few minutes and is very simple to do. Expect horsepower increases of approximately five percent. Costs range around $200 uninstalled.

Harmonic Balancer/Crankshaft Damper: A harmonic balancer evens out the rotary motion of the crankshaft by actually adding weight. Its presence lowers bearing load, helping protect the crankshaft from excessive wear. It is easy to install because in most cases there is a single bolt that holds it onto the crank. Harmonic balancers must have an SFI rating of 18.1 and prices range from $150 to $450 uninstalled.

Rear End

Gears: Lower ratio rear end gears are worth the money to install. Lower ratios (which have higher numbers) allow the car to accelerate quicker. Very low ratios are for strip use only and on the street will be impractical. Prices run in the $200 - $500 range.

Axles: It is advisable to replace axles before breaking them. If using a Ford rear end, go to at least 31-spline axles or bigger, especially if running slicks. Using slicks without bigger axles will sooner or later cause the stock axles to break. Cost is around $200 apiece, but front wheel drive axles are much more.

Aftermarket Axles: Aftermarket axles and C-clip eliminators are required on cars running 10.99 and quicker or on any car with a spool (locked rear end). These are used because stock axles could twist and break under shock loads. Approximate cost of axles and spool is $600 uninstalled. C-clip eliminators uninstalled are approximately $150.

Chassis and Suspension

Urethane Bushings: Stock rubber suspension bushings can be replaced with urethane to improve the steering and handling capabilities of the car. Due to their lack of flex, they are unsuitable for use in street vehicles. Kits are available for many applications and price is a little over $50 uninstalled.

Adjustable Anti-Roll Bar: Installing a rear anti-sway bar helps keeps the car straight and level, reduces tire shake and improves the 60 foot times and consistency. Prices are generally under $300.

Wheelie Bars: Wheelie bars allow the car to keep going straight and propel in a forward motion. It keeps the front end from lifting, which loses valuable time and energy. It allows better car control and prevents damage to the undercarriage of the race car. They are a chassis safety device.

Some classes limit the length of the wheelie bars. All bars must have non-metallic wheels (i.e. rubber, plastic) and the wheels must turn freely at the starting line. They are made out of 4130 chromoly tubing for lightweight strength and weigh approximately 18 pounds. Most allow ample room for floor jacks. They cost approximately $300 to $400 uninstalled.

Wheelie bars help keep the front end down and allow for better elapsed times

Subframe Connectors: Any race shop can install subframe connectors. They connect the front and rear subframes on unibody cars making the chassis stiffer to allow for better traction, make the car more stable and reduce body flex. The subframe connectors should be welded into place and not bolted. After installation, the welded areas should have paint applied to prevent rust. They are generally priced under $100 per pair and add another couple hundred for installation.

Torque Boxes: The torque box is found by removing the back seat. It is located next to the lower control arm. The factory spot welds this piece. It is much better and safer to bead weld and add reinforcement to this box which strengthens it, resulting in less flexing. Pre-fab kits are available, but most chassis shops make their own.

Electronics

Knock Sensor: This is a sensor that is mounted on the engine which detects engine knocks or detonation. If it does, a warning light on the dashboard will light up brightly. When this happens, it is advisable to immediately back off the gas, and turn the engine off.

Computer Chip: A modified computer chip replaces the stock chip and can change the fuel curves and timing. They should be installed after bolt-on modifications have been added; this allows them to be specifically selected based on the fuel curve, timing and tune level of the engine. They will significantly increase horsepower. Prices are approximately $260 - $300 and several companies like Superchips, Diablo and Hypermex will custom program a chip for about $100 more.

These custom chips, which are designed specifically for each application, can be downloaded to certified shops so the chips may be picked up locally. This allows customers to have custom chips that are ready very quickly.

Two-Step Module: A low cost addition is a two-step module. This gives the driver two rev limiters, allowing him to concentrate on the light and not have to concentrate on the tachometer. The system is activated by staging, pushing the button, flooring the throttle and waiting for the lights to activate. At this time it will hold the rev limit to a specified lower level. When the button is released, the two-step switches to the higher rev limiter for protection against missed shifts and will not allow your engine to rev beyond a certain rpm. On the line it gives the car a loud, stuttering sound and allows the car to leave the line pretty violently.

Tachometer: A large, easily read tachometer and shift light should be mounted in a prominent location. They can be programmed to any specified revolution count. When the engine reaches that rpm, a bright light flashes alerting the driver to shift. This may seem unnecessary, but in the heat of competition a reminder is often helpful. At a cost of $200 - $400, it is inexpensive engine insurance.

Delay Box: This is a timer that sets the *transbrake* to release after a specified delay. It is set by the driver to coordinate to the lighting of one of the amber lights on the Christmas Tree. Just wait for the light, let go of the button (which is usually mounted

Programable tachometer with large shift light at upper left

on the steering wheel), floor it and wait for the car to take off automatically. Each driver must learn how to set the delay from different amber lights to determine the best combination for his race car. Usually on a Pro Tree light system, it should be set for the very first glimpse of the first amber bulb. It helps to establish better reaction times and also helps eliminate red lights. Delay boxes are illegal in many classes and are only effective in bracket racing.

Cross Over Delay Box: This unit is similar to a delay box, but the driver can enter both his dial in and his opponents during eliminations. The delay box will figure out the handicap so the driver can leave using his opponents starting lights. These are only used in bracket racing.

Line Loc: While performing burn outs, the Line Loc allows you to keep the front brake pressure activated to keep the car still and steady. This is an inexpensive way not to burn up the rear brakes by having steady pressure on them.

Computer System: Some electronic and fuel injection systems allow quick and precise adjustments to tune for timing, fuel and rpms. Between runs, a laptop computer can be connected to the control units to change settings. These are made by F.A.S.T. (Speed-Pro), Electromotive, Motec and others and replace the standard factory fitted computer which maps fuel and timing. Prices run from $1000 to $8000.

An Electromotive aftermarket computer system set up

Transbrake: This locks an automatic transmission in first and reverse gear under load. When leaving the line, the transbrake is released and the car takes off like a bullet. When the switch is pressed in and held, the car will not roll at all, even if floored.

Tires and Wheels

Tires can be specialized racing rubber or may be D.O.T. approved street tires depending on the racing class. In this book we will confine the discussion to rear wheel drive cars. Tires are checked at technical inspection.

Front Tires: The pressures in the front tires can help with reaction time. The reaction time will be slower if you deflate the tires to 25–35 psi which shrinks the tires and aids against red lighting (crossing the starting line before the green light is displayed). The reaction time will be quicker if the front tires are inflated to 40 psi. Front tire pressures lower than 25 psi result in erratic handling and steering and can be very dangerous.

Using *skinnies* (15 x 3.5" tires) up front helps lighten the front end and reduces rolling resistance. This will allow for quicker times and help with the weight transfer to the rear tires. Weld and Centerline make wheels can be used with these tires.

Rear Tires: The better the traction, the faster the tires can turn without spinning. Traction is the ability of the tires to grip the road without slipping. A tall, narrow set of rear tires will help on launch and wide ones will hook more consistently. If the tire width or diameter is changed substantially, it may be necessary to also change the rear end gear ratio to maintain optimal ET.

Each drag racer needs to decide which tire will be the best application. D.O.T. drag radials can be driven on the street and they look like street tires. These are great tires for a sleeper. Their tread compound is a little softer than regular street tires and because of this, they have a shorter life span than a regular

Slicks with approved screws in rims

tire. If raced frequently they have a much shorter life span. All street tires must have a minimum of 1/16-inch tread depth.

There are street slicks which are called ET street tires. Basically they are slicks with only a few grooves in them. They are D.O.T. approved so they can be driven on public roads. They hook up very well but are lousy daily driver tires. They are also very dangerous in wet weather. They can be driven to and from the track; however, it is not really wise since inclement weather could send your car into a frenzy.

There are slicks which are made out of a super soft compound with no grooves on them on all. They are for track use only, never for highway. They are very easy to puncture and very unsafe with moisture and wet roads. They should be inflated between 10 and 14 pounds per square inch tire pressure. Anything less than ten pounds may adversely affect the handling of the race car. Slicks should also be balanced.

When running slicks, it is best to run tubes and screw the tires to the wheel rims. If run tubeless, slicks often leak air through their thin sidewalls. Screws should be installed on both the inner and outer flange of the rim and the tire should be screwed to the rim to avoid damaging the tubes. Installing tubes also strengthens the sidewall of the tire making it stiffer. Incorrect tube size may cause a bulge in the sidewall. If you are undecided about using tubes, ask the guys who sell tires at the track.

Metal valve stems are stronger, don't rot and are mandatory on cars faster than 11.99 ETs

Be ready to change tires when 60 foot times are starting to become inconsistent. This is a sign that your tires are becoming worn. Depending on the power of the car, a set of slicks can have a life as short as five passes to well over 25.

If you are driving your race car to the track, load your slicks in the back seat and/or trunk, along with a jack. At the track, head to the pits and change tires, but when you go through the tech line and to the starting line, make sure you have a safe, secure place to leave your street tires. When the racing is over, simply replace the street tires on your car and re-pack the slicks.

Sun shields for tires are available. Sitting in the sun changes tire pressures and these reflective covers help keep temperature and pressure consistent. The shields are held on by magnetic strips and are well worth the money.

To store slicks follow these tips. Keep them away from direct sunlight and fluorescent lights. Cover them and keep away from extreme hot or cold temperatures. If mounted, raise the car up and drop the tire pressure to 5 psi. Keep the tires away from any electrical devices, i.e., air compressors. Only clean your tires with a mild detergent and water, then rinse.

Metal, screw-in valve stems are mandatory in tubeless tires, front and rear, on cars which have 11.99 or quicker ETs.

Exterior Modifications

Air Foils/Wings/Spoilers: These aerodynamic devices are designed to force the body of the car downward as it passes through the air to load the suspension and the resulting increase in traction allows for a faster run. If used in the front they are used to help with steering. Airfoils, wings or spoilers may not be adjusted while the car is in motion.

Spoilers can be mounted to allow air to pass over the top, underneath the device or both. Sometimes

Aluminum race wings on production based cars are bolted to the existing bodywork

Large wings on dragsters are positioned well above the bodywork to take full advantage of air free from turbulence to help keep the rear end planted during the run

Hood scoops increase airflow to the induction system at speed

they also have vents in them allowing air to pass through the middle, as well. They can be mounted on the bodywork of the vehicle or may be placed on struts, pedestals or stands. Prices vary drastically, but start at approximately $400.

Hood Scoop: The opening for a hood scoop may not extend more than eleven inches above the height of the original hood surface. These are inexpensive and readily available from many suppliers or can be fabricated.

10

Power Adders

There are three main power adders used in the drag racing world and they are as follows: superchargers, nitrous oxide and turbochargers. Whichever one you choose to use, it is all a matter of preference. There are many racers who swear by nitrous and would not use anything else. There are those that only use superchargers. It is just a matter of what you feel comfortable with, can afford or simply prefer to use.

Superchargers

Superchargers produce additional power by forcing air and fuel into the engine via a belt driven blower. The extra volume of air and fuel introduced into the cylinder results in raising the compression ratio without having to alter any mechanical components inside. Often supercharged cars run lower compression pistons than normally aspirated ones. Running stock pistons may result in damage to the engine or blown head gaskets. Switching drive pulley diameters will radically alter boost and as a result, performance.

Fuel flow is instrumental to successful power production in these engines. Ignition timing and fuel mixture may need to be adjusted with the higher volume of air for engine longevity and it is always better to run a little rich than lean. It is important to have the correct jets or injector size, fuel pump flow and charge temperature.

Fuel pressure and boost gauges are very important to monitor supercharged engine performance. Stock

fuel pressure runs around 28-32 psi., but supercharged cars run approximately five to ten pounds higher. A fuel pressure regulator allows adjustment to maintain the appropriate level.

Belt slipping, which results in inconsistent pressure, is a common problem and can be eliminated by using an eight-rib belt drive belt system. Installation requires replacing all the belt drive and driven pulleys. Price is approximately $600 for belt and pulleys.

This Vortech supercharger mounts to the front of the engine allowing a lower hood to be used; great for street applications

Belt failure can result in significant damage to external engine components resulting in possible fluid spillage or fire. Due to this, rules require that all fuel and oil lines must be shielded where they pass the supercharger drive belt by using a fuel/oil line guard or belt guard for all cars running 9.99 seconds or quicker.

An electronic boost retard box helps with combustion of the air/fuel mixture. It is necessary to adjust ignition timing for effective use.

Superchargers are street legal, easily installed and provide reliable performance. The main advantage of supercharging is that the power is always available, though under normal driving conditions, the supercharger is not providing boost. As the revs pick up, then the power kicks in, smoothly and progressively. Fuel economy is likewise unaffected at low revs, though it becomes geometrically poorer at high RPMs, since fuel is being forced into the combustion area.

For high boosted applications, an intercooler/aftercooler can be used for even greater performance and safety. It lowers the temperature of air entering the engine. The cooler, denser air charge allows less fuel to be used, which along with altered timing reduces chances of inappropriate detonation and results in significant power increases. Most conventional intercoolers are air-to-air, but a more efficient air-to-water aftercooler, which uses ice water, is commonly used for drag racing.

Anyone with basic mechanical skills and common hand tools can install a supercharger. They cost approximately $3500 for complete kits. Prior to purchase make sure that your internal engine components are compatible with the higher induction pressures that the supercharger generates. The manufacturer and/or your race shop should be able to advise you.

NOS (Nitrous Oxide Systems)

Nitrous Oxide (N_2O) is a non-toxic, colorless gas composed of nitrogen and oxygen, which when added to the air/fuel mixture in the combustion chamber, results in a substantial increase in horsepower generation. Though it was discovered way back in 1772, the Germans were believed to be the first ones to use nitrous to enhance the power of fighter planes during the second World War.

There are two types of nitrous systems. In the first, called the dry system, nitrous enters directly through the intake manifold. The fuel is then added by injectors. In the second type, called the wet system, gasoline and nitrous are mixed together prior to entering the intake manifold.

As with any type of induction system, the engine must have correct amounts of air and fuel supplied. By adding nitrous the engine actually burns more fuel and oxygen, which generates additional horsepower. Higher octane fuel must be utilized and ignition timing needs to be retarded to prevent improper combustion or detonation. It is best to initially set the car up to run rich and gradually lean it out. When running too rich with nitrous, black smoke will come from the tailpipes. It is extremely important to have large amounts of fuel though, because running too lean will result in serious engine damage.

In addition to fuel management, ignition settings are critical on a car using nitrous. Using colder plugs and retarding the timing is necessary because nitrous generates more heat than standard combustion. Reading the spark plugs after each run is helpful, but true readings can only be obtained if the engine is shut off at the finish line and the car pushed or towed back for plug removal. Specks on the porcelain insulator indicate detonation.

Detonation is caused by increased pressure within the cylinder. A high performance electronic ignition and timing retard module will help prevent it. It is usually recommended to retard the ignition timing by approximately two degrees for each additional 50 horsepower generated by nitrous use. When driving the car without nitrous, a timing retard module will restore the normal ignition timing and allow the engine to run smoothly.

Nitrous bottles set up in the trunk of a race car. It is always good to carry an assortment of bottles so you don't have to fill them up between rounds at the track

Always start with a small shot of nitrous and work up to larger shots. Resist the temptation to add too much and get carried away with the great power increase. If using extreme amounts of nitrous, it is necessary to have a good aftermarket fuel system, good rods, forged pistons and a steel crank.

Nitrous bottles are made from aluminum or carbon fiber and weigh between two and one half and 25 pounds. A DOT-1800 pounds rating should be stamped on each bottle along with nitrous oxide identification. A 10 pound bottle should be good for five to six runs.

Locating nitrous bottles in the trunk helps put weight over the rear wheels. If the bottle is installed in the drivers compartment, a pop-off relief valve must be on the bottle. This valve opens automatically if bottle pressure exceeds the safe limit and vents it outside of the compartment. It is important that nitrous bottles be securely mounted in case of an accident or roll over.

The bottle pressure should always be monitored, because this is very important for production of maximum horsepower. For peak performance, the

Your local speed shop carries nitrous fittings, equipment and will refill your nitrous tanks

optimal pressure is between 850-1000 psi. If pressure is too high, the air/fuel mixture could lean out and result in engine damage. By changing the temperature of the bottle, the pressure can be controlled. A pressure gauge should be installed so you can tell the pressure at a glance.

Bottle pressure can be stabilized via use of a bottle warmer and blanket. Blankets help keep heat in and also contains the bottle and keeps it from getting beat up. Most blankets have insulated lining and attach with velcro fasteners. Bottle warmers are used to heat bottles to their desired pressures and come in 12-volt in-car and 120-volt plug-in styles. Heating bottles with a torch can cause an explosion, but believe it or not, many racers still do this!

An electric bottle opener allows the valve on the bottle to be opened or closed via an electric motor at the touch of a button. Remote shut-off valves can also be installed. After every run it is best to shut off the nitrous flow immediately to prevent leakage, which can cause frostbite on the skin.

The most popular and most easily installed nitrous system is called a plate injection system. The plate mounts between the carburetor and intake, between the upper and lower intakes, or between the throttle body and upper intake. It allows nitrous to be introduced into the induction system through the plate.

The fogger or wet system produces more power. Nitrous and fuel are pre-mixed and supplied to individual ports in the intake manifold by using a central fuel and nitrous block with individual spray nozzles for each cylinder. It can be activated in three stages, which can be activated at different times.

A NOS purge system is used to remove the gas and air from the system. With this in place when the driver hits the nitrous button, the car will receive a fresh shot of nitrous and it will flow through the motor and up to the solenoids. The purge system adds an extra solenoid which lets the nitrous pressure vent.

The solenoids in the system allow the flow of nitrous and larger solenoids produce greater flow. It also lets the driver lower the bottle pressure if it becomes too high. It is also a crowd pleaser when a blast of white smoke at least 15 feet in the air is released from a car before a run.

It is best to weigh bottles before having them refilled, so you know how much to add. A 10 pound capacity bottle which weighs 15 pounds when empty will weigh 25 pounds when full. Nitrous refill pumps are also available.

Before each run, it is a good idea to check all nitrous lines, wiring and switches for damage. Broken or clogged fuel lines can cause fuel loss and possibly a fire or even an explosion. Always use top quality fuel lines, braided hoses or triple insulated hoses.

Multiple nitrous purging in a parking lot – must be a guy thing!

Using nitrous on the highway is not recommended. Not only is it a waste of money, but if used when cornering, it can cause sudden loss of control.

Finally, if you start your engine and then shut it down, do not re-start your engine if you have NOS in the lines. It can cause a huge nitrous backfire or explosion. The explosion pictured here blew the intake apart and even cracked the windshield. Instead, remove the plugs and coil wire, then crank the engine over to clear the nitrous from the engine. This way, you will prevent damage to your engine.

The aftermath of an NOS explosion

Nitrous kits start at $500; they can add 50-175 horsepower in unmodified cars.

Turbocharger

The oldest form of forced induction is the turbocharger. A turbocharger uses exhaust gases to spin a turbine. The turbine in turn spins a compressor, which compresses the intake air. Just like a supercharger, this makes more power and improves the fuel efficiency, because it increases the volume of the air/fuel mix in the combustion chamber.

Turbochargers are very efficient, quiet in operation and can be quite compact and lightweight. The turbo consists of turbine housing, exhaust turbine, compressor wheel (impeller), and compressor housing. It generally is incorporated into the exhaust manifold or header.

Turbos do not create boost at low RPMs enabling turbocharged vehicles to sound almost stock at idle. The turbo unit actually quiets exhaust noise, since the exhaust gases go through the turbine housing before passing through the rest of the exhaust system. These turbo cars sound harmless at idle, but take off as the boost builds at higher revs and the turbo starts to whine.

It is important to run an aftermarket ignition/fuel system and an engine management system such as F.A.S.T., Electromotive or Motec, designed to be used

Turbocharger set-up in a small engine bay can be a tight fit

with a turbocharger. Using an intercooler/aftercooler, makes for more efficient combustion, as with a supercharger. Twin-turbo systems are more efficient and have better response than single turbocharger set-ups.

Turning high RPMs immediately after starting will lead to excessive turbo bearing wear or failure, because it is forcing the turbocharger to operate at less than optimum temperature. Also, it is best to allow the engine to idle for a few minutes prior to shutting it off. This allows for reduction of the turbocharger temperature, which gets very hot during operation. Most turbocharger failures are caused by bearing failure or foreign objects going into the compressor.

Safety Equipment

Drag racing can be dangerous. It is up to the driver to be ready for these dangers and deal with them the best way possible. Anything can happen at speeds in excess of 100 mph. For example, a small animal could run down the track in front of you. How would you react? If there is oil or fluid on the track, your car could go into the wall, crash into your opponent, or even roll over. It is important to adhere to the following guidelines for vehicle and personal safety. They could mean the difference between life and death.

I want to dedicate the Safety chapter to my racing friend, Jimmy Heavner. Jimmy was involved in a 160-mph death-defying crash into the cement retainer wall at Moroso Motorsports Park in Palm Beach Gardens, Florida. His beautiful ice blue Mustang was poised to break into the 6-second zone in the quarter mile. Jimmy was air lifted to the local hospital where he survived life-threatening head injuries, eye, nerve and muscle damage. He is recovering from these injuries at this time.

SFI Rating

All safety equipment must be labeled with an SFI rating. In 1963, a group called the Speed Equipment Manufacturer's Association, *SEMA*, was formed by racing parts manufacturers*. The main purpose was the development of product specifications for use by the suppliers of racing equipment. Over time the specifications were determined and various rule books were compiled.

*SEMA still exists, but its name reflects a broadening in direction. It now stands for Specialty Equipment Market Association and includes a wide array of performance and accessories manufacturers.

Car owners could be denied participation in a racing event if certain products do not meet the SFI specs. Therefore, a rating program was initialized and has continued as a result of this ruling of the SEMA founders.

The SFI Foundation, Inc. (*SFI*) is a non-profit organization founded to administer and issue standards for automotive racing equipment and performance components. It was originally set up by SEMA and the letters *SFI* stood for *SEMA Foundation, Inc*. Though no longer directly administered by SEMA, SFI continues to set the recognized levels of performance and quality for various racing and high performance products.

When the race sanctioning body rule books are compiled, SFI ratings on various components are specified. The manufacturers will supply products for the racer that are in compliance with the specifications required by the sanctioning body.

Driver Equipment

Safety Harness: A 5-point seatbelt with a quick release for emergencies is the minimum requirement for this important component. It serves to keep the driver in place and secure inside the roll cage, where the least amount of injury will occur in a crash.

The safety harness consists of three-inch wide lap and shoulder belts with an SFI specification of 16.1. The webbing in the straps of the restraint assembly must be replaced or re-webbed two years from the date of manufacture. Belts degenerate from exposure to the weather and if you have old, weak belts, they could easily snap or break under the harsh loads imposed on them from an accident situation. Failure to properly restrain the driver in a crash could have deadly consequences.

There must be one strap for each shoulder, intended to restrain movement of the upper torso and shoulder regions. An optional cross strap across the chest can be used to hold the shoulder harness together. The lap belt restrains movement of the pelvis and a two inch crotch strap prevents the pelvis from slipping forward from under the lap belt in the event of a frontal impact.

The belts are attached together with a buckle that has a quick and easy release mechanism so the driver can escape quickly from the car in case of emergency. There are three types of buckles to choose from: latch/lever, turn/push, and cam lock. The latch type restraint system is where you simply unlatch the system to release the five-way harness.

Simpson produces the Cam-Lock buckle which is made from billet aluminum alloy. It has steel tumblers that lock the belt and harness into the buckle by snapping them together. The driver pushes the handle forward to release the belts.

Latch-type 5 point safety harness. Notice also the foam rubber roll bar padding: a good idea to help prevent injury in places where the driver is in close proximity to the roll bar or cage

The correct installation of the restraint system greatly affects the reliability of the product. It is extremely important to follow the manufacturer's installation instructions. Safety harnesses run from $100 to $200 uninstalled.

Helmets must be approved by the Snell Memorial Foundation and manufactured within the past ten years to be legal.

Helmets: You will need a Snell 95 or newer approved and certified helmet. They are usually made with a thick Lexan shield and lightweight Kevlar glass composite for the outer aerodynamic shell. This hard outer shell of the helmet is filled with Energy Absorbing Material (EAM), which protects the head against violent impacts. The padding does not help with the initial impact and is only for comfort and to fit your head comfortably. Nothing but the padding and the EAM in the helmet will touch the driver's head. They are covered with a fire-retardant lining. Helmets range in price from $300 to $800.

You will need to find out the proper size helmet to wear. If the helmet is too large, it will simply slide over your head with no resistance. A loose fit can lead to injuries in the event of a crash. It is a good idea to go to a speed shop or karting track, where different size helmets can be tried on prior to purchase. The top edge of the liner padding should be just above the eyebrows. If glasses are worn while driving, they should be put on while wearing the helmet.

A clear Lexan shield provides facial protection on a full-face helmet. Drivers of any open-bodied car wearing an open face helmet must wear face shields or protective goggles. If you are ever involved in a crash with your helmet, it should never be used again, no matter the appearance.

Air Conditioned Helmets: Air conditioned helmets provide clean air, ventilation and cooling in all facets of racing, including quarter mile runs in a dragster. They give the driver a racing edge and are quite a luxury on humid days, when the track temperatures can be in the 130 degree range. Sometimes drivers sit in their cars ready to race, only to be delayed while track personnel clean debris off the track. During this time it is easy to become dehydrated and even suffer from heat exhaustion. Many drivers are also claustrophobic and these helmets may help alleviate the closed in feeling with low steady tone and light breeze.

There are different types of air conditioned helmets designed for all types of motorsports, including circle track, road racing and drag racing. Circle track and road racing versions utilize air intakes vented outside of the vehicle to pick up clean air. On drag racing applications, most use a blower system, which attaches to a lightweight cooler, filled with ice and water.

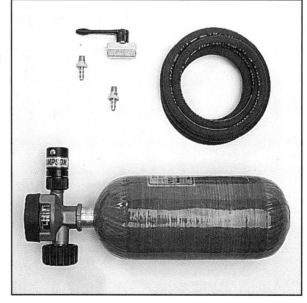

Air conditioned helmet components for compressed air system. Photo courtesy Simpson Racing

Another type of external air system utilizes a composite

bottle with approximately 8-10 minutes of compressed air, connected to the helmet with a fire rated hose and controlled via a pressure regulator for proper air flow. Helmets for this system are constructed with a built-in headsock.

Prices vary significantly. Some systems are added to your existing helmet, while others come as a complete unit. Expect to spend from $600 uninstalled to $1150 for a version including helmet.

Head Protector: To prevent whiplash or head injury, a padded head protector must be mounted on the roll cage or roll bar at the back of driver's head. This is unnecessary on cars with high backed seats.

Neck Collar: A neck collar with a 3.3 SFI rating is mandatory in cars running 9.99 or quicker to help lessen the immediate impact of the launch. It is a foam support surrounding the neck which serves as a shock absorber for the head and neck. It also helps reduce neck fatigue. Price is around $35.

HANS® Device: The HANS® device was invented by Robert Hubbard, PhD., Professor, College of

Engineering at Michigan State University, along with his brother-in-law, Jim Downing, a long-time IMSA sports car driver. It was designed to reduce the chance of serious injury caused by the violent movement of the unrestrained head and helmet combinations in an accident. It helps to prevent the type of sudden-stop injury that occurs in serious car crashes. Race car drivers are most severely disabled by head and neck injuries, which are less frequent than other injuries, but have devastating results.

Helmets and cockpit padding help protect drivers from direct head injuries, but drivers necks still allow largehead motions and their necks still carry the impact load. It will help alleviate neck strain when decelerating the end of the run. The HANS® head and neck support reduces extreme head motions and neck loads that injure race drivers. It utilizes a collar and yoke system constructed of carbon fiber and Kevlar. The device is worn on the upper body under the shoulder straps. It is connected to the helmet by two flexible tethers which allow normal movement of

The HANS® Device prevents forward neck and head extension to help minimalize injury. Photo courtesy Vince Tidwell, Hubbard/Downing Inc.

head (left, right, up, and down) but limit extreme head motions and neck loads.

The HANS® device is shipped with a kit which allows the customer to install the helmet attachment hardware himself. Installation prices range from $975 to $2000 with Jr. Dragster devices selling for $675. Contact www.hansdevice.com or call (770) 457-1046.

Driving Suits/Jackets: A SFI Spec. 3.2A/1 fireproof jacket is needed for running speeds of 11.99 or quicker. It needs to have a Thermal Protection Performance (TPP) rating from 6 - 80. The higher the number, the higher the thermal protection. The black and white SFI patch on the drivers' left shoulder means that the jacket is SFI certified through their lab testing and passed the test requirements. The suits are made out of gabardine nomex. Nomex undergarments/socks are recommended to wear under all racing suits to create air gaps.

How the suit fits is of utmost importance because if a suit is too tight it will compress the air gaps. This means, it will allow heat to reach the skin faster. Some suits are machine washable; others have to be dry cleaned, this can be determined by looking at the tag affixed to the suit. Properly maintaining the suit will extend its life and provide years of protection.

If ever involved in a fire or the suit is torn or otherwise damaged, always throw it away and buy a new one. Even if the suit does not look damaged, it could still have a bad spot in the material and may not perform properly if exposed to fire again. Prices for jackets range from $200 and up; full racing suits range from $300 to over $800.

Head Sock: These are designed to be worn under most helmets. They are made of fire-resistant Nomex material with either dual or single eye-ports. Price range is around $35.

Fire protection from head to toe is provided by a professional driver's suit, such as this. Photo courtesy Simpson Racing

Racing shoes are necessary in cars that run 9.99 or faster. Gloves not only protect your hands from fire, but also help you hold onto the steering wheel

Gloves and Heat Sleeves: SFI 3.3/1 gloves and heat sleeves should be used to protect hands and arms from burns. They are made from fire-retardant Kevlar and are padded, three-ply mesh gloves with an elastic wristband with padded layers of Nomex on top of the hand. Leather palm gloves without a full layer of Nomex separating leather from driver's hand are prohibited. They also ensure a non-slip grip on the shifter.

Racing Shoes: These shoes are extremely comfortable for racing with Nomex linings and have an SFI 3.3/5 rating. They are also fire-retardant and meet SFI and FIA ratings. They are available in high or low top. They have sensitive grips that allow for good driving control. They are required in cars that run 9.99 or faster ETs. Prices range from $80 to $100.

There are also heat shielded shoes which allow air to pass between the heel and the floorboard to evacuate heat. They have heat deflecting, aluminized Kevlar shields with heat absorbing foam.

Seat Belt Cutter: It never hurts to carry a seat belt cutter within reach. These can be bought at any fire equipment company for under $10. They allow a quick escape if for some reason the seat belt malfunctions or is jammed.

Center Punch: This is recommended in case of a crash where you cannot open your door or window and you need to immediately exit the vehicle because of fire. It should be mounted within reach so it can be easily grasped and used to hit the side window (not the windshield which is laminated glass). When struck, the tempered side glass will shatter into small pieces. A center punch can be purchased from any home improvement or hardware store for $15 or less.

Car Equipment

Roll Bar: Roll bars/cages will prevent the driver from being crushed in the event of a crash. They are made from strong metal tubes and encase the driver in a safe little environment. The roll bar must be adequately supported or cross-braced to prevent forward or lateral collapse. All roll bars/cages should surround the driver, but allow them to comfortably reach all the controls and be able to quickly exit the vehicle when needed. A roll bar will also add stiffness to the vehicle. They are required in vehicles running 10.00 to 11.99 and convertibles running 11.00 to 13.00.

Roll cages are mandatory in all cars quicker than 9.99

Most, if not all, sanctioning bodies use the roll bar and roll cage specifications of the NHRA. Per these specifications, all roll bars must be within six inches of the rear, or side of the driver's head, extend in height at least three inches above the driver's helmet with driver in normal driving position, and be at least as wide as the driver's shoulder, or within one inch of the driver's door.

Rear braces must be of the same diameter and wall thickness as the roll bar and intersect with the roll bar at a point not more than five inches from the top of the roll bar. Sidebar must be included on driver's side and must pass the driver at a point midway between the shoulder and below. Swing out sidebar is permitted.

All roll bars must have a cross bar for seat bracing and must be installed no more than four inches below, and not above, the driver's shoulders or to side bar. All vehicles with OEM frame must have the roll bar welded or bolted to frame; installation of frame connectors on unibody cars does not constitute a frame, therefore it is not necessary to have the roll bar attached to the frame.

Roll bars are available with a swing-out version. This is where there is a swing-out bar for the driver's side door to enable easier access to the seat, however, this may make a somewhat weaker connection between the main hoop and the front of the car.

Roll bars must be padded anywhere the driver's helmet may contact it while in driving position. Adequate padding must have a minimum of one quarter inch compression or meet SFI Spec. 45.1. Pre-fab roll bars are available starting at about $120 uninstalled. Most race and chassis shops prefer to make their own.

Swing out roll cage element allows easier access to and from the cockpit

Roll Cage: Roll cages are mandatory on convertibles 10.99 or quicker and all cars 7.50 – 9.99. Also, if the ET is higher than 10.00 but the car hits speeds over 135mph, the same safety rules for cars running quicker than 10.0 apply.

Per NHRA Specifications, all cage structures must be designed in an attempt to protect the driver from any angle, 360 degrees. All 4130 chromoly tube welding must be done by approved TIG heliarc process; mild steel tube welding must be by approved MIG wire feed or TIG heliarc process.

Additionally, the roll cage must be padded anywhere the driver's helmet may contact it while in the driving position. Cages must also be NHRA certified and must be renewed through re-inspection every 3 years.

External electrical cutoff switch allows safety personnel to disable fuel pumps and other electrical equipment quickly

Battery Disconnect Switch/Master Cutoff Switch: When relocating the battery to the trunk, a master cutoff switch should be mounted on the rear of the car which is easily located and accessible from outside the car. This allows emergency personnel to easily shut the switch off, immediately turning off all electrical components including fuel pumps. It must be clearly marked *on* or *off* regardless of if it is a *push/pull* or *twist* type. It must be connected to the positive side of the electrical system. Approximate cost $30 uninstalled.

Driveshaft Loop: A driveshaft loop is a loop of steel strap that surrounds the driveshaft and protects the driver if the driveshaft breaks or u-joints fail. In case of driveshaft breakage, the loop holds the driveshaft up in place and does not allow the driveshaft to hit the ground. If unrestrained, you could flip or the driveshaft

Driveshaft loop protects the driver in case of driveshaft breakage

could tear through the floor and enter the cockpit. It is required on cars that run 13.99 or quicker and recommended on all other front engine, rear drive cars.

The loop should be 360 degrees around the driveshaft, one quarter inch thick by two inches wide steel and mounted within six inches of the front universal joint. Price approximately $50 uninstalled.

Fire extinguishers should be mounted within reach of the driver for emergency use

Fire Extinguisher: A fire extinguisher should be mounted securely and within hands-reach of the driver. It is recommended that each driver carry a fire extinguisher both in the race car and tow vehicle. Dry chemical or CO2-type extinguisher B/C or A/B/C , 2 1/2 pound minimum size, are recommended.

Dry Chemical System/Halon System: This is a more sophisticated on-board fire extinguishing device, built into the car. The extinguishing agent is dicharged around the engine and driver's compartment to put out flames. They are easy to install and do not require special wiring.

Activation of this type system can be either manual, automatic or both. A heat detection cable can detect temperature increase and will automatically activate the extinguishers. If there is a manual control, the driver can activate the system by hitting a switch, if it does not work automatically. These need to be serviced every couple years to make sure they continue to function properly.

Halon is one of the more popular and vehicle friendly extinguishing chemicals. Though no longer produced, this allegedly environmentally unfriendly gas fights fire by depriving it of oxygen, quickly eliminating flames without leaving chemical residue. It is also colorless, so it does not obstruct the driver's vision. Systems are rechargeable and recycled Halon continues to be available, though it becomes more and more expensive as time goes by. Cost for a complete system at the time of this printing ranged from $300 to over $500 uninstalled.

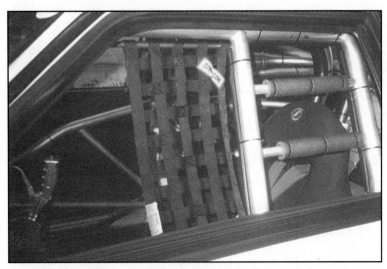

Window nets are designed to keep the driver's arms inside the car in the event of a roll over

Window Net: A window net, with an SFI 27.1 rating, keeps the driver's head and hands inside a closed car in case of a roll over and is permanently mounted to the inside of the roll bar. A net is mandatory for a car that is required to run with a roll cage. All attachments must be put together in an attempt to protect the driver and not allow contact with the outside surfaces. Like seat belts, they must be replaced two years from the date of manufacture. They should be installed in compliance with the manufacturer's recommendations. Prices range from $20 to $60 uninstalled.

Quick Release Steering Wheel: Some cars have quick release steering wheels that can easily be removed to allow the driver to quickly exit. One type features hard anodized aluminum outer boss designed for maximum strength and durability. Price for the quick release is approximately $170.

Fuel Cell: A safe way to control fuel is to install a puncture resistant fuel cell in the trunk with a 28.1 SFI rating. They are available in a number of standard sizes including 4, 5, 8, 12 and 15-gallons. The mounting straps provided are one or two inches wide and 1/8 inch thick. This allows the fuel tank to be located in the trunk and eliminate the need for your original, factory fuel tank located underneath the car. This will also eliminate some unnecessary weight.

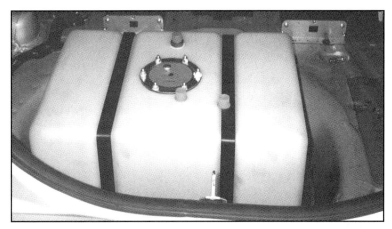

Fuel cells can be safely mounted in the trunk and come in an assortment of sizes and configurations

Some are made from clear, thick polyurethane compound, which resists flexing and sagging. The clear poly material eliminates the need for a gauge. Others are made from opaque materials or aluminum with a rubber bladder. Filling the cell with foam will help control fuel sloshing and will help increase fuel flow. Most tanks include a vent with a positive ball type check valve to prevent spilling in the event of a rollover. Costs start at $130 and can be much more expensive in custom applications.

Throttle Return Spring: A throttle return spring is required to be attached directly to the carburetor or injector throttle arm. There is nothing worse than having the throttle hung wide open at the top end. Not only scary, but can potentially blow up your engine. They're cheap, why not use two?

Scattershield/Transshield: A scatter-shield or transshield with a 4.1 SFI rating protects the driver in the event of clutch or transmission explosion. It is a flexible blanket shield that will contain shrapnel if the transmission blows. A transshield is mandatory on cars running 10.99 or quicker. A scattershield is mandatory for cars running 11.99 or quicker.

Flexplate: An SFI 29.1 specification is required for a flexplate of an automatic transmission car running 9.99 or quicker. A flexplate is for the drivers own personal protection to guard against an exploding transmission. Prices range from $80 to $250.

Scattershields are commonly made of thick steel plate to contain the powerful explosion of a clutch or transmission

Flywheel/Bellhousing/Shield: An SFI 30.1 rating is required for a bellhousing on an automatic transmission to avoid physical harm if the transmission explodes. This is installed when your transmission goes into the car. An SFI approved flywheel is mandatory if you run 9.99 or quicker and can be made from mild steel, chromoly or aluminum. An SFI 30.1 approved flywheel shield is also required. It mounts to the outside of the bellhousing. The flywheel shield will protect the driver and spectators if the flexplate fails.

NOS Safety: If using nitrous as a power adder, there should be a sticker in the rear window that simply states *NOS*. If the nitrous bottle is in the driver's compartment, it must have a relief valve vented outside of the compartment.

Radiator Overflow: All cars must have a radiator overflow catch can, which is a minimum of 16 ounces, to prevent cars from dropping coolant under the tires or on the track.

Parachute packed and ready to race on the Frank Hawley Super Gas Firebird

Drag Parachutes: For all cars exceeding 150 mph, parachutes are mandatory as brakes are not enough to slow down these *bad boys*. They are reliable and durable. Tech inspectors will check for worn or frayed shroud lines, ripped canopies and worn pilot chutes. Parachute cable housing should be mounted to frame tube or other suitable member, no farther back than one inch.

Parachutes have quick-release mounts that allows the packs to detach from the back of the car. Cable ties hold the cable securely and prevent an accidental opening of the parachute by tire shake. Different sizes are available based on the terminal velocity of the car.

If the car is supercharged, it is mandatory that the parachute pack and shroud lines be protected with fire-resistant material. Parachutes run about $250 each.

Racing Seats: Racing seats are designed to accept racing seat belts, offer good lateral stability and support the spine in its natural shape. Some professionally designed racing shells are made with ultra-lightweight carbon fiber, Kevlar material which possesses great strength. Other aftermarket seats available are made from aluminum, fiberglass or double layer poly and must have reinforced head rests. Magnesium seats are prohibited.

Seats need to be bolted in on the seat bottom and back to the frame or cross member. Prices range from $500 to $2000 uninstalled.

Jacks & Jack Stands: No work may be done in the pits with only one jack under the car. Jack stands are mandatory to provide extra protection in the event the jack fails. Failure to adhere to this rule is grounds for immediate disqualification.

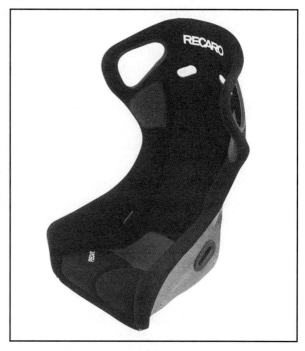

Recaro professional lightweight racing shell is durable and comfortable for racing

Car Prep

A lot of preparation is needed to change your car from regular street use to a race car. Weight reduction needs to be addressed to lighten your vehicle which will result with faster speeds. You need to become familiar with reputable race shops, unless you intend to master the mechanical aspects yourself.

Talk to other racers with similar type race cars to find out what is needed for your own application. You need to decide how far you would like to go into racing, for instance, what speeds, what class, etc., and build your car accordingly. If you want to run in a certain class, make sure your car is set up properly so you can legitimately race in that class.

Weight Reduction

As a rule of thumb, every 100 pound reduction in weight results in a one-tenth reduction in ET. It is also important to remove as much weight from the front of a rear wheel drive car, as possible. A 50/50 weight distribution or a little more bias toward the rear improves traction.

A good way to start on the weight reduction is to strip the matting or deadener that is underneath the carpeting in the interior. If appearance is important, some or all of the carpet can be reinstalled. It is surprising how much the matting weighs. If the car has one, remove the back seat to get rid of additional unnecessary interior weight. This is generally fairly simple, so it can be replaced easily, if desired, when not at the track.

A lightweight aftermarket racing seat can be very expensive, especially when looking for comfort too. They must be attached to the roll bar at the top and on the seat bottom. Some classes allow the passenger's seat to be removed and if so, this should be done.

Removing the heater and its hardware will reduce the weight by approximately 20-plus pounds. If the car is for strip use only, there is no real use for the air conditioning unit and the stereo system either.

This car is in the process of being gutted. The dash was pulled out to reduce unnecessary weight from the interior

Removing the front sway bar saves weight and frees the control arms which allows them to drop easily on the launch and also is important for weight transfer needed for traction. On the other hand, an anti-roll bar in the rear is quite important since it acts to equalize traction, reduces chassis flex or side to side roll and will improve your sixty foot times and produce more consistent ETs.

Installation of a tubular k-member, adjustable coil over shocks and tubular control arms will reduce weight on the front end of the car. A tubular k-member will also give extra room to install headers and provides for increased caster angles to add stability to maintain a straight line down the track. Approximate price uninstalled is $270. The coil overs help to adjust the ride height. Aftermarket struts with softer shocks allow the car to launch quickly lifting the front end slightly.

An aluminum radiator will reduce the weight of approximately 25-plus pounds. They are usually made of 1 5/8 inch thick core and are engineered for maximum air flow. Dimensions vary with application, but a 21.5 by 13 inch radiator only weighs approximately eight pounds when full. Cost is approximately $250. An aluminum water pump will reduce the weight by another ten pounds or so.

An aluminum driveshaft not only saves weight, but also reduces vibration. Cost is approximately $160 uninstalled.

It is especially important to cut weight up front, so consider a fiberglass hood, light wheels and skinny tires. The hood alone will lighten the weight by 45-plus pounds. Remove the front bumper support, but not for street use, just strictly racing it on the track.

Lexan or plexiglass windows are lightweight

Lexan, Plexiglas or another shatterproof material for windows is an excellent way to save pounds. The windshield will need to be a minimum of 1/8 inch thick. This eliminates some weight and also in case of an accident, there will be no shattered glass to contend with.

Take the spare tire, jack, and insulation out of the trunk. Relocating the battery to the trunk shifts at least 30-50 pounds from the front to the rear, which helps to increase traction and causes the front end to lift a little better. The battery needs to be a larger deep-cycle type and secured in place with metal hold-down straps. A battery box, made from either steel or aluminum is required if the battery is in the passenger's compartment and not a bad idea if located in the trunk. In all cases it should be fastened to the frame and located as far to the right as possible to counter balance the weight of the driver. An aluminum battery box is priced at approximately $90 uninstalled.

Last, but not least, never go to the track on a full tank of gas. This is too much unnecessary weight.

Chassis Shops

There are many reputable chassis shops and it is necessary to compare and ask around for shops in your area. In South Florida, my personal choice is Keystone Race Cars which has been owned and operated by Emile Rayot for over twenty years.

A competent chassis shop can build anything from a complete chassis to roll cages, subframes and suspension components. They can install roll bars, ladder bars, 4 link suspension and any high tech aftermarket suspension components.

Race Shops

If you do not plan to do all the work yourself, look around and find a reputable race shop which is familiar with the type of car you have. The primary function of a race shop is to maintain and fine tune the car, both in the shop and in some instances at the track, as well. They also install and modify components and make necessary repairs. They maintain the computers and complete the final assembly of the race car.

I use Super Street Racing, from Miami, Florida. This race shop is owned and operated by Richard Martin and Javier Gottardi. Not only are they are expert engine technicians and race car builders, they are both active racers.

Engine Builders

Some race shops have their own engine builders in house and others farm out this important specialty. As with others involved in the service aspects of drag racing, it is a good idea to ask around and do a little research when selecting someone to occupy this position of trust. There are many different choices involved when building an engine and the professional builder will know the options and costs to fit the aspirations and budget of each individual racer.

My personal engine man is Ronnie Crawford who has been professionally building engines for over thirty years. Ronnie originated, designed and popularized the Ford Stroker 347 engine (a 302 stroked to a 347). He works very intricately with his engines, paying special attention to minute details. He takes pride in every engine and builds each one according to the owner's specifications and desires.

A number of race shops and racers feel extremely confident with his high-quality engines and will run them to their utmost because they are very strong and durable. In my opinion, he is the best engine builder in the world.

Chassis Dynomometer

A chassis dynamometer (dyno) measures vehicular power at the drive wheels. They are much more practical than engine dynos, which require removal of the engine from the car. Many race

Straps are needed to securely tie down race cars while on the dyno

shops now incorporate dynos in their shops to receive accurate readings and help in trouble shooting.

Placing the car on a chassis dynomometer allows you to find out pertinent information which will aid in the optimization of the car's performance. It measures, analyzes and spots problems with vehicles, and can be used to diagnose performance and driveability problems. Dyno runs can be done safely and reliably at speeds up to 200 mph without leaving the shop.

An atmospheric sensing module measures absolute pressure, air temperature and relative humidity. By making changes and comparing dyno runs, the optimal settings for fuel mixture, jetting, timing and various other modifications can be determined to maximize torque & horsepower.

The dyno can also detect problems such as belt slippage. The dyno print out should show horsepower and torque curves rising smoothly. If they are not smooth and are bouncing around, then you might have a belt slippage problem.

Chemicals

Painting the brake calipers, brake drums and suspension components will make the car look professional and appealing. You can also either paint the fuel tank or spray on a little Armor-all to keep it clean.

Water Wetter and Armor All are two indispensible products

If you spray a little Armor-all inside the boot and on the wire, the boot will slide easily over the spark plug wires. Dropping light oil on electrical connections helps with corrosion and keeps them clean.

Water Wetter in the cooling system and intercooler breaks down the capillary action of water, so it helps the water stick to the metal surface of the radiator and engine to increase heat transfer. It contains an anti-corrosion agent and mixes with antifreeze well (only street racers are allowed to use conventional antifreeze). Cost is approximately $8 a bottle.

For use at the track, there is a spray called Geddex Burnout Guard in which you apply to the back quarters of the car before burnouts. It is so much easier to clean the car afterward because the tire chunks wipe right off. Just hose the chunks off with water after your run.

Another track chemical tip is to use Dial In instead of shoe polish to write car numbers on the windows. It wipes off much easier.

Cleaners/Waxes

You never know when magazine photographers might want a picture of your vehicle and they don't pay much attention to dirty cars. A number of manufacturers make these products and for the most part, prices are reasonable allowing experimentation and comparison.

A pre-wax cleaner prepares paint for glazing or waxing by removing oxidation, dirt, stains and old wax. It restores the color and luster to paint. It can be applied to clear coat paints, lacquers, enamels, pearls, candies, urethanes and all other paint types.

A wide assortment of Mothers cleaners and waxes

A sealer/glazer fills and hides scratches, swirl marks and spider webbing. It will not streak, smear or finger-print and it can be used over existing wax.

Yellow carnauba wax is a very hard natural wax which is often compounded with other chemicals to allow greater ease in application. Remove the haze and enjoy the most spectacular shine you will ever experience.

Car wash formulations are pH balanced to protect the car's finish while washing away dirt, road film, bugs, bird droppings and other contaminants. They will not resist water spotting and remove wax. Dishwashing liquid and detergents can cause substantial damage to automotive finishes.

Clay bars incorporated with cleaning solutions are a recent addition to the chemical collection designed to remove paint damaging contaminants such as embedded metal particles, tree sap, paint over spray and haze.

Wheel cleaners come in many types; read the fine print carefully, because they are specifically designed for different wheel materials and finishes. A wrong choice here can permanently damage wheels.

Magnesium and aluminum polishes can be used on non-coated aluminum wheels, manifolds, valve covers, brass and other metals.

Chrome cleaners can be used on wheels, bumpers and other chrome accessories. They generally remove contaminants and rust, as well.

Leather cleaners soften and moisturize leather upholstery and other leather items such as clothing, luggage and other types of smooth leather. They may be used to clean vinyl, but they do not provide any softening or preservation to non-leather upholstery.

Carpet and upholstery cleaners remove dirt and stains from upholstery and carpet, including velour, vinyl and cloth. Convertible top cleaners are also available for both cloth and vinyl convertible and vinyl tops.

Oils/Synthetics

Synthetic Oil, like Mobil 1 and Amsoil, is manufactured from synthetic base stocks and special additives. Using it will better protect moving parts of the engine at lower engine temperatures, will cause less engine wear and allow easier cold weather starts. Synthetic oil reduces friction for quicker engine response and resists oxidation and thermal breakdown, common with petroleum based oils.

Be aware, though, that synthetic oils may not be compatible with engines that are not freshly rebuilt. If synthetics are tried in engines, which have previously been used with conventional motor oil, many times serious oil leaks will occur.

Race Fuel

Sometimes it is necessary to take several containers of race fuel when traveling out-of-state as some race tracks do not have the correct octane fuel or carry different brand names than what you are used to utilizing in your race car

The higher octane number of racing fuel increases the resistance to detonation during combustion. High-octane fuel burns slower, but it does not make the car go any faster. Actually, on cars that are stock, it could actually slow it down. Race fuel only reduces engine damaging detonation which occurs due to high compression and makes it safer to run. Buying a higher octane for a lower compression engine is simply wasting money.

Race fuel is available at most tracks with a variety of octane ratings. It is nearly always fresh, due to the volume that they sell. Some tracks even provide self service pumps that take credit cards, but expect to spend at least $5 per gallon. Buying race fuel from a known and reputable race shop or gas station can save some money, but be careful. Fuel will go stale when it starts to oxidize. It changes to a much darker brown, cloudy color and will not perform well. Most race fuels will stay fresh for six to twelve months, as long as it is stored properly. Do not place it in direct sunlight and never store your race fuel in light colored or white plastic containers.

This paintwork is a real show-stopper! Marc Dantoni's '41 Willys Pro Mod which is an NOS & EFI equipped 707-inch bullet from Pat Musi Racing Engines. Photo courtesy of Brian Wood.

Miscellaneous

Using an automatic transmission helps you to be more consistent. No more missed shifts; however, you might be a little bit slower. It is very important to change your fluid and filter quite frequently (maybe every few runs).

If you decide to paint your race car, pick a unique paint scheme. It is always interesting to go to the tracks and see what kind of wild murals show up on these tricked out race cars. Paint jobs do not come cheap. You must pay good money to get a top-quality, unique paint job.

Sponsorship

As you get more and more involved in racing, you will realize how expensive the sport is. Some racers are self-supporting and do not need to seek out sponsorship; however, most racers could use a little extra money and that is where sponsors come into play. Sponsorship is the fastest-growing form of marketing with billions spent on drag racing each year.

To get sponsorship, it is as simple as asking local and/or major companies to sponsor your racing effort. Whether it is free nitrous fills for a year, free or discounted parts, money, traveling expenses or anything else, offsetting your expenses is the key to the racer. Present your portfolio to the person in charge of marketing with the prospective company. Then, schedule an appointment to meet or speak with him. Take your race car/trailer, if possible.

Your portfolio should include the following items.

Desired Compensation: In other words, what you would like to get from the sponsor. You do not have to be entirely specific because this is something you can negotiate once you find they are interested in sponsoring you.

Photographs: A collection of large format color photos make a professional impression. Be sure to include trackside pictures, burn out or other action photos and a picture of you in your drivers uniform. It would also be advantageous to have at least one professional photograph of you with your race car, preferably with a few trophies.

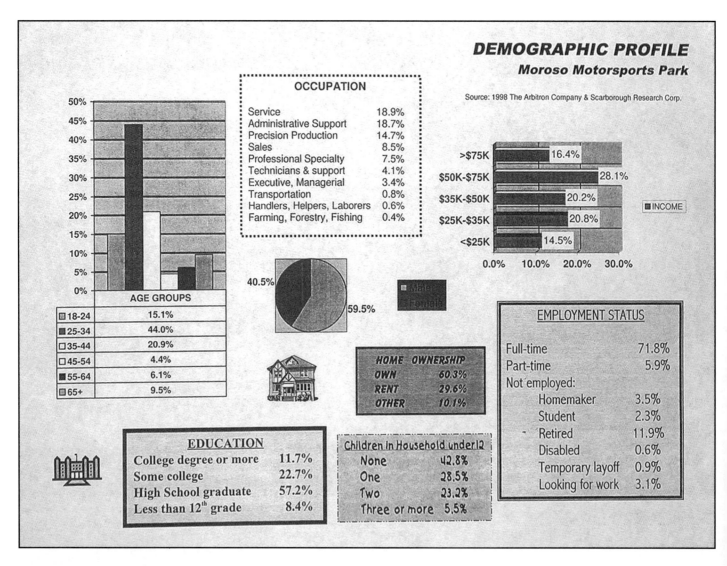

DEMOGRAPHIC PROFILE
Moroso Motorsports Park

Source: 1998 The Arbitron Company & Scarborough Research Corp.

OCCUPATION

Service	18.9%
Administrative Support	18.7%
Precision Production	14.7%
Sales	8.5%
Professional Specialty	7.5%
Technicians & support	4.1%
Executive, Managerial	3.4%
Transportation	0.8%
Handlers, Helpers, Laborers	0.6%
Farming, Forestry, Fishing	0.4%

INCOME

>$75K	16.4%
$50K-$75K	28.1%
$35K-$50K	20.2%
$25K-$35K	20.8%
<$25K	14.5%

AGE GROUPS

18-24	15.1%
25-34	44.0%
35-44	20.9%
45-54	4.4%
55-64	6.1%
65+	9.5%

Male 40.5% / Female 59.5%

HOME OWNERSHIP

OWN	60.3%
RENT	29.6%
OTHER	10.1%

EMPLOYMENT STATUS

Full-time	71.8%
Part-time	5.9%
Not employed:	
Homemaker	3.5%
Student	2.3%
Retired	11.9%
Disabled	0.6%
Temporary layoff	0.9%
Looking for work	3.1%

EDUCATION

College degree or more	11.7%
Some college	22.7%
High School graduate	57.2%
Less than 12th grade	8.4%

Children in Household under 12

None	42.8%
One	28.5%
Two	23.2%
Three or more	5.5%

Magazine/Newspaper Articles: Keep a scrapbook of anything that has been published about you and your race car. Some magazines will offer reprints or back issues, which will offer a professional look. At the very least utilize high quality photocopies or laser prints.

List all your winnings and trophies to your prospective sponsor

Track Demographics and Statistics: Track demographics include attendee gender, age, household income, education, marital status, household size, vehicle ownership and vehicle maintenance. This will show the company what type of people frequent the race track and some statistics to help in their decision making. You can ask tracks where you will be racing for a copy of these demographics and statistics for each year.

Event Schedules: List the locations and dates of all racing events you plan to attend for the upcoming year.

Awards/Trophies/Winnings: List any winnings you have received racing, including any monies, trophies, plaques and special awards.

Sponsors: List all of your sponsors, who they are and where they are located. Make sure their logos are visible in the photos of your car included in the portfolio.

Time slips: Include your best time slips which show great reaction times.

Vehicle specifications/modifications: List all modifications performed on your race car and any dyno sheets that are available.

Accomplishments/Goals: Include information about what has been accomplished for the present year and since you have been racing, what your goals have been, what goals you have attained to date, why they are important to you and what your future goals are.

Expenses for the year: Total up and itemize expenses for your racing season, including, travel expenses, fuel, meals, lodging, admissions, race fuel, nitrous refills, engine/transmission/chassis repairs and spending money.

What you will do for them: This is the most important area! You need to explain how sponsoring your car will help increase sales for their company. Explain how you will help promote their company, including their name and company logo on the car, mentioning their name in magazine articles and always recommending them to everyone. Their company, with banners or flags, can be displayed in the pits along with an area to showcase their business cards, products and brochures.

Terms of Agreement: Set your terms out on the table and, if possible, have a contract written up. That way, no one will be disappointed and there will be no disputes. Record how much money will be involved, how long this sponsorship will last and any other conditions.

When you receive sponsorships, you need to place all the companies names on your race car and trailer

Car shows are an excellent way to showcase your race car

Donations: Not everyone has a racing cause or a place they wish to donate their winnings to; however, if you donate your winnings, you may want to tell the company about this. I donate some of my winnings to the *Lupus Foundation of America*. Lupus is a chronic autoimmune disease which causes inflammation of various parts of the body. I, personally, struggle with Systemic Lupus Erythematosus and it is very rewarding to donate some of my winnings to them. I always carry an assortment of pamphlets and literature, while in the pits. Sponsors may be very interested if you are racing for a certain cause as they may have someone in their family or a friend who may be dealing with similar issues.

A portfolio looks more professional if the information is in a binder or multi-compartmented folder. Plan to present this to several companies and do not become discouraged when you are turned down. This is to be expected and there are always more companies to ask.

After landing a sponsor, proudly display their name and logo on the race car. Hopefully their marketing department can provide you with decals or artwork. Show them how pleased you are by presenting them with a plaque that was made up thanking them for their sponsorship, along with a picture of the race car on the plaque. These can be made at local trophy shops for $30 - $40.

If articles are written about you or if you are in appropriate public situations, always mention your sponsors. This is good advertising for their business and they will greatly appreciate it. Keep them up-to-date on your racing results, promotions and future race events on a weekly or monthly basis.

Keep all the promises you have made to these companies. For instance, if you did not totally fulfill your contractural obligations and missed a few races because of illness or mechanical problems, advise the company that you acknowledge this missed time and will make it up to them by giving them credit or some special accommodation.

Make sure you personally use all their products or services and always present a professional appearance and image to the companies. Remember you are marketing yourself. Any financial arrangement made between you and the company should remain confidential at all times.

Team uniforms give a sense of pride and professionalism. Photo courtesy Jackie Ling, UrbanRacer.com

Professional Racing Look

Many teams are very professional in appearance: wearing matching shirts, hats and pants with their logos and sponsor's names on them. This presents a favorable appearance for the fans and spectators. Many race teams have business cards made up and hand them out at the track and other social events. Team graphics are also incorporated on the race car, tow vehicle and trailer. Most have meticulously clean equipment and team members are encouraged to be outgoing and friendly to fans at the track or at shows where the car is displayed. Professionalism is really an attitude that has little to do with the amount of funding behind the effort.

Make up a professional web site of your racing team. My personal racing website is www.gocindy.com. I post a little bit about myself, my accomplishments, personal notes, and my racing sponsors and race crew. Included are my vehicle specifications, pictures and a message board. Stickers are made up of my web site address to hand out to racing friends and fans. This allows a little exposure to the race car and team, plus allows you to make many, many friends.

Tow Vehicles & Trailers

Driving your car to the local track is what most first time racers will prefer, but as time goes on it becomes more practical to consider buying a trailer and something to pull it. If you have a trailer, you can already have your slicks on the car and be race-ready when you arrive at the track, saving both time and effort. Since you never know when your race car will break, it also gives you a way to get home. If you do not have a trailer, always have enough money to be towed home if necessary.

The choices for tow vehicle and trailers range from a mid-size sedan with a single axle open trailer to an eighteen wheeler that requires a Commercial Drivers License (CDL) for operation. Something in the middle will satisfy most racers. Before making the decision of which suits you best, take a walk around the pits and talk to the teams about their rigs. Trailer regulations are not the same from state to state, so it is also a good idea to check with your local motor vehicle department or AAA.

Trailers: In many cases the trailer selection dictates the tow vehicle. Open or flat trailers can be pulled by anything from mid-sized cars and minivans to pickup trucks and SUVs. They are inexpensive and easy to maintain. Avoid single axle trailers and tandem axle trailers without brakes.

Also, pay careful attention to the ramps and deck height. Trailers with high decks require long ramps. If the ramp is not long enough the car can bottom out or *high center* during the loading process. To alleviate this, many trailers have a sloping area or *beaver tail* at the rear. These trailers can utilize much shorter ramps, which also makes loading more convenient.

Ramp mounting and storage are also important. In many cases ramps are stored externally or under the trailer and get covered with road grime, meaning you get dirty during loading and unloading. Tie down hardware is also susceptible to weather and road dirt, as is the race car, so that arrival at a distant track is often followed by a lengthy cleaning session.

Wiring and lights on open trailers are often exposed and vulnerable to damage. This is a problem that seems to be compounded if you loan your trailer to friends, or worse, friends of friends.

The positive features of open trailers, aside from low cost and flexibility of tow vehicle, include maneuverability, ease in backing and storage concerns.

Slummin it. Flat trailers are inexpensive and easy to maneuver. They are also easily stolen as was the one above belonging to this book's publisher

Enclosed trailers come in many shapes and sizes and are made from a variety of materials. Unless they are not weatherproof, your car (and tie down hardware) will arrive clean and ready to go. Most use a reinforced back door as a ramp, though the really fancy ones have rear mounted elevators, two levels for car storage, workshops or apartments.

Enclosed trailers also provide a secure location to keep your tools and other equipment. In addition, your car can be stored or worked on out of the weather. Depending on the trailer size, you can also bring all the comforts of home, picnic tables, grilles – even ATVs and golf carts, if the tracks allow them. Some new trailers are constructed from composite outer materials so that they do not have rivets on the exterior. This allows for easy application of your logos and graphics.

Smaller enclosed trailers can be pulled by the same tow vehicles used for flat trailers, but taller ones and ones with greater gross weight will require larger and more powerful haulers. Larger trailers are also awkward to maneuver and store. When traveling with a larger trailer, fuel and food stops will frequently be dictated by the length of the rig.

Dually with 24 foot tag along trailer. If you really get involved in the sport of racing, you will eventually need to purchase a truck and trailer

Enclosed trailers come in three basic types defined by their hitch configurations. Tag along trailers have a bumper level hitch behind the tow vehicle. There are three different hitches which are bumper, receiver and weight distributing types. The basic bumper hitch is rated at 5000 pounds. Receiver types are rated 2500 to 8000. With the receiver type, a weight distributing hitch can increase the towing capacity from 5000 to 12,000 pounds. Use of an anti-sway bar can reduce the trailer from fishtailing and the same with a weight equalizer (hitches that have equalizing devices). It allows for more stable steering and less rear end sagging.

If greater capacity is required, both gooseneck and fifth wheel hitches are rated at

Gooseneck hitch has little effect on the trucks utility. Some have a feature where the ball can be rotated under the bed surface

Tri-axle gooseneck trailer with hauler. Due to the height and weight of this size trailer, a dually or larger truck is required for on road stability, especially at highway speeds. Note air-conditioner on the forward roof of the trailer

10,000 to 30,000 pounds. These require pickup trucks (dually rear wheels highly advised for stability) or larger commercial grade trucks to pull them. The difference between these two higher capacity hitches is that the gooseneck uses a large trailer ball on the tow vehicle mounted at the mid-bed level of the pickup, while the fifth wheel has a greased mounting surface similar to a semi-tractor. The gooseneck hitch in a pickup truck allows normal use of the bed, but mounting the trailer can be time consuming due to the precision needed when dropping the trailer. The fifth wheel pretty much renders the truck bed useless, but it is much simpler to hook up the trailer than the gooseneck.

Tow Vehicles: In most cases the choice of tow vehicle initially is related to what you or a close relative or friend already owns. If it is not yours, it helps if this person has a keen interest in your new racing hobby. Sooner or later, though, it will be time to select what you think is the best vehicle for your situation. Again, walk around the pits and look at what other people use and ask the crews about their choices.

In many cases there will be a need to balance your trailer pulling needs with other family uses. SUVs and pickups tend to be popular choices. Not only do these vehicles fit in well at home, but they are also useful at the track for trips into town for replacement parts or food. Bigger trucks or motorhomes can be considerably less convenient trackside, but this is resolved if one of the crew drives separately. If your tow vehicle is in the pits, it must have the driver's competition number displayed on the vehicle.

Diesel trucks are a popular choice since they are long lived and economical to operate. Another way to help with the rising costs of fuel involves mounting a wing on the truck so air will rise over the top of the rig.

Make sure your trailer (and race car) weight is within the towing capacity of your tow vehicle. This can cause mechanical damage to the drivetrain and suspension and can also raise safety concerns if you are pulling too much weight. Duallies are safer for towing heavy loads like the enclosed trailers while single-wheel trucks are good for open trailers.

Trailer Use and Maintenance: Use safety chains, which are located on the front of the trailer. They should be hooked to the hitch, so that if the trailer comes off the tow vehicle, the chains will hold it. You should cross your safety chains at all times. If there is a breakaway box, make sure to clean the connections and check the grounds. If the trailer becomes unhitched from the tow vehicle, this box automatically locks up the trailer brakes.

Application of WD-40 on the trailer pin that plugs into your tow vehicle keeps it clean. Periodically check your trailer wiring for broken or damaged wires and repair them as needed.

Running and brake lights are very important, so other drivers can see you. When hooking up the trailer, check all the lights before you travel to make sure they are working correctly. Check your lights periodically through your trip also. Federal Regulations state that a series of red lights must be on the rear of trailers and yellow running lights along the front and sides.

Use reflective strips on both enclosed or open trailers. These strips should line the bottom area of the trailer on the rear and both sides of the trailer. This allows the trailer to be easily seen at night to help avoid accidents.

Reflective strips allow your trailer to be better seen at night for safety

Most trailers require specific trailer tires, not ordinary car tires, so it is wise to carry spares since these tires are often not readily available. Make sure to keep the proper air pressure in them. Check them occasionally on your trip. Don't forget to bring a jack and appropriate sized lug wrench in case roadside repairs are necessary.

The race car should be secured to the trailer properly with four tie downs, two for the front and two for the rear. It helps to have brackets installed on the car where the tie downs can be easily attached. Before each trip, make sure the tie downs are not worn or frayed and that the ratchets are working. You should also check your trailer tie downs shortly after leaving and at each fuel stop, to make sure they are still attached and tight.

Your trailer will not wander as much if you have greater weight at the front. When driving, watch your mirrors and look far ahead of you on the highway so you will be able to judge distances for lane changes and braking. Always brake much earlier than you would with driving a normal car, the extra weight means you will need more time to stop than normal. Be aware that many people will pull in front of you and create potentially dangerous situations, underestimating your vehicle's limitations. Always drive defensively.

Anti-Theft Devices

Theft is very common with expensive race cars and trailers. Thieves know that an substantial amount of money is tied up in these cars. Unless you have excellent records and a clear understanding with your insurance carrier, it is possible that a claim will not recover what the owner has invested in the car.

An electronic location device such as a Lo-Jack is the best way to recover a stolen vehicle and is the only universally accepted device of its kind. It is placed in an inconspicuous place in or under the car or trailer and when the car is stolen, the owner simply calls Lo-Jack and the police. Through their tracking abilities, they usually locate the car within an hour or two. This will not allow much time for the thief to take your car to a chop shop, which is a warehouse or shop that strips your car of all the *goodies*, and leave the bare shell. Cost of the Lo-Jack system is around $500.

Alarm systems that simply make an alarm noise are not sufficient. How many times have you heard alarms going off and ignored them? There are systems that have a pager feature which immediately informs the owner of the theft.

The Club and other steering wheel locking devices are also available. While they

The Club can be inexpensive insurance, protecting your car from being stolen

will not prevent a thief from stealing a car, they may not want to be *bothered* by the extra effort and leave it alone.

Kill switches are fantastic and will deter the would-be thief while trying to figure out where the switches are located. Consider two switches or even a starter switch. This is one of the lowest price anti-theft investments you can make.

Common Sense Strategies: Always remember to take the keys out of the ignition. This makes it pretty enticing for someone just thinking about stealing a car, including teenagers going for a joy ride. Park in highly visible areas, under a street light, or around a crowd of people. Do not park in underground garages or unlit parking lots.

Simply locking your doors is a minor deterrent, but is still helpful. Most thieves will carry a *slim jim*, which is a device used to break into cars. Locking your car will, however, add more time for the thief to get into the vehicle. As your car becomes more race than street, locking doors are often abandoned, but the theft risks are also enhanced by the car's obvious *look at me* appearance and noise level. Placing the car in a garage does not mean it is safe. Lock the door manually by pulling the release lever on the overhead door. Remove the battery if you will not be driving your car for a long period of time. You can also drain the fuel from the fuel cell or tank.

If the thief has a tow truck, make it harder for them to steal the car by turning the steering wheel to full lock with the wheels to the extreme right or left.

Do not keep registration, insurance information and title inside the vehicle. This will give the thief unnecessary information about you and the vehicle. You will also need to have this information to inform the police about your stolen vehicle. Carry around in your purse or wallet all relevant information about your vehicle, so in case it is stolen, you will have it on hand at a moment's notice.

Remember a thief can and will go to any length to take a car. All you can really do is slow down the process and make things very difficult for them to buy some time for them to get caught. It is possible that the thief will become so frustrated that they will leave your car alone and give up. Remember, though, virtually nothing can stop a professional car thief.

Driver Prep

Driver Aids

Portable Christmas Tree: At a race shop buy a handheld portable Christmas Tree practice light. For a couple hundred dollars you can practice your reaction times for hours on end. Program it for 0.400 (Pro Tree) or 0.500 (Sportsman Tree) and also use the transbrake button, gas pedal or clutch. It will also average your reaction times automatically. Remember, most races are won or lost at the light. Plus, it is actually fun to play with this device with your friends and/or racing buddies.

NHRA Rule Book: Pick up, read and keep on hand a NHRA and IHRA rule book. These are available at the tower at your local race track for $10.

Auto Mechanics: It never hurts to take a basic course in auto mechanics. It sure helps keep costs down if you can do some of the work yourself. However, race shop mechanics/engineers are trained and are very knowledgeable when it comes to engine installation and engine modifications.

Competition License

Drivers running 9.99 or quicker will need a valid competition license. First, you will need to pass a physical examination and driving test. This license is valid for two years and expires on the anniversary of the physical examination.

The driving test consists of completion of two 1/8 mile passes and one 100 feet pass, followed by completion of one 1000 feet pass and two 1/4 mile passes. At this point you can send in your license application listing your runs to NHRA. Your competition license will arrive by return mail.

Professional Training

If you have the opportunity and the money, attend a drag racing school. Top drivers attend these schools to brush up on their racing skills. You could greatly benefit from them.

Frank Hawley's Drag Racing School is without question the oldest and most respected school on the planet. Frank has won two Nitro Funny Car World Championships and numerous National Event titles in Top Fuel Dragster. Frank started racing when he was 16 years old and it has been his life ever since. He started his school in 1985 in Gainesville, Florida and in 1996 opened a second location in Pomona, California. More than 10,000 sportsman and professional racers and race fans have chosen Frank's Drag Racing School. He has a staff of seasoned racers who are very good at what they do.

There are a few other schools that have opened up since then. You can search the web for more information depending on where you live. Some drag race enthusiasts would rather wrench than drive. Frank Hawley also offers a Race Tech Program centered around his Alcohol Dragster and Funny Car classes to prepare someone for an entry level position on a race team.

Students range from 16-80 years of age. The experience level ranges from someone who has never seen a race to current Top Fuel competitors. Novice racers attend to live a long time dream of driving a race car either as a one-time event or to prepare to start racing. Age, gender, physical size or strength are not factors. Almost anyone can drag race.

Drag racing is much more a mental sport than a physical one. Veteran racers usually attend schools to learn mental programming and focusing techniques to make better decisions and cut a better light off the starting line. They teach you the importance of visualization, dealing with your unconscious mind and practice techniques. There are thought provoking classroom sessions on psychology and physiology.

Many top drag racers return to fine tune their racing skills and keep on top of things. It is always possible to return to drag racing school again and again to perfect technique and skill. Most racers realize the tremendous value in attending a drag racing school. Proper training will help you to become a safer, more confident and more competitive driver.

Not only do they discuss the way to have the confidence needed to race and to win, they teach the skills to have patience and not be overwhelmed or nervous when it comes to making a run. They demonstrate how to visualize and concentrate; not to worry about the competitor in the other lane.

They teach necessary driving skills which can help utilize the full potential of the car, including control mechanisms such as transbrake, two-step, line lock, etc. and they make it fun and entertaining. Individual instruction is given on all facets of training. The drag racing school will provide all the necessary equipment needed and makes sure the car provided is completely race ready and safe.

Students are given hands-on experience and step-by-step instruction. Everything from getting into the car and strapping in, to proper braking in the shutdown area. These schools will help you learn the skills to become a very talented and winning drag racer.

I was given the opportunity to attend the Frank Hawley two-day classroom school and it was quite an experience. This class was the Super Comp Gas Dragster and Super Gas class. Before class, the students were sent a Gas Course Manual to review so they would have some knowledge of what

Classroom instruction is a very important part of any racing school. Not only are the hardware and physics of racing explained, but also the psychology of the sport

to expect. We started at 7:30 am with five students. Frank started out with introductions and went straight into talking about what to expect from his school, to the steps of how to strap into these fast race cars.

From there the students were fitted with their safety equipment: racing jackets, pants, head sock, helmet, neck brace, gloves and arm restraints for the drivers of the dragster. The instructors taught the students how to strap into the race car or dragster. They were given a blindfold test to make sure they were acclimated to all the controls in the cars. The students were strapped in one-by-one. Each would perform a burnout, run to the 200 foot mark and drive back to the staging lanes.

The equipment room provides racing apparel for students who do not yet have their own

Once all of the students had taken a run down the track we would go back to the classroom and Frank would critique the runs which were videotaped. Once the students learned from their mistakes and were praised for their accomplishments, it was back out to the track. If the students succeeded in running the 200 foot mark then they would proceed to the 600 foot mark, then back to the classroom to critique and learn from these runs.

In our case the rain started falling mid-afternoon which quashed the final run for the day. Frank was prepared to handle anything, even an untimely rain storm, so we stayed in the classroom to receive additional information. Much to my surprise, Frank did not speak about racing as a whole. He taught about mental preparedness, visualization techniques and the importance of rehearsing the steps over and over again to make it permanent in your unconscious mind. He related many important issues of human behavior, visualization and techniques to use.

Out of the classroom and onto the track to get a closer view. Frank explains the procedures for the cones and what you are supposed to do while driving these cars

The second day we went back into the classroom for more discussions. Frank is an excellent motivational speaker and interacts very well with his students. He gave the students a lot of pertinent information to use on and off the track, detailing information on the chalkboard to illustrate what subject he was speaking about and citing examples in his own personal life.

The students completed all their runs on the second day. At the completion of the program, two of the students received competition licenses.

In my class, each student who attended was thrilled with the school and mesmerized by Frank's speaking ability. There are a number of other options available at the school.

Super Comp Dragster and Super Gas Pontiac Firebird - The most popular of Frank's course offerings is the 2-day licensing course for Super Comp Dragsters or Super Gas bodied cars. They provide an outstanding training curriculum which includes safety procedures, driving procedures, timing systems, mental preparation and reaction time. They provide all of the driving equipment and, of course, the race cars.

The Super Comp Gas Dragster has an McKinney Corp Chassis, 229 inch wheel base, weighs 1550 pounds and will run 8 second elapsed times at about 155 mph. The Super Gas Pontiac Firebird has a Chassis Engineering chassis, 106 inch wheel base, weighs 2300 pounds and will run mid 9 second elapsed times at about 145 mph. The Super Comp/Super Gas Class rates are $1795.

All programs include classroom instruction, safety discussions, runs down the track and video reviews to critique your runs. You will learn basic techniques and procedures on how to deal with the mental challenges.

Two Super Comp Dragsters and Super Gas Pontiac Firebird school cars

After each run, session drivers go back to the classroom to review the runs. Your instructor will help you to improve your driving skills with each run.

The school cars are built with adjustable controls and can accommodate most any size driver from 100 to 300 lbs. There are some limitations.

During the two day class, each driver will make six runs. Additional runs are available on a pay per run basis. If you drive well and complete the required runs mandated by the National Hot Rod Association, you will earn your NHRA Competition License.

Frank has developed a system to teach a lot during the two day class and more than 10,000 graduates will tell you it works. Earning an NHRA competition license is a very attainable goal for most students. If you want to try to earn it, you will need an NHRA physical form completed by your physician. Completion of one 1/8th mile pass, three moderate runs, and 2 full 1/4 mile passes. Then send in your license form, medical and original time slips to NHRA. Your competition license will arrive in the mail.

Frank offers graduate races and race car rentals for licensed graduates.

Bring Your Own Car - You can take the same two day course in your own race car. You can bring your own car and your own safety equipment (drivers uniform) if you prefer. The Bring Your Own Car class rates are $895.

Saturday Night Special Bracket Racing - Once you are a licensed graduate you can continue your training at an actual race. You can rent a dragster and a crew chief. The only thing you need to do is drive the car, the crew chief will help you learn to dial the car. He will coach you through everything and make sure you and the car are ready when they call you to the staging lanes.

Adventure Program - Adventure programs are offered as a very inexpensive way to get into a dragster. The cars are slowed down some which is a good thing. A half day program is only $139 and a full day is $398.

Super Ride - You can let one of the professional drivers take you for the *thrill of a lifetime* ride full throttle to the 1/8th mile mark in a 700 horsepower car. This super ride costs $99.

Corporate Programs - The school also provides corporate group programs to provide you the opportunity to offer your prospective customers and clients the thrill of driving a race car.

Race Tech Training Program - In this class you will work side by side with NHRA National Event winning mechanics and drivers in their race shop. You will assemble a Top Alcohol Funny Car or Top Alcohol Dragster from the ground up. Then you take this car to the track and race it. You will perform maintenance between rounds and prepare for the next round. The experience you will receive from this class is incredible.

Alcohol Dragster and Alcohol Funny Car - Frank Hawley offers two day licensing courses for Alcohol Dragster and Alcohol Funny Car. The Alcohol courses are considered advanced courses. Racing experience is strongly recommended or you can prepare for an alcohol course by attending a Super Comp course first. The Alcohol Dragster and Alcohol Funny Car course is $4995.

Pro Stock Motorcycle - Frank offers this Pro Stock Motorcycle two day licensing course. This is considered an advanced course. You will learn to ride and race 7-second motorcycles with 250 horsepower 4-valve Suzukis. Prior racing experience is strongly recommended. The Pro Stock Bike course is $1995.

Please note that these course descriptions and prices were current at the time of publication and are subject to change. Legal Requirements include, a parental consent form for students 16 –18 years of age, a valid driver's license for Adventure Programs and an NHRA physical for licensing classes only. Additional infomation can be obtained from: Frank Hawley Drag Racing School, PO Box 484, La Verne, California 91750, by calling 888-901-7223 or the website: www.frankhawley.com.

Attitude

Racers are certainly a different breed of people. They love to thrill an audience; they dare to stand out from the crowd. Think of all the positive things you can do as a racer to help the community, fellow racers and spectators. You can not only make differences in your life, but also in the lives of others. You have the abilities and powers deep inside you to give a positive outlook on life as a whole to others that view you.

Children look up to drag racers as role models. Let young fans sit in your race car. Have your picture taken with them. Let them know that they can do anything they put their minds to.

Respect yourself and treat others with respect, especially your opponent. Treat your body well, do not get into drugs, alcohol or cigarettes. Always present a respectable and professional appearance on the track and off, so people and children will admire you. Take responsibility for your actions, never be untruthful, and always act with class and dignity. Walk with your head high, be proud of what you do, and try to be a good example to everyone.

Always be willing to help others less fortunate in your community and at the track. Raise monies for charities that you believe in; donate your winnings to a special group or foundation for a special cause. Be a good, honest, respectable person. Value your friends and treat them well. Be a good listener and look at people when they are talking to you. Give them your full attention. Always be there to lend a helping hand to someone in need. Comfort and lend an ear when they are hurting inside.

Take time to learn by reading about drag racing, talking to people, and learning automotive technology. Do whatever you can to enhance all your skills and better yourself in any way possible. Dedicate your life to being the best possible person you can be.

Learn from your mistakes but do not dwell on them. As long as you learn something from them, then it is not a total loss. Every day at the track plan to learn something new.

Losing with dignity and maturity makes you a winner every time. Lose gracefully. Always congratulate the winner of the race. Be happy for them and their abilities. Realize that you tried your best.

Be humane, sincere and compassionate. Compliment others and use kind words. Never gossip or talk badly about anyone behind their backs, especially other teams; this makes you look and feel very bad. Appreciate people for who they are. It is okay to be scared at a race or nervous, it is a common reaction. People like to see that you are a normal human being and have feelings, just like everyone else.

Racers are one big family - always thinking of a fellow team member

Set goals and challenge yourself on a daily basis. Figure out how you will go about attaining them. Do not make such a huge goal that it is too hard to obtain. Take baby steps, that is, small steps that lead to higher goals. Remember, anything is possible if you put your mind to it. Dreams can come true especially when you have a positive outlook on life!

Take all these qualities to the track with you at all times and live your life abiding by them. Be a law-abiding citizen and be a great American. Be patriotic, love your country, and cherish family values and traditions.

At the Track

This section will provide familiarization with the track facilities and surroundings. This is basic information for novice racers or anyone wanting to learn all about the racing facility. It will help acclimatize you when arriving at the race track.

Entrant's Gate/Ticket Counter

When arriving at the track, there will probably be a long line at the entrance. At the front of this line there is the ticket counter, where racing fees are paid and a tech/waiver sheet is given out.

This tech sheet needs to be filled out by the driver and has a place for a signature at the bottom. This is an agreement/waiver that states that if injury occurs at the track, the track owners are not responsible. The tech sheet includes areas for name, address, age, phone number, work number and racing class.

Tech

After filling out the tech sheet, next up is the tech line. Officials from the drag race sanctioning association inspect the car to see if it meets all the safety requirements. A racing number is assigned, if one is not present on the car, and the racing class is assigned. Have your competition license and chassis certification numbers on the tech sheet, if required. This will make the tech inspector's job much easier. Always have your safety equipment up-to-date. A sample inspection sheet is on page 44.

The ticket counter where you pay to spectate or race is located at the entrance gate of the track. This is where you receive your tech/waiver sheet

ETI Serial Number _____ ETI Expiration _____

Driver _____ E.T. Limit _____ MPH Limit _____

Vehicle Year _____ Make/Model _____

SFI Inspector _____ SFI No. _____ Inspection Date _____

1:1 COOLING SYSTEM
1:2 ENGINE
Harmonic Balancer SFI Spec. 18.1
Manf. _____ Ser. # _____
1:3 EXHAUST
1:4 FLASH SHIELD
1:5 FUEL SYSTEMS
1:6 RACING GASOLINE
1:7 LIQUID OVERFLOW
1:8 METHANOL
1:9 NITROUS OXIDE
1:10 OIL SYSTEM
1:12 SUPERCHARGER
1:13 SUPERCHARGER RESTRAINT DEVICE
SFI Spec. _____ Manf. _____ Exp. Date _____
1:14 THROTTLE
1:15 VENT TUBES, BREATHERS
2:1 ANTI-BLOWBACK DEVICE
2:2 AXLE-RETENTION DEVICES
2:3 CLUTCH
SFI Spec. _____ Manf. _____ Exp. Date _____
2:4 DRIVELINE
2:5 FLYWHEEL
SFI Spec. _____ Manf. _____ Exp. Date _____
2:6-10 FLYWHEEL SHIELD
SFI Spec. _____ Manf. _____ Exp. Date _____
2:11 REAREND
2:12 TRANSMISSION
SFI Spec. _____ Manf. _____ Exp. Date _____
2:13 TRANSMISSION
Type _____
Neutral Safety Switch
Reverse Lockout
TRANSMISSION SHIELD
SFI Spec. 4.1 Manf. _____ Exp. Date _____

2:14 TRANSMISSION, Automatic
FLEXPLATE
SFI Spec. 29.1 Manf. _____ Exp. Date _____
FLEXPLATE SHIELD
SFI Spec. 30.1 Manf. _____ Exp. Date _____
Ser. # _____
3:1 BRAKES
3:2 SHOCKS
3:3 STEERING
3:4 SUSPENSION
3:5 TRACTION BAR ROD ENDS
3:6 WHEELIE BARS
4:1 ALIGNMENT
4:2 BALLAST
4:3 DEFLECTOR PLATE
4:4 FRAME
Chassis Spec. _____ Serial # _____ Exp. Date _____
4:5 GROUND CLEARANCE
4:7 MOUNTING HARDWARE
4:8 PARACHUTES
4:9 PINION SUPPORT
4:10 ROLL BARS
4:11 ROLL CAGE
4:12 WHEELBASE _____ IN.
5:1 TIRES
5:2 WHEELS
6:1 DRIVER COMPARTMENT
6:2 UPHOLSTERY, Seats
6:3 WINDOW NET
SFI Spec. _____ Manf. _____ Exp. Date _____
7:1 ADVERTISING
7:2 AIRFOILS, WINGS
7:3 COMPETITION NUMBERS
7:4 FENDERS
7:6 FLOORS
7:7 HOOD SCOOP
7:8 WINDSCREEN
7:9 WINDSHIELD
8:1 BATTERIES
8:2 DELAY BOXES/DEVICES

8:3 IGNITION
8:4 MASTER CUTOFF
8:5 STARTER
8:6 TAILLIGHTS
8:7 SWITCHES & BUTTONS
9:1 COMPUTER
9:2 DATA RECORDERS
9:2a TELEMETRY DEVICES
9:3 FIRE EXTINGUISHER
9:4 JACKS & STANDS
9:5 LIFTING DEVICES
9:7 PRESSURIZED BOTTLES
10:1 APPAREL
10:2 APPEARANCE
10:3 ARM RESTRAINTS
Manf. _____ Ser. # _____
10:4 CREDENTIALS
Category _____ Code _____ Number _____ Exp. Date _____
STATE DR. LICENSE (10.00/6.40 & slower)
Lic# _____
10:4a NHRA MEMBERSHIP
Memb # _____
10:5 DRIVER RESTRAINT SYSTEMS
SFI Spec. 16.1 Manf. _____ Exp. Date _____
10:6 HEAD PROTECTOR
Ser. # _____
10:7 HELMET/GOGGLES
Snell/SFI Spec. _____ Manf. _____ Exp. Date _____
10:8 NECK COLLAR
SFI Spec. 3.3 Manf. _____
10:10 PROTECTIVE CLOTHING
HEAD SOCK SFI Spec. 3.3
JACKET Manufacturer _____
PANTS Manufacturer _____
SFI Spec. _____
GLOVES Manufacturer _____
SFI Spec. _____
BOOTS/SHOES Manufacturer _____
SFI Spec. _____
10:11 SEAT BELTS
SFI Spec. _____

Extended Tech Sheet

VEHICLE INSPECTION CLASSIFICATION FORM
PLEASE PRINT - FILL OUT COMPLETELY

MOROSO MOTORSPORTS PARK
THE PALM BEACHES OF FLORIDA

Number	Class

Driver _____ Date _____

Street _____

City _____ State _____ Zip _____

Home # _____ Work # _____ **E-mail** _____

Social Security # _____ State Driver's License # _____

Employed by: _____ Occupation _____ Age _____

Year & Make of Car _____ Make of Engine _____ No. of Cyl _____ C.I. _____

Check the following if applicable and O.K.

_____ Belts	_____ License Expires
_____ Belt Expires	_____ Jacket/Pants
_____ Balancer	_____ Helmet 90-95-2000
_____ Trans Shield	_____ Gloves
_____ Flex Plate Shield	_____ Neck Collar

Notable Facts/Announcements/Sponsors _____

_____
_____
_____
_____
_____
_____

Inspected and Approved By _____

ENTRY & ADVERTISING RELEASE: In consideration of this entry, vehicle owner and spouse or guests permit Moroso Motorsports Park, Inc. the use of their names, pictures, and pictures of their vehicles, for publicity, advertising and commercial purposes without limitation before, during, and after the event, and do hereby relinquish any rights whatsoever to any photos taken in connection with the event, and give permission to publish and sell or otherwise dispose of said photographs to Moroso Motorsports Park, Inc.

Signature _____

Number

_____   _____
Description and Location of Scheduled Event(s)   Date Release Signed

IN CONSIDERATION of being permitted to compete, officiate, observe, work for, or participate in any way in the EVENT(S) or being permitted to enter for any purpose any RESTRICTED AREA (defined as the advance staging area, burn out area, competition area, shutdown area, staging lanes, return road area, and any other area within the barriers, fences, and/or structures separating the general public from racing activities), EACH OF THE UNDERSIGNED, for himself/herself, his/her personal representatives, heirs, and next of kin:

1. Acknowledges, agrees, and represents that he/she has or will immediately upon entering any of such RESTRICTED AREAS, and will continuously thereafter, inspect the RESTRICTED AREAS which he/she enters and he/she further agrees and warrants that, if at any time, he/she is in or about RESTRICTED AREAS and he/she feels anything to be unsafe, he/she will immediately advise the officials of such and will leave the RESTRICTED AREA and/or refuse to participate further in the EVENT(S).

2. HEREBY RELEASES, WAIVES, DISCHARGES AND COVENANTS NOT TO SUE the promoters, participants, racing associations, sanctioning organizations or any subdivision thereof, track operators, track owners, officials, car owners, drivers, pit crews, rescue personnel, any persons in any RESTRICTED AREA, promoters, sponsors, advertisers, owners and lessees of premises used to conduct the EVENT(S), premises and event inspectors, surveyors, underwriters, consultants and others who give recommendations, directions, or instructions or engage in risk evaluation or loss control activities regarding the premises or EVENT(S) and each of them, their directors, officers, agents and employees, all for the purposes herein referred to as "Releasees", FROM ALL LIABILITY TO THE UNDERSIGNED, his/her personal representatives, assigns, heirs, and next of kin FOR ANY AND ALL LOSS OR DAMAGE, AND ANY CLAIM OR DEMANDS THEREFORE ON ACCOUNT OF INJURY TO THE PERSON OR PROPERTY OR RESULTING IN DEATH OF THE UNDERSIGNED ARISING OUT OF OR RELATED TO THE EVENT(S), WHETHER CAUSED BY THE NEGLIGENCE OF THE RELEASEES OR OTHERWISE.

3. HEREBY AGREES TO INDEMNIFY AND SAVE AND HOLD HARMLESS the Releasees and each of them FROM ANY LOSS, LIABILITY, DAMAGE, OR COST they may incur arising out of or related to the EVENT(S) WHETHER CAUSED BY THE NEGLIGENCE OF THE RELEASEES OR OTHERWISE.

4. HEREBY ASSUMES FULL RESPONSIBILITY FOR ANY RISK OF BODILY INJURY, DEATH OR PROPERTY DAMAGE arising out of or related to the EVENT(S) whether caused by the NEGLIGENCE OF RELEASEES or otherwise.

5. HEREBY acknowledges that THE ACTIVITIES OF THE EVENT(S) ARE VERY DANGEROUS and involve the risk of serious injury and/or death and/or property damage. Each of THE UNDERSIGNED also expressly acknowledges that INJURIES RECEIVED MAY BE COMPOUNDED OR INCREASED BY NEGLIGENT RESCUE OPERATIONS OR PROCEDURES OF THE RELEASEES.

6. HEREBY agrees that this Release and Waiver of Liability, Assumption of Risk and Indemnity Agreement extends to all acts of negligence by the Releasees, INCLUDING NEGLIGENT RESCUE OPERATIONS and is intended to be as broad and inclusive as is permitted by the laws of the Province or State in which the Event(s) is/are conducted and that if any portion thereof is held invalid, it is agreed that the balance shall, notwithstanding, continue in full legal force and effect.

I HAVE READ THIS RELEASE AND WAIVER OF LIABILITY, ASSUMPTION OF RISK AND INDEMNITY AGREEMENT, FULLY UNDERSTAND ITS TERMS, UNDERSTAND THAT I HAVE GIVEN UP SUBSTANTIAL RIGHTS BY SIGNING IT, AND HAVE SIGNED IT FREELY AND VOLUNTARILY WITHOUT ANY INDUCEMENT, ASSURANCE, OR GUARANTEE BEING MADE TO ME AND INTEND MY SIGNATURE TO BE A COMPLETE AND UNCONDITIONAL RELEASE OF ALL LIABILITY TO THE GREATEST ALLOWED BY LAW.

PRINT NAME	SIGN NAME HERE	PRINT NAME	SIGN NAME HERE

Vehicle Inspection Classification and Waiver

Cindy Crawford
Tech Inspection

Harmonic Balancer
SFI SPEC 18.1
S/N C5320
PIN 0245
A170466

Bellhousing
SFI SPEC 30.1

Transshield
SFI SPEC 4.1

Flexplate
SFI SPEC 29.1

RCI Racing Harness 5 way system
SFI 16.1/ manufactured 10/99

Roll Cage
Certified /

Tires
Metal valve stems
Long studs

Window net
Fuel Safety Switch – Push off label
Radiator catch overflow
Driveshaft loop

**SFI approved Shoei Helmet, snell rating, Model RF-8000
Serial #BA478683, manufactured 6/98, Model W-I**

SFI approved pants, MTO 22, SFI 3-2A/5, S51574

This laminated sheet of paper lists all safety equipment and necessary SFI ratings, serial and model numbers

Permanent racing numbers should be placed on your car

At major meets, this tech line can be very long and waits can be several hours. Before getting into line always make sure that all your necessary safety clothing and equipment is present and the tech card is filled out in its entirety. Samples of the Vehicle Inspection Classification Form and a Release and Waiver of Liability are shown on page 45.

To make the tech inspector's job a little easier, carry a laminated sheet of paper with all of the safety equipment listed. This list will include all of the mandatory safety equipment, SFI ratings, serial and model numbers and date of manufacture. Keep this paper in the glove box of the car at all times. Also, keep it on file in your computer, so it can be updated as needed.

Make sure you have a permanent racing number or dial-in number on your window, along with your class and car number. The tech inspectors will use white shoe polish to mark the car's class on the windshield. It is also necessary to clearly mark NOS (Nitrous Oxide Systems) on your back window when utilizing nitrous at certain tracks.

Do not tell the tech inspector that your car is slower than it really is. They check your safety equipment based on the speed your car is capable of.

Be respectful of and never argue with tech inspectors. They are doing their job and do not want to see anyone hurt from faulty or missing safety equipment. If proper equipment is not there, you will not race. However, once you are told what you need or what is defective, head to the pits and try to rectify the problem. Get back in the tech line once changes are made and go through tech again.

At most tracks, they are now including extended tech inspection. This was set up by NHRA so that the drivers who participate on a regular basis in the same car need only be teched once a year, or on an *as needed* basis. This is something new and is quite advantageous to racers. There is a lengthy inspection form to be filled out. However, once you pass through tech, you will receive a serialized NHRA ETI sticker for that car. It will be good until one or more of the inspected items expire. This saves a great deal of time and aggravation waiting in the long tech lines. It costs nothing additional for NHRA members. Forms are available from tech inspectors at most tracks.

Scales/Weigh-In

Certain heads-up classes require cars to be weighed. There will be a weigh-in area where the car can be driven on a scale. The scale gives the combined weight of car and driver. Certain classes have weight restrictions and it is necessary to abide by them or inspectors will not allow cars in violation to race.

Pits

After tech, go to the pits and inspect and prepare your car for racing. Change your tires if you are switching over to slicks, and check everything on your car to make sure it is race-ready. The pits are where the driver and crew perform any required car preparations. In the pits, one can change tires, change spark plugs, check timing, replace transmissions and perform any other necessary work on the car. A lot of frantic engine work goes on in the pits between races and it can be quite a hectic place.

Always pit in a comfortable place, whether it be close to the staging lanes, close to the restrooms, close to the public address system, close to friends, away from the noise of the generators or other preferences. Once a place is staked out, it is usually not possible to move because by then the pits will be packed with other racers setting up their own areas. Many people bring campers, trailers, barbeque grilles, tents, generators and canvasses for cover, to allow them to be as comfortable and relaxed as possible.

If you do not have a lockable trailer, it is a good idea to pit adjacent to a fence. This allows valuables, tools etc. to be attached to the fence using a cable and lock when the car is in line waiting to run or be teched. This can be avoided if someone stays to watch over the area, but then they miss the action. If your tow vehicle is in the pits, you must display the driver's competition number on it.

Some people even stay in the pits over night if they have properly equipped campers, motorhomes or pop-up tents. Most people, however, head to their motels after the race, leaving their race car and trailers at the track, so that they do not have to lug them all around town.

The pits is a great place to glimpse a favorite driver or favorite crew chief and say hello. Take pictures of your favorite cars up close and maybe get autographs of

Scales are located at all tracks in order to make sure your car is within the necessary weight limits to run a particular class. Some cars are weighed after each run down the track

Some tracks carry race fuel, but not all tracks will carry the correct octane that your car requires

The pit area takes on the character of a tent city for the weekend activities

Staging towers come in all sizes and shapes throughout the country

There can be as many as 150 cars in each staging lanes at some point

Mike Murillo performing a burn out in his Texas Jam Mustang.
Photo courtesy Andrew M. Wood/Icecold Images

your favorite drivers. It is also a meeting place for representatives of big companies, manufacturers, major car owners, potential sponsors, magazine/newspaper editors and television crews.

Wait in the pits until they call your class. When they call your class, make sure your car is ready, that you have all your necessary safety equipment and head to the proper staging lanes.

Staging/Control Tower/Timing Tower

The announcers and track officials sit upstairs in a tall building directly over the burn out box (where drivers clean debris off their tires and heat them up). They get a bird's eye view of the track, while they announce what class and who is racing. In the big racing events, they may also give a little background on the individual driving the race car, name some of their sponsors and may throw in additional comments.

The results of each race are relayed from the control tower to the timing shack where the time slips are picked up. The announcer has this information and gives the crowd the name of the winner, the elapsed time and the top speed.

They also make sure that the track is clear and safe for the racers. They do not allow any cars to stage on the line, if there is trouble down at the end of the track. They closely monitor the track to make sure it is free of debris, that the last racer is completely off the track and that no animals have wandered onto the track.

Staging Lanes

The staging lanes are where drivers line up with other racers who are in the same class. The announcer will call each class over the loudspeaker when it is time to line up.

Drivers in the staging lanes should always stay with their car so they do not block other racers. When the starter calls the class onto the track, each car will slowly inch up until it is finally time to race. Sometimes drivers can be in line for hours.

Burn Out Box

A burn out is a process of spinning the rear tires. This makes the tires hotter and thus stickier for better traction. It also cleans any debris off the tires picked up in the pits or staging lanes.

The burn out box is at the end of each staging

lane. Here you do a burn out by placing your rear tires in the liquid traction compound (VHT) and/or powdered rosin (gold dust) or water, which is poured on the ground. Unlike pro drag racing, burn outs do not consist of trips across the starting line and part way down the track.

Staging Area

After the burn out, the drivers *bump* or inch up very slowly to the beam that activates the Christmas Tree. This is called the staging area and is immediately before the starting line.

Christmas Tree

This is an electronic light system with photo-electric beams set up between the two driver's lanes and is twenty feet beyond the starting line. It is activated when the drivers *stage* their vehicles. First is a *Pre-Stage* indicator light, which is yellow and warns that you are getting close to the starting line. It lights when the front wheels cross over the beam of light. Second is the *Stage* bulb, which is also yellow and is illuminated when the front wheels cross a second beam closer to the start line. When it is lit, you are in the location to start the race. When the car leaves this beam at the start it triggers the timer which records the run.

The Christmas Tree is where the race begins. It is controlled by an electronic light system that is activated as drivers stage their vehicles

There are three more amber or countdown lights; however, they can be used in two different ways. A Pro Tree light has a .400 second difference between the amber and green lights and flashes all three amber lights simultaneously. A Sportsman Tree or .500 light means that it flashes one light down at a time with .500 difference between the last amber light and the green light.

The green light is the start light. Most drivers have their car in motion before the green light comes on and try to leave when the last amber light goes off.

A final light is a red light and it is only activated if the driver takes off from the line prematurely, before the green light is activated. This results in disqualification and loss in that round.

Drag Strip

The drag strip begins at the *Christmas Tree* staging area and ends at the *traps* at the far end of the track. The drag strip is a straight paved track used for drag racing.

The most popular drag strip is usually a one-fourth (1/4) mile track which is 1320 feet in length. A 1/4 mile is the equivalent to the length of four football fields laid end-to-end. There are also one-eighth (1/8) mile mini-drag strips, which are 660 feet in length.

Close up view of the Christmas Tree

Beyond the finish line, is a shut down area which is an extended road or sand trap at the end of the drag strip to allow fast cars to safely slow down.

The time that it takes to get from start to finish lines on the drag strip is called the *elapsed time* or *ET*.

Traps

Traps are electronically timed speed zones on each side of the finish line. They consist of an area between two light beams at the end of the drag strip. The two beams are spaced 66 feet apart.

Once you pass through the second of these light beams, it will stop the ET clock and it will display your ET on the scoreboard. The time between the breaking of the first and second beams is used to calculate the speed at the finish line, where the second beam is located.

Traps are located at the end of the track where you begin to slow down after the race. The scoreboard at the traps displays your times. Photo courtesy Rich Barry

Shutdown Area

The shutdown area is after the finish line where drivers safely slow down the vehicle. It is at least a quarter-mile in length and most tracks have a sand trap or field at the end of this road to safely stop you in case of brake failure, stuck throttle or if the parachute does not engage properly. Always try to get off the track as quickly as possible to avoid the following cars.

After your race you will pick up your time slip from the timing shack located on the return road

Return Road

This is the road you return on after making a run down the track and through the traps. It is important to obey the 15 mph speed limit on the return road for the driver's safety and the safety of others. This is also the same speed limit in the pits. This is strictly enforced and you could be ejected from the track if you do not comply.

After racing down the track and making the trip back on the return road, there will be a timing shack to the left-hand side of the road. When the racers break the photoelectric beam at the finish line, the information is flashed electronically to the control tower back at the starting line. The control tower informs the timing shack of your time. The driver collects the time slip at this location.

Spectators/Fans

Many people attend the races so that they can enjoy the noise, smells and the spectacular ground shaking on some fast runs.

The fans and spectators are protected by guardrails, concrete walls, and heavy fencing to separate them from the cars racing. Some fans line up near the staging line and burn out area to get a really close view of the cars. However, most fans go up into the stadium seats, sit and enjoy the races. They have a great view of all the action of the races and can still hear the noise that the louder cars make.

Spectators enjoy the heart-stopping, exhilarating speeds of the race cars

Grandstands

The grandstands are where race enthusiasts, spectators, fans and friends sit and enjoy the races. They are usually stadium seating, as found in a football arena. There are concrete walls and tall fences separating the racers from the people sitting in the grandstand seats. This way, spectators are out of harms way and away from any flying debris that might come from the race cars.

Race Crew

The race crew consists of the crew chief, mechanics (wrenches), car owner, driver, friends and other members of the racing group. Everyone works as a team to prepare the race car for the drag racing event.

The crew also helps to transport the race car to the track. When traveling to out-of-state events, everyone on our crew takes turns driving. Some teams who do not have a lot of money to spend on motels, may drive to out-of-town races straight through without stopping. This cuts down on expenses, but there have to be sufficient drivers available to do this safely.

The race crew is there to repair the car if it breaks or needs adjustments. This may involve engine repairs, transmission repairs or whatever is necessary to make the car have a good solid run down the track.

Race crews plan their strategy for the day by having a pow-wow

One of the race crew members can help stage (line up the car) in racing events. This helps greatly as it gives the driver one less thing to worry about and allows them to concentrate more on racing.

Entry Fees

Please note, the fees listed are accurate as of the publication date, but are subject to change by the sanctioning bodies at any time.

Pricing at the Fun Ford events and NMRA events is pretty evenly matched, but there are some differences. For instance, to race Pro 5.0 with Fun Ford for car and driver is $200, for NMRA it is $150.

All Fun Ford Heads Up classes, Bracket Racing and Modular Motor classes for car and driver are $60. The cost is the same for all of NMRA's classes, except for Super Street Outlaw, which is $100 for car and driver to race. The cost for NMRA Bracket Racers 1 and 2 for car and driver is $50, and $35 for Bracket 3 racers.

For Super Chevy Shows, most race classes for all car and drivers are $55. For GM shows, car and driver is $45 for the weekend. For the Mopar Nationals, car and drivers are $75.

The price for Fun Ford and NMRA spectators and crew for each day is $18 each or $30 for both days. Children under 12 are free.

Most NHRA race classes for Friday night Test & Tune are $15. Saturday and Sunday each are $60, for car and driver. The Outlaw Class is $60, for car and driver. The Quick 16 Class (one day) is $45, Combo (each day) is $45, Sportsman (each day) is $35, Pro Bike (each day) is $35 and Jr. Dragster (each day) is $20.

Spectator and Crew for NHRA events are $10 for Friday, $20 each for Saturday or Sunday, or a combo (Saturday and Sunday ticket) for $35.

The price for PRO Fastest Street Car racers for each day is $20. The price for PRO Fastest Street car spectators and crew for each day is $20 each or $30 for both days.

Spectator and crew for GM shows are $5 on Friday, $20 on Saturday, $20 for Sunday, or Saturday and Sunday combined is $30. If you go to all three days combined, the total is $35. Juniors (age 13-16) pay $10 per day and under twelve is free. The crew for GM races pays $30 for the full event.

Spectators for the Mopar Nationals pay $35 for both days or $18 each individual day. The Regular car show admission is priced at $60 and the Judged Car Entry for Certification is $150.

Tow Trucks

Tow trucks are always on hand to assist the racers who break on the track.

Safety Crews

Safety crews are standing by in case of emergencies to help injured drivers or spectators. They park their safety vehicles towards the end of the drag strip near the traps so they can respond within seconds of a crash.

Tow trucks are available at a moment's notice if you break down on the track

Paramedics/EMTs (Emergency Medical Technicians) are always ready and available in case of such emergencies. These professionals carry all the necessary equipment to aid injured drivers, including the *jaws of life*. These paramedics are well trained to handle serious racing accidents and are highly skilled. It is nice to know that they can react at a moment's notice, especially when those precious seconds count.

Fire Truck equipment – located in the bed of the truck:
Full water tank - 100 gallon F500 Foam (which breaks down the gasoline so it does not ignite)
Nitrogen for water tank – Air pressure tools
Spare Nitrogen- For air pressure tools
Nitrogen Bottle for air tools
Booster hose with nozzle
Cribbing – Blocks of wood placed to stabilize things spaces so they will not crush anyone
Air bag system – Hook up to hoses and they expand up to lift up things.
Air chisel
Hurst Power Unit – Jaws of Life
Hurst Spreader – Hydraulic Jaws of Life
Hurst Cutter - Hydraulic cutter for Jaws of Life
Hurst Ram – Post that expands and spreads open to push open small spaces into bigger ones
Chains for Spreader – For steering wheel
Foam System
Piercing Nozzle – Has a narrow nozzle to bust in hoods, etc. to get water in
Flat & Pick Headed Axe – Break into anything on a car or rip anything out
Haligan Tool – Pry bar
Crow bar
Glassmaster with center punch – Bust out windows
Two come-alongs
Pike Pole – Used to pull stuff out
Tow strap
Saw-saw – Reciprocating Saw

The paramedics/EMT's with their Fire Rescue truck carrying an assortment of safety equipment located in the bed of the truck. From left to right, EMT Mark Perkins, FF/EMT Jim Howard, FF/PM Eric Price

Bolt cutters – To cut heavy chains, metal
Two Dry Chemical Extinguishers – Puts out fires and takes the oxygen out also
Two AFFF Extinguishers with Foam
Two – CO2 Extinguishers – Used for fuel fires

Fire Truck & Rescue Truck equipment that is kept in their cab for easy use:
Exam Gloves – Used for safety
Fire Gloves – Used near or in fire
Extrication Gloves – When cutting or extricating a victim out of a vehicle
Helmet – Head protection
Nomex hood – Fire protection
Log Books – Make notes
Cell Phone
Flashlight
Binoculars

Rescue Vehicle equipment located inside compartment of truck:
Stretcher – To carry injured patients
Backboard – For use with back injuries
Spare Backboard – For use with back injuries
AED (Automatic External Defibrillator) – Shock system to bring a non-breathing victim back to life
Red bags – Biohazardous bags
Suction Unit – To clear airways
Igloo cooler – To keep things cold and iced
Medical waste garbage can – To be disposed of after use
EZ Up Canopy – For sun protection for the rescue personnel
Fully Stocked C Collar bag
Mast Suit – military anti-shock trousers worn by the victim to push the blood back up to the patients heart and vital organs. Used more for hip fractures. It is basically a full body splint that pumps up.
Ferno Traction Split – Keeps broken bones straightened
Padded Board Splints
Vacuum Splints with pump – Forms to the patients body part for padding and suctions out air
Two Keds – Very rigid, hard board
Pediatric Board – For children
Adult VM

Airway Bag:
EOA – Esophageal Airway
Blood Pressure Cuff, adult, large, child
Stethoscope – To measure heart rate
Portable O2 with regulator above 500 PSI
Non-Rebreather Masks for patients
Nasal Cannula for oxygen
O2 Tubing – Oxygen tubing
Oralpharyngeal Kit – If victim is not breathing
Bite stick – To keep patient from swallowing their tongue
Thermometer – Check temperatures

Trauma Bag:
Seat Belt Cutter – Cut seat belts away from victim if they will not release
Ring Cutter – To cut victims rings off if needed
Triangle Bandages – For making slings
Ammonia Inhalants – To wake someone up
Trauma Shears – To cut someone's clothes off in emergencies
Assorted gauzes, pads, peroxide, burn sheets, tape, ace wraps, sting kill, band aids, trauma, dressing, eye wash, eye shields and Penn lights.

Rescue Truck equipment located in outside compartment of truck:
One CO2 Extinguisher – Used mainly for fuel fires

Five 10-pound Dry Chemical Extinguisher – Puts out ABC Fires; A being wood and paper; B being fuel; and C being electrical fires.
One Halon Extinguisher
Broom – Sweep up debris on track
Yellow Road Course Flag
Red Road Course Flag
One can oil dry – Clean and dry up spills on road surface
Portable Generator – Which is tested daily
Fuel can
Funnel
2 Spare Portable O2 Tanks – Oxygen tanks

Your Personal Checklist for the Track

Always be prepared and bring everything you will need – and then some. This will cause less headaches and aggravation if a problem arises. If you do not need it, maybe someone else at the track needs it, so bring whatever you think is necessary. It is better to be prepared than not. Make a list each time you go to the track of what you bring and while at the track, jot down what you wish you would have brought. This will help you remember all the necessary equipment when you go to the next race. Keep it on your computer so it can be updated. Here is a sample checklist:

Sunscreen
Bug/mosquito spray
Food/cooler/ice
Hat for shade
Sunglasses
Camera/VCR
Portable practice tree
Ear plugs/mitts for children
Long pants/race pants
T-shirt and/or race jacket
Jacket (if cool at nights)
Business cards to pass out
First aid kit
Medications/tylenol
Driver's license
Competition license (if needed)
NHRA/IHRA Rule Book
Umbrella/tent
Chairs
Grill
Helmet
All safety equipment needed
Mechanix gloves
Fire extinguisher
Towels, rags
Hand cleaner
Dial in/shoe polish
Waxes/cleaners
Portable weather station/weather radio
Tie wraps/racers tape
Misc. tools needed
Jack and jack stands
Hand winch/come along
Tire pressure gauge
Tire/track temperature gun
Air compressor
Extra spark plugs
Extra blower belt (if supercharged)

Spare NOS bottles (if using NOS)
Bottle warmer/blanket (if using NOS)
Sunshields for tires
Spare tires/slicks
Burn-out guard
Spare oil/filter
Race fuel/jugs (if needed)
Car cover
Log book to record runs
Log book to record tire pressure/temp/air pressure
Tow vehicle or trailer
Golf cart/moped/ATV
Generator, if needed
Chain and lock so you can chain your toolbox to a post or fence while you head to the lanes
Money
Big smile!!

Miscellaneous Track Tips

Attend a drag racing school to brush up on your techniques or to earn your competition license. This will help you learn all the necessary components and skills to become a qualified drag racer.

Rent the local race track. They are available usually four nights a week for a nominal fee, which includes a safety crew and functional timing lights. Get a few buddies together to offset the price. You can practice the Christmas Tree lights, work on reaction time, set up different modifications or actually just learn how to drive your car without a crowd around.

You look like a rookie if you use the last four numbers of your social security number for your racing number. Pick a number that you like and post it on your tech card. The tech inspector will place the number you picked on your windows instead of the last four digits of your social security number.

When making modifications on your car, try to do only one modification at a time in order to see what a difference it makes in the car. If you make more than one change, you may not be able to tell if it made a difference or not.

To read your spark plugs at a drag strip, you need to do it after your quarter mile run, but, you need to have the car towed or pushed back to the pits. If the car is driven back to the pits, you will not get a good reading from the plugs. Specks on the tip indicate objects airborne in the cylinder. The whiter the porcelain area, the engine is running lean and you need more fuel pressure or less timing. If you have a black, sooty plug, you have excessive fuel in the engine.

Remove anything in the car that could become airborne in case of an accident. You do not want flying debris in your car which could injure you.

If your engine runs hot after a run down the track, turn the heater on. This will cool the engine quicker.

Some event sponsors pay prize money, called contingency, to anyone who wins and is using and advertising their product. When racing in an event, be sure to place the contingency stickers on the car for the entire event. Have the product on your car to collect contingency money – some companies check to make sure. You can pick up these decals when you go through the tech line.

Make sure your firewall, floorboard and trunk are free of holes. These can allow

Make sure you place all your contingency stickers on your car before your first race down the track

fumes, fluid and flames to enter the car and are forbidden in most rule books. A roll of duct tape can be an inexpensive remedy.

Do not use a big heavy key chain for the ignition key. The weight will wear down the switch and may cause the key to get stuck or break.

Learn the different tracks, their rules, conditions and accommodations. Jot down some notes about things that affect you and your team. This will allow you to know the important aspects of the surroundings so you are acclimated to them and you have one less thing to worry about.

Have someone videotape your launch and run, so you can evaluate it at a later time. This will help tremendously when you have time to sit back, check it out and critique it on your own.

You always have the right to protest if you believe someone is running illegally. There is always a small protest fee involved.

Keep a log book and record tire pressure and track/weather conditions. If you record the results for each run, you will learn the best tire pressure to use. If you do not have a log book, simply jot this information on the back of your time slip.

Invest in a weather gauge which records temperature, barometric pressure and humidity. Elapsed time slows when the temperature and humidity go up and when the air pressure goes down. Weather gauges range in price from $100 to $800.

Two-way radio systems are allowed in all classes allowing the crew to communicate with the driver. Some systems broadcast up to five miles. A scramble feature makes the signal unintelligible to other users or eavesdroppers if they turn to your channel. They have voice activated systems for hands-free operation. Motorola makes many different styles. Price starts at approximately $50.

Keep a log book with your times recorded from your time slips. These will include date, dial in, reaction time, 60 feet, 330 feet, 1/8th mile, MPH, 1000 feet, 1/4 mile and MPH. Put this in a chart format.

Make any adjustments to the car after each race in the pits. Allow your car to cool down, make the necessary adjustments and get ready for the next race. You should always bring the necessary tools to the track in case repairs are required.

Make sure you eat something to have energy. You do not want to be lethargic and sleepy. You need to be wide awake and ready to rock.

Get to the track early. This way you have time to get the car race ready, relax and focus on racing.

It is very important to make sure you listen to the announcer to hear when they call your class. Most times it is very difficult to hear the public address system. You could miss your race completely. Pit near a loudspeaker to avoid this problem. Some tracks announce the races over an AM or FM radio station.

Pit near adequate lighting at a night race.

Ask questions of other racers and track officials. Always make it a point to learn something new each time you visit the track.

Always wear comfortable clothing to the track. There are usually very long days in the hot and humid weather. However, if it is cold weather, make sure you bring the appropriate jackets,

Try to pit near the lighting system and the loudspeaker so you don't miss your class when it is called to the staging lanes

sweaters, gloves and blankets. Dress appropriately. Sneakers are preferred and comfortable for the long walks in the pit area.

Bring sunscreen and a hat. Sometimes you are out in the sun all day long. Mosquito repellant is good to have on hand also.

Do not borrow someone else's tire gauge unless you plan on using it exclusively. Each individual gauge may read a little differently. A good tire pressure gauge is needed at all times and is very crucial in producing good and consistent runs. A typical street tire gauge cannot deliver accurate readings.

Do not have your radio playing loudly in your car nor in the pits. Be respectful of others.

Watch other racers. Observe how they perform their burn outs and launch off the starting line. Study the Christmas Tree and watch the lights come down and other racers reaction times. Try to learn from them.

Use the same tire pressure gauge at all times as some read differently than others. It is very important to keep track of your tire pressures and make the necessary adjustments as needed

Get with your race crew and plan the week-end's strategy. Set up new combinations, discuss who has what duties, going over all details for the entire race event, making sure everyone is on the same page and doing his own part to help out.

Set goals and challenge yourself on a daily basis. Figure out how you will go about attaining them. Do not make such a huge goal that it is too hard to obtain. Take baby steps, that is, small steps that lead to higher goals. Remember, anything is possible if you put your mind to it. Dreams can come true especially when you have a positive outlook on life.

Take time to learn by reading about drag racing, talking to racers and learning automotive mechanics. Do whatever you can to enhance all your skills and better yourself in any way possible.

If there is a fire in the engine compartment, do not open the hood unless you have a fire extinguisher. It will give the fire more oxygen and will make it burn faster. Turn the ignition off, unlatch the hood and either use a fire extinguisher or wait for the fire truck.

In bracket racing, the fastest car usually has the advantage. The reason is that the faster driver can always see the other car going down the track and can tell firsthand if they red light. The other reason is the faster car gets to *catch up* to the slower car and keep it in sight. This makes it much easier to judge the finish line. The slower car has to anticipate the other car coming up on them, which is much harder.

Save up your money, cause if you get *bitten by the bug* you are going to want a truck, an enclosed trailer and all the goodies to go along with it.

And sorry, guys and girls, but do not leave the track with all your buddies racing down the highway. Your adrenaline may still be high, but save it for the track. Remember, street racing can kill!

Tips for Having a Good Time

After the races, it is fun to go out to a local restaurant, meet up with some buddies, talk racing, brag a little about your car or complain, whatever the case may be. Drink modestly because drinking a lot and partying heavily will take its toll on you the following race day. Racers need an adequate amount of sleep and good hydration to make it through the day.

Sometimes the racing event holds a car show and autograph session at a local restaurant the night before the race. This is really fun and you get to mingle with all the racers and fans.

If a child shows an interest in your race car, take the time to show it to them. Let them sit in your car or take a picture of it. I love to see a youngster looking at a race car with a twinkle in their eyes.

Make it a family affair and bring your family and friends and enjoy their company. It makes for a very fun day to share it with everyone. Plus, it is fun to have your family and friends encourage you on to win.

Meet and make new friends with business associates, race officials, etc. All you need to do is walk up to any person in the pits and you will find that most racers love to talk about their cars with you.

Race at your local track ahead of time to practice the Christmas Tree light. That way you will have better reaction times at the event and will stay in competition longer and have more fun.

Challenge yourself to see how well you will do when you are trying new modifications. Maybe you have added an extreme amount of horsepower and are anxious to try it out, your first time trying out slicks, your first time trying new wheelie bars or your first time trying to learn to activate a parachute. All of these can be very exciting.

Make sure you bring refreshments to quench your thirst and food and snacks for nourishment. Some racers bring their own grilles to cook hot dogs, hamburgers, steaks and/or chicken.

Meet up with your fellow racing friends. It is exciting to see them all in different race locations in different states all the time. Catch up on gossip and the latest news, make sure they are healthy and doing fine and enjoy your conversations with them.

Bring your video recorder and take pictures. Nothing is better than a lasting memory of the event and the good times you are having.

Shop at the vendors, get souvenirs, shop for car parts and buy t-shirts. Attend the car show and see all the beautiful, tricked-out cars. Visit the racers in the pits and check out all of their cars.

Cheer on your friends and fellow racers. Congratulate them if they do well and encourage them if they do not do well.

Make sure you get to watch all the spectator and exhibition cars. Jet Cars and Funny Cars are very exhilarating to watch. The Jet Cars, Back up Pick Up Trucks, Wheelie Cars and Motorcycle Trick Riders are all very entertaining to watch.

If you cannot attend your Sunday morning church service, most tracks schedule a *Racers For Christ* service, which is held on Sunday mornings. This is a non-denominational service which usually lasts an hour.

Children look up to drag racers and it is up to them to be their role models. Let them know that they can do anything they put their mind to. Always present a respectable and professional appearance on the track and off, so people and children will admire you. Take responsibility for your actions and always act with class and dignity. Walk with your head high, be proud of what you do and be a good example to everyone.

Hotels

Hotels can be very costly, so many racers *buddy-up* and get a few people in one hotel room to save on costs. Many racing circuits involve traveling every two weeks to out-of-state races.

You may be able to get a special rate if you stay in the *host hotel* through your racing organization. Sometimes this is fun because most racers stay there and it is a lot of fun hanging out poolside at night or in the parking lot by the race cars and trailers and talking.

It is also possible to save some money by simply finding cheaper motels. After all, you spend the whole day and some of the night at the race track. The only reason you go to the motel is to shower and sleep. Unless your spouse or significant other stays at the motel all day while you are at the race track to enjoy the pool and sun, look for the best deal.

Driving Technique

This chapter is to familiarize you with the steps to actually drag racing down the track: from waiting in the staging lanes, to performing burn outs, staging at the Christmas Tree, racing techniques, driving the race and after you hit the traps.

Staging Lanes

Sometimes the staging line can be very long. While waiting there are a number of things you can do or check.

As the person in line in front of you moves up, move up behind him. Do not leave spaces in between until you get close to the water box, also known as the burn out box, which is the puddle of water where burn outs are performed.

Make sure the seat is adjusted properly and the controls are within reach. Do not recline your seat to be comfortable during the wait. Instead, sit upright and concentrate on your run.

Make sure you check your tires and lug nuts before each run. Check to make sure you have no fluid leaks.

Idle your car's engine a minute or so before each run. This will warm up the engine and circulate the oil which is better for your car's performance. Cold oil blows oil coolers and causes bearing wear.

Never run the air conditioning even if it is very hot weather. This can be very dangerous because condensation leaks on the ground could potentially cause loss of control when racing with water on the tread of the tires.

If you ice down your intake, put a towel underneath the ice pack. Otherwise, it will leak water on the ground.

Do not perform mechanical work on your car while it is in line. This should have already been done.

Do not have a favorite lane. Drive in both lanes to convince yourself that both lanes are equal and whichever lane you have to race on will be fine. The reason for this is if the staging director points you to race the right lane, when you feel more comfortable in the left lane, this will automatically psyche you out to think, "I hate that lane, I know I will not win." You need to have a positive outlook in either lane.

Make sure you check your gauges prior to running your car

Check all your gauges and make sure you have the proper readings. If anything reads improperly, do not race.

When they call your class be ready to race and in the proper lane. If you are in competition and you are lined up against a competitor, walk over, shake hands and tell the racer good luck. Good sportsmanship counts.

When lining up in the staging area always have a tire pressure gauge. Get a professional type dial gauge that reads in one pound increments, not a silver pencil one. Check your tire pressures while waiting in line. Hot temperatures cause the tires to raise and cold temperatures cause the tires to lower. You may have to adjust the tire pressure, if the temperature changes.

Make sure you have a bottle of water in your car. It is very easy to become dehydrated. Some days you wait in line while the sun is beating down on you for hours.

Stay with your car in the staging lanes and sit in your car when the announcer calls your class. Buckle up with a seatbelt or safety harness. Put on your helmet when they announce your class is ready.

When you are putting on your safety equipment, if people are telling you to move up, do not rush. Take your time always and make sure you are safe. That's number one!

Let your pit crew know if you do or do not want to talk with them while in line before racing. This may deter you from focusing on your run.

It is okay to be scared or nervous at a race, it is a common reaction. People like to see that you are a normal human being and have feelings just like everyone else. Your butterflies will ease up after you take a few runs down the track.

As you approach the burn out box, clear your mind of clutter. This will allow you to feel refreshed. Remain calm, but be ready. Do not think about what happened that day, a fight with your girl/boy friend or whatever, just visualize your upcoming run.

Be calm and others will be intimidated by you.

Burn outs

Burn outs can be the difference between a great launch and a bad launch. Make sure you heat up the tires to get the rubber sticky and knock off any debris that might be on the tread. This will give you maximum traction so you will not spin your tires.

You can have your crew chief go up to the line with you. He can place you in the burn out box to get the maximum burn out and then inch you towards the

Stay comfortable in the staging lanes with a cool drink and shorts, if possible

staging lane. This gives you, as the driver, one less thing to worry about, allowing you to concentrate more on your run.

If you are driving on drag radials, do not go through the water box. Go around it. Sometimes you can back up towards the water box but do not go into it and do a quick burn out there.

If you are driving on regular street tires, go around the VHT and water and pull ahead of it. With street tires it is not necessary to do a burn out.

Do not pull up behind someone who is doing a burn out in the burn out box. Not only is this dangerous, as flying debris can hit you or your car, but you need to allow the racer some room in case the racer backs up and performs a second burn out. Sometimes when a vehicle does not get a good burn out, they want to back up and do it again.

There are actually great reasons to do burn outs, but they also look cool and are fun to do

To properly perform a burn out in a car with an automatic transmission, press lightly on the brake enough to keep the car still without burning out the brakes. You will have to practice to get the feel of it. Press the gas pedal with your right foot to get the car tires spinning, using light to moderate pressure on the gas.

With a standard transmission, you need to press the clutch down with your left foot, hit the brakes lightly with your right foot (the heel part) and at the same time rev the engine with your right foot toe part. Releasing the clutch will start the tires spinning. It is a little tricky maneuver but once mastered it is quite fun.

Engage the line lock if you have one. As you do your burn out, learn the correct rpm's that warms/cleans the tires the best. You need only see a small smoky haze, not big clouds. When you learn the correct rpm, use it consistently. It usually only takes a few seconds in the water box to achieve maximum heat.

Long burn outs will wear out the tires. They may look impressive and can be a crowd pleaser, however, they can prove to be very expensive. You want to see a small amount of smoke not a massive burn out. Normally, on your first and second pass each day, you should do a fairly long burn out. Afterwards, a light burn out is all that is needed to heat up your slicks and soften them. This will increase the life of the tire also.

Some people use second gear, others use first gear during their burn outs. It is a matter of preference. In second gear you can do a longer burn out.

You can roll through or drive around and back into the water box. By backing in, the front tires do not get wet and pull water to the starting line.

If, after your burn out, you feel something is wrong with your car, motion to the Starter (who is located in front of the Christmas Tree between both race cars) to let him know you are backing up. Do not be embarrassed, it is better than wasting a motor and spewing oil all down the track. If the car cannot be backed up, do not turn your car around and face in the direction of the oncoming race cars. If it is disabled, it will either be pushed backward or a tow truck will take it off the track.

Never do a burn out across the starting line, it will upset the Starter and he may disqualify you.

Nobody is allowed to hold or touch the cars during burn outs.

Crossing the centerline during a burn out is not a disqualification.

Christmas Tree Behavior

Staging must be done under the vehicle's own engine power. No push starting is permitted. Stage the same way on each run to be consistent. Try to line up at the same place each and every time.

Never let anyone rush you. Stage your car when you are ready, but do not be discourteous and take extra time by playing mind games with the other driver.

If you have nitrous, purge your system before you activate the first beam. This is usually done by pushing a button or hitting a toggle switch within your reach. It emits a white cloud of smoke, which is a definite crowd pleaser!

Slowly inch or *bump* your car up to the line which will activate the first small yellow light on the Christmas Tree. This is called the Pre-Stage indicator light.

Then you move seven inches more until you activate the second light which is the Stage Indicator Light.

Do not move forward to light up the second beam until the other driver activates his top light. This is called courtesy staging.

Some racers prefer to *deep stage*. This means the front tire rolls to where the Pre-Staged bulb is activated and then the Stage bulb. By pulling a few more inches ahead, the tree's top bulb goes out. This will cause reaction time to be lower, but it is much easier to red light and be disqualified.

Some racers with automatic transmissions put their foot on the gas pedal to raise the revs and pump the brakes to get lined up into the beams. This takes some practice to not cross over the beams. Then roll-in slowly and activate the second light just barely turning on the next yellow.

The official Starter will give the drivers a reasonable amount of time to stage. If you fail to stage at the Starter's request, you might be disqualified. Re-staging is prohibited.

There are two different Christmas Tree light systems, Regular/Sportsman and Pro Tree light. Sportsman lights the top two bulbs as you stage, then it slowly blinks third light, fourth light, fifth light, and then to green at half-second intervals. The Pro Tree light activates all three amber lights simultaneously with a 0.4-second difference between the amber and green light.

The driver's reaction time is the time between the appearance of the green light and when the tires pass through a third light beam, called the guard beam, which is 16 inches from the stage beam. A perfect light is a 0.400 on the Pro Tree and 0.500 on the Regular or Sportsman light.

Never wait to see the green light. On a Pro Tree light, you need to leave at the first sight of any amber light or even after the second racer lights up the Stage light. On the Sportsman light, react to either the second or last amber bulb, depending on your car's speed. You will have to experiment with the lights and see what gives the best reaction time.

First timers are usually a little shaky. This is normal; do not think anything is wrong with you. After each run you will become more and more relaxed. It becomes quite a rush after you get over the butterflies.

If the starter holds up the race for some reason, back up behind the burn out box. When the race commences you can do your burn out again and stage as you normally would. This way you will not lose your concentration. You want to try to keep everything in the normal sequence. This will minimize distractions and help to keep your mind focused.

If both drivers of a race leave the line before both staging lights are lit and the start system is activated, both racers are disqualified.

Driving the Race

As you drive down the track, stay as straight in a line as you can. Look straight down the center of the track;

do not let your eyes stray. You lose valuable time when you shift if you are jerking and moving around in the car. Notice that some top drivers rest their left elbow on the windowsill, reducing unwanted movements.

Try side-stepping the clutch. This is done by taking your left foot and placing it on the clutch pedal. When you go to shift, let your foot simply "slide" off the side of the pedal. This allows the clutch to disengage quickly.

Do not worry about who you are racing. Do not look over at them. As far as you are concerned, you are racing yourself. It does not matter if the other driver is faster than you or slower than you.

Do not look at the crowd, your friends, or anything else. Be oblivious to everything except racing. Taking your eyes off the track for one second could have devastating results.

Consistency means everything. The key to being consistent is doing the same things each and every time you come up to the line. Always stage exactly the same way, unless you are trying something new.

Go up to the line and watch the other racers. Try to learn how they do their burn outs and launch their cars. Study the Christmas Tree and watch as the lights activate.

Read any material on drag racing that you can get your hands on. There are plenty of magazines, articles and books on drag racing.

Always use focus, use discipline and visualize each run.

Be confident in yourself and don't fear anything. Never worry about who you are up against or which lane you have. So what! Use intimidation techniques, don't let them intimidate you.

Pay attention to what you are doing. Focus straight down the track and watch the Christmas Tree in your peripheral vision. Don't let your eyes wander.

Rehearse in your mind all the steps you will go through from the burn out to winning at the finish line. Using positive reinforcements will program your mind and you will actually be going through the motions.

Go home, sit in your room in a chair and visualize a full race in your head. From putting on your race equipment, maneuvering the controls in the car, burn outs, staging, the run and shutting down. Doing these steps in correct order in your mind over and over again sends signals to your unconscious mind. Your goal is to get into your car and unconsciously know what to do without concentrating. When it becomes natural then you will become a better and more focused and relaxed racer.

Never rehearse in your mind what you don't want to do. Rehearse only the steps you want to remember.

Never be aggressive or fearful. Remain calm. If you have rehearsed the run 100 times in your mind then you should have nothing to worry about.

Practice, practice and practice. That is what makes a winner. Practice in your car and practice visualization techniques at home.

If you have a standard transmission, never grasp the lever or knob tight and smother it. Instead just place the fingers and the palm of your hand on the shifter pulling it back. Pushing forward is done by pushing your palm on the shifter.

Learn how to speed shift. This is where you up shift without lifting your right foot off the gas, then go to the next gear. In other words, you keep your right foot firmly planted on the throttle without releasing, then with your left foot, jab the clutch pedal each time the gears need changing. This takes a lot of practice and you have to be careful not to break anything.

If your engine has a problem or is leaking oil, pull over immediately to the side of the track. There is nothing worse than having to clean up oil spills all the way down the track. The track announcer will also usually complain about such behavior over the public address system.

Front end lift may look neat, but it isn't necessarily the fastest way to the finish line

To avoid wheel spin, the car needs to launch putting equal amount of weight on both rear tires. If the front end lifts, yes, it is a crowd pleaser, however, it is just wasted time and effort. It is much quicker to see a car simply *rocket* off the line.

If you are losing control of your car and it is getting out of shape, lift off the accelerator. A true racer knows when to lift. Being willing to back down on the power takes a lot of discipline and maturity.

When bracket racing, do not lift the throttle if you are ahead of the other car. Just quickly jab the brakes for a second to allow your car to slow down. Sometimes you brake too much and the opposing racer might pass you by.

After The Race

After you go down the track and through the traps, do not slam on the brakes. Slow down gently; do not worry about your stopping distance as there is plenty of room.

Never turn around at the end of the track and come back in the opposite direction. This was done many years ago at Miami/Hollywood Speedway and several spectators and racers were killed.

Never exit from the track in front of your competitor. It is often difficult to estimate his speed or it is possible that his brakes may fail. If the turnoff is in his lane, always wait for him to exit first.

Pull around the return road to the shack and pick up your time slip. Keep a log of all information. A time slip records your reaction time, 60 feet, 330 feet, 1000 feet, one-eighth (1/8) mile, one-fourth (1/4) mile ET and trap speed.

If you notice an animal or debris on the track, immediately notify the person who hands out the time slips. They will notify the tower to stop the racing and check out the track. This is for the safety of all concerned.

Always compare your time slips and note the differences between them. Make sure you jot down the time and the temperatures.

Don't be afraid of losing or screwing up. Everyone is human. Take responsibility for your run, good or bad. If you did screw up, admit it. So what! It's a drag race. No Excuse. Tell yourself that you tried your best and will do better next time. There is no need to beat yourself up over a loss or making a mistake.

If you lose a race, do not get mad and blow through the timing shack without getting your time slip. This shows that you have a bad temper and poor sportsmanship. If you see your competitor, give a thumbs up, a smile or say, "good run." This will show that you are a good sport.

If you are called for a tear-down after a race, you must comply or face disqualification. You will have to tear-down your engine for inspectors who want to make sure you are running legally. This can happen because officials think your car is running faster than it should or someone has made a protest against you and your car.

Women in Racing

Drag racing is predominately a male-dominated sport. It used to be in the *old days* that men were ashamed to lose a race to a woman. However, today's men are more open to change and realize that there are many excellent female drivers competing in drag racing. There are husbands who totally support their wives in racing. One that comes to mind is Curtis Moore. He admires his wife Michele's skills and qualities to drive a fast race car and stands behind her one hundred per cent.

There are also a number of husband and wife teams. The most famous of couples is Barry and Roxanne Shepard. They live in Michigan and race in the NMRA and Fun Ford Events. They have each won many races. They truly support each other in drag racing and are both very competitive and excellent racers. When I started out racing in the Modular Motor Class with both of them, Barry took me under his wing and helped me learn drag racing. I thank him for that from the bottom of my heart.

Today, women are involved in all aspects of drag racing. There are women mechanics, women pit crew members and women race car drivers. There are many famous women out there racing drag bikes, jet cars, dragsters and many other racing vehicles.

Angelle Monique Savoie, formerly known as Angelle Seeling, is at the time of this writing a three-time NHRA Pro Stock Motorcycle Champion. Angelle is the first female NHRA Pro Stock Motorcycle Champion. She is the second professional female champion in NHRA's 49-year history. This Louisiana lady has surpassed Shirley Muldowney's NHRA record for career wins by a female racer. She has run a career best of 7.049 and has driven to speeds up to 190 mph.

Angelle began racing motorcycles at the age of six. She earned her competition license while attending the

Frank Hawley Drag Racing School in 1995. There she set the school's elapsed time and speed records. That same year George Bryce of Star Racing Squad invited her to their team. The rest is history.

She was married in the off season to former NFL player, Nicky Savoie, who is a tight end for the Birmingham Bolts. She graduated from the Charity School of Nursing in 1995 and served as an Intensive Care nurse until 1996, when she decided to begin her drag racing career.

Angelle is one of only six women to capture an NHRA World Drag Racing National Title event and she has claimed the number one spot 24 times thus far. In 2001, Angelle launched her own Suzuki Motorcycle dealership, *Angelle's Motorsports* in Houma, Louisiana, which was a dream come true for her. She is truly a leader and role model for all women in drag racing.

Angelle Savoie at work. Photo courtesy Rich Barry

Prior to Angelle, there was Shirley Muldowney. Shirley is a wonderful inspiration to everyone and she is still racing and turning some remarkable times. It is ladies like this that give us the will and inspiration to know we can do it ourselves. I commend them for their skills and accomplishments in drag racing and in life.

Years ago there were powderpuff derbys where the females would race against females. Often there were only one or two women competing, so they ended up being placed in the men's classes. Over the years it has been proven that women can be just as competitive as men in drag racing. In racing events these days, women are not segregated from the men and compete against them as equals.

The competitor's typical view of Angelle. Photo courtesy Rich Barry

It is not unusual to see a woman putting on a driver's suit, donning the helmet and climbing into her race car these days. Women are extremely competitive and are known to have good reaction times. Females are not there to be scrutinized or to look pretty for anyone. They are there for the same reason as men, to have fun, to compete and to win. They get the same adrenaline kick and rush from competing that men do.

Sometimes it seems that women still have to prove themselves to the male population, though. They need to show men that they are competitive, persistent, consistent and dedicated to the sport of racing. When I first starting racing, I received mixed reactions. At the beginning, some men thought it was a *waste* to race me. I only had one problem at a track and that was when someone told me, "I didn't come all this way to the track on a trailer to be beaten by you (meaning a girl)!" and started cussing. I was so astonished that I could say nothing in return.

For the most part, though, once men see that women have that *inner drive* to win, they will be welcomed as *one of the guys* and be treated as equals. Women can breathe, eat, sleep and dream drag racing just like the men. Once drag racing gets under your skin, it stays in your mind on a permanent basis. If you go to a restaurant, you are thinking, "Maybe they would like to be a sponsor." Your mind is always full throttle thinking of how you can improve your racing abilities.

My father was a stock car driver and my mom always enjoyed watching racing. I guess it was congenital. I was always thrilled as a youngster to watch stock car racing, drag racing, thrill shows and demolition derbys. I always dreamed of becoming either a stock car racer, drag racer, or some kind of thrill seeker or daredevil. Most racers are usually born with this inspiration to race, the thrill of speed and the *racer's high*.

If you are female and have been contemplating racing for some time, my advice is "get out there and start racing now!" Do not be afraid to make that first move and head to the track. Men will look at you and see your positive self image and they will look up to you. Most husbands and boyfriends will be proud to talk about you to their friends and boast of your abilities. Once you start, you will find that it is very addictive and really kicks your adrenaline into high gear.

DRAW (Drag Racing Association of Women)

DRAW (Drag Racing Association for Women) is a drag racing charity that provides financial and emotional support to individuals involved in drag racing incidents. Membership is open to men, women and even children. DRAW is an all volunteer organization whose motto is "Fast Help For Fast Friends."

Following a 1984 fundraiser for injured racer Shirley Muldowney, members of the drag racing community were encouraged by the support of racers and fans. As a result, DRAW was created in 1985. It provides financial support to individuals involved in drag racing incidents and helps racers in all drag racing categories and sanctioning bodies.

DRAW's ten female founders were Gere Amato, Penny Beck, Holly Beadle, Laura Earwood, Pat Garlits, Etta Glidden, Diane Hedrich, Linda McCulloch, Janie Oswald and Lynn Prudhomme. The governing body is elected by the membership. DRAW geographically divided the United States and Canada into seven different areas and each area is guided by a Area Coordinator. There are also track representatives, who work at local tracks to recruit volunteers, report injuries and keep DRAW informed of happenings in their area.

Thousands visit the DRAW booth at NHRA and IHRA events where they can purchase clothing, jewelry, decals, pins, earplugs and memberships. There are also fundraising events held each year, including auctions, barbecues, label program and a golf tournament. One other important activity is the *cards and letters* program. Each month's newsletter includes a list of injured racers, their needs and concerns, with addresses. DRAW suggests that members send cards and letters to brighten the day of someone in recovery or to comfort those who have suffered a loss.

DRAW membership information can be found on their web site: www.drawfasthelp.org. Dues are $30 individual, $50 family per year in the United States, $45 individual, $75 family outside the US. Members receive a DRAW name tag, decal and monthly newsletter, *DRAWing Attention*.

WAAI

The Women's Automotive Association International (WAAI) is dedicated to promoting the role of women in the automotive industry, encouraging entry through scholarships and the retention of women leaders. The association focuses on education in automotive issues, recognition of women in the automotive industry for their contributions and professional growth through networking.

The WAAI was established in the United States in 1995 by Lorraine Schultz. They have chapters in Ohio, Michigan, Canada, New York and California. They plan on adding the National Racing Division this year.

Their purpose is to network with one another, promote personal growth through motivation, further education and establish a scholarship fund to encourage women to enter the automotive field. The WAAI's objective is to support both women wishing to further their education toward an automotive-related career, and those with established careers in the industry.

Membership in WAAI includes an invitation to all speaker series and special series, an opportunity to actively participate on committees, scholarship program, free subscription to newsletter and membership directory.

Sponsorship of Women

Women make up half of the auto racing audience, both on television and trackside. Therefore, it makes sense to sponsor a female racer. Women actually draw more attention to themselves and the companies they represent. They seem to receive more free magazine and television coverage and are in the publics' eyes more often then men. An American tradition is to root for the underdog, including female competitors in a male-dominated sport. Female spectators seem to admire and respect a woman who *races with the boys*. Companies can benefit as this draws a huge clientele into their business, as sponsor loyalty in auto racing is the highest of any sport.

There are many accomplished women race drivers in the world. There are many benefits to sponsoring a female, however, there are some companies who have objections to sponsoring them. Some think that they are good just for showcasing them. For instance, placing them next to their race cars for publicity. Others think women simply can't win a race against all those hardcore racing men. Others are afraid they might get pregnant or might have men trouble. Others are afraid that if a woman racer is killed on the track, it would look bad for their company, letting a poor little defenseless girl drive.

So to remedy these objections, women have to make sure they get their meaning across. They have to show the sponsors that they are not simply a showpiece to put up on a pedestal; that they are there to race and not only to race, but to win. They need to show the sponsor that they are hardcore racers, that racing is in their blood and their motivation is the thrill of speed. Females need to talk up front to potential sponsors about anything in their personal life that might keep them from attending races. They need to quote any and all statistics regarding females and racing. Explain to them that women can be killed in a race car the same as any man. That is something no company would like to deal with, whether male or female, and in no way would this hinder a company's reputation.

So never rule out a woman as a potential driver to sponsor as you might just have the best representation tool in the World. Thanks to T.W. Theodore, President, Thunder Valley Racing, website of www.thundervalleyracing.com for providing this information.

Today's Women Racers

Check out these women race car drivers and their stories.

Nicolle L. Douglas – '93 Mustang, 550 horsepower

Nicolle L. Douglas lives in Dallas, Texas. She is an Office Manager for Lone Star Performance and serves as

Editor of Girls Can Too section for Mustang Works Magazine web site. She races and shows a 1993 Mustang GT with 550 horsepower.

She is a ten times Fun Ford Weekend Car Show winner, subject of many magazine articles, Main Coordinator for the Mustangs & More Car Meet and first generation member of DFW Stangs. She is a moderator on the Stangs website and is involved with their charity events. She is married and has one daughter.

The women in her family passed down the gene for speed. Nicolle relates that after years of watching them own a variety of hot rods, she began racing at 14, after learning to drive in a '65 Mustang at age 11. The street races were her playground and she was there every weekend pulling in bet money using a family friend's '85 LX, followed by racing Chevys for more years than she cares to admit. After owning a slew of Camaros, she finally decided to go back to her roots: the Fox-body Mustang. Although she's never had a speeding ticket, Texas premiums are high on Mustangs. In 1994 when her insurance rates dropped, she sold her slick '92 Camaro, and she was able to begin the search for a Mustang.

She spent the next seven years devoted to her 1993 Mustang GT and the hobby that gave her so much pleasure. On top of racing her home built, heavily modified, show/race GT every weekend at the local tracks, she would spend many nights at the local hot spots, meeting others who also participated. With her outgoing personality she be-friended many and, within one year of painting a personal signature on the back of her car, it seemed everyone knew who *Girls Can Too* was. Although Nicolle is modest by nature, it was obvious the recognition she and her car had achieved. She decided then to build a website to, not only discuss her Mustang, but also featured the Dallas racing scene.

The website (www.girlscantoo.net & www.girlscantoo.com) received so much exposure that *Muscle Mustangs & Fast Fords Magazine* did a full feature on it in their Cyber Stallions column. One month later Dan McClain, owner of *Mustang Works Online Magazine*, contacted her about heading up the first ever Ford enthusiast section geared towards women. To be chosen as a spokesperson for all ladies who are active in this great hobby was certainly an honor. Her goal with the section is to make sure there is a place for women to meet and befriend others, where they can be featured, not only because of the modifications to their vehicle, but also for their participation in a hobby once dominated by men.

Although racing has been her strongest passion, over the years she has found that participating behind the scenes has been the most rewarding. She thoroughly enjoys coordinating charitable events and being active in the Ford community. She has made numerous friends and has gained respect for her work. Besides her family, she does not think anything could provide her more pleasure. She hopes to be the Internet voice of women in this great hobby for many years to come.

Kim Kasye Jones – '99 235 inch wheelbase dragster

Kim Kasye Jones' dragster runs 8.70s @ 155 mph in the quarter mile, but Kim wants to pilot a top fuel dragster and it is just a matter of securing a sponsorship deal. She already has her racing team set up, her car and enclosed trailer. She is in the process of getting her licensing completed.

Kim is the owner, host and producer of Racer's Edge, a television show which airs on Fox Sports Net on Sundays. She is the owner of Dragonlake Media and Agency, which is a production company.

She has a degree in media communications from Brookdale College in Lincroft, New Jersey and she was formerly a Production Assistant on the Geraldo Rivera Show in New York City. She also worked for Mark Weiss at Weissguy Productions working closely with high profile clientele.

Kim's husband, Todd Jones, is her Crew Chief he and her daughter, Britny, are her biggest supporters. Her racing team consists of Todd, Gordon Dibattisto, Jr., her brother, Robert Kasye, Jr., and Harvey Spencer.

Michele Moore – Thunderfoot Motorsports - 250" wheelbase rear engine dragster

Curtis and Michele Moore live in Katy, Texas and have two children, Heather and Aaron. They have been drag racing as a couple for six years at various tracks in the southern United States and they are IHRA, NHRA and DRAW Fast Friends members.

Curtis introduced Michele into the world of drag racing, not only to the mechanics of the sport, but also as a driver. In 1999, Michele was hired to take over the driving duties for a local race car owner/driver, who had seen her driving skills, her reaction times and the professionalism she showed while under pressure. Michelle, while driving this full race, 145 mph 1969 Camaro, not only won, but in her first year as a *hired gun* she finished in the top ten and was nominated for *Rookie of the Year* in Division 4.

In the 1999-2000 season, Curtis drove the Thunderfoot owned 1966 Chevelle. He competed against Michele many times which made for an excellent day at the races, but many a silent trip home. Neither admits who has the better win/loss record.

The 2000/2001 season was a milestone for the Moores. Curtis stepped down as a driver, put Michele behind the wheel of their 250" wheelbased rear engine dragster and became her crew chief. The choice was a wise one as Michele has become a very successful, accomplished and safe driver.

Michele would like to compete at this level for another year or two and then take the next step into a top alcohol dragster. This is a planned stepping stone towards reaching her goal of climbing behind the wheel of nitro gulping, fire belching top fuel ride.

Her current sponsors are FM Motorsports, Royal Purple, Lucas Oil, Con Net, Ramblin Rose Racing Transmissions, Fields Racing Service, Clifford Custom Welding Unlimited, Fantasy Automotive and Badger Boat & RV Storage.

Kim Morrell - '84 Suzuki Pro Drag Bike

Kim Morrell is a single working mother and has three children, who are truly her inspiration. She attends the Palm Beach Community College where she is studying to become a paramedic. Having a full time job, being a college student, raising three children and racing is quite a feat for this young lady.

In 1998, a co-worker asked Kim to race his '72 Chevy Luv Truck at the local race track. Her first run down the track was recorded at 10.60 @ 135 mph. Needless to say, Kim was hooked and felt like she could never walk away from something this exciting. At this time she knew that racing would become a part of her life.

Kim took her first check home from the All Chevy Show at Moroso Motorsports Park. However, as she observed all the different racing vehicles and trucks, she came to realize that she seemed to have a love for the drag bikes. Eventually she fell into the hands of Anthony Girardi, owner and racer for 15 years of T.G. Racing Team. Anthony decided to give Kim an big opportunity by placing her on an '84 Suzuki drag bike.

Her first run was 9.22 @140 mph and she remembers this run clearly because it was such an amazing feeling to her. She was in the staging lanes thinking that perhaps she really didn't want to do this. Anthony reassured her, telling her to just hold on and she would do well. After her first run on the drag bike, she knew this was where she wanted and needed to be and instantly developed a new love of life.

After becoming more familiar with the bike and attending some test and tune events, Kim entered her first drag bike race at the Pepsi Jet Car Nationals at Moroso

Motorsports Park in 2001 and she came home with the win. She was very proud as this was the beginning of a winning team effort between her and Anthony Girardi of the T.G. Racing Team.

Believe it or not, this young lady is a mere 111 pounds of might and muscle driving this powerful and dangerous drag bike. It is quite a sight to see this little lady overpower this drag bike to run at such fast speeds. She has definitely made quite an impression on her sponsor of T. G. Racing and all her fans that come to watch her.

Kim's dreams are to move on to bigger and better opportunities and perhaps procure a Pro Stock racing bike and sponsorship. She receives support from all her family and friends, including Anthony Girardi, Crew Chief Matt Utt and especially her three children who are her biggest fans!

Angela Samanick – '85 Mustang GT, 306

When Angela received her driver's license at the age of 17, her father, John, gave her his gray '90 Mustang LX 5.0 coupe. John had always taken excellent care of it, since he bought it new in 1990. After owning this muscle car for approximately 5 months, her dad suggested that she try racing it. So in early August of 1999, Angela and her dad took the LX to E-Town (Old Bridge Township Raceway Park) in Oldbridge Township, NJ. Angela was apprehensive but listened to her father's directions of how to stage and leave the line and at the completion of her first round, she was thrilled and knew she was hooked.

A class called High School Eliminator was running that day so her dad suggested that she race in it. The class was created for high school kids who wanted to try their luck racing and was limited to street legal tires with no electronics. There were 4 boys running in the Eliminator class that day and Angela made it to the final round and won her very first race! She won a trophy and her picture was put in the track papers.

For the next two seasons Angela raced in High School Eliminator and won a few races. In March of 2000, Angela and her dad installed some parts which turned the car from 15's to 14's. Towards the end of the 2000 season, her dad decided to let her try his '85 mustang, which had been sitting and collecting dust for quite a while, in which she flew through the quarter mile at 110 mph. They then decided that starting in 2001 that Angela would begin using the '85 as her race car and leave the LX as her daily driver.

Angela joined NMRA in 2001 and competes in the Open Comp class. In her first year she was eligible to compete in the Mean Street finals in September. She was consistently running 11 seconds flat without the aid of any power adder.

Her dad constructed the motor and installed all the safety equipment, along with a 10-point roll cage. He also does most of the "wrenching" but makes sure Angela understands everything that is being done to the car and how everything works. Angela works part time at an auto parts store, which has increased her knowledge about cars immensely.

Angela's goal is to race in the NMRA and Fun Ford Weekend events. They are beginning to work on a new 351 SVO block and billet crank, which will become a 396 Hot Street motor. She will be getting her competition license, so she can begin running NOS on the current motor, which will dip her into the 9's. Angela and her dad recently incorporated their racing operation as JACS Racing, Inc. She is a student at Monmouth University and her education in business and accounting will assist in their new business.

Nika Rolcze – '85 Ferrari 308 GTS

Nika Rolcze, age 34, was born in Toronto, Ontario, Canada. Her hobbies include cars, racing, travel and wine collecting. Nika has had a love for cars and racing since childhood. As a regional racing license holder, she has been involved with the industry, working with racers, teams, journalists and automobile manufacturers in sponsorship solicitation, logistics, hospitality, road show and communication program implementation.

With over eleven years of Investor Relations and Corporate Communications experience with public companies, Nika is currently Manager of Investor Relations for a mid-sized company, based in Toronto. She has traveled from Monza to Homestead to satisfy her love of racing and now with racerchicks.com, her focus will be to bring together other women with the same passion for the sport. Her website provides an informative and entertaining look at women and their passions for cars. Nika drives a 1985 Ferrari 308 GTS and the loves of her life are her dogs, Fangio and Misha.

Corinne Livengood – '96 Mustang GT

Corinne enjoys entering her '96 Ford Mustang GT Coupe into car shows and cruises; however, she also races her car at Keystone Raceway in Pennsylvania. Her car is known as *SHO PONY* which is how her vanity plate reads. Her email is sho_pony@hotmail.com and she gets her racing spirit from her dad who used to own a '69 Z-28 Camaro, a sixties Mustang and a seventies Corvette.

Corinne started showing horses at the age of five with a Shetland pony named Care Bear. She won the 4-H High point award every year she competed and had a different horse each time. When she was thirteen she took on a project horse to show and then sell for profit. The horse cost $2500 and when he was sold about a year and a half later, he turned an impressive $18,000 profit. This exceptional horse named TKO is still showing and winning. Corinne still shows her horses, but her schedule is a lot lighter because of her automotive activities.

Corinne's car is equipped with 17x8 Premium Alloy Wheels, keyless entry, AOD-E 4-speed transmission, 4.6 liter, SOHC, with her best ET of 13.9 in the quarter mile. She has made numerous modifications to her car, including 4.10 gears, Flowmasters 2 inch cat-back exhaust, H-pipe with high flow cats, and a NOS dry kit with purge. She plans on making more modifications in the

future. Her car is also set up for car shows with numerous interior and exterior modifications, along with many audio components.

Tiffany Charise Guidry – '98 Camaro Z28

Tiffany started an interest in cars back when she was 9 years old. Her brother-in-law introduced her to racing by allowing her hands on experience and watching him build his '69 Chevelle. He took her to Houston Raceway Park and from there she fell in love with cars and racing.

She started out a Ford girl, learning all the mechanics of a 5.0 Mustang and then decided she wanted to learn something new and purchased a '95 Z28 LT1 which was a lot of work, moving up once again to her current '98 Z28 LS1. Tiffany performs all mechanical work on her race car.

She is a moderator/event coordinator for the Houston-F-Body.org which is a Houston car club. Her club races in the Car Club Bash, a bracket racing meet between major Houston area car clubs once a month and holds onto the title. She plans to expand her racing schedule this year.

Her car is a '98 Red Camaro Z28 with quarter mile times recorded at 11.5 @ 118mph, dynoed at 376 horse-power and 409 Ft. Lbs. Torque, Modifications include IRS Stage 2 Heads, 215/221 114 Comp Cam, LS6 Intake, Comp Cam 7955 pushrods, Comp 26915 valve springs, ASP pulley, Borla Catback, Mac Headers w/off road y-pipe, ported MAF, air lid, free mods, 2800 Vigilante converter, aluminum driveshaft, 3:42 gears, Custom LS1 edit programming, Pro-Kit springs, Lakewood control arms and IRS Subframe Connectors.

Carly Smith – '96 Pontiac Trans Am

Carly Smith was always interested in cars. Even though she was never a *gearhead* per se, she loved to watch drag racing and was always around men who raced. Her first car was a Chevy II with a 327 engine and a 4-speed Hurst speed-shifter. One of her first boyfriends took her to a West Texas track, which had fuel dragsters running. She was mesmerized by the awesome display of power and little did she know that this would set the stage for what has become her passion in life.

Her ex-husband was a car hobbyist, racer, and weekend mechanic, and Carly became well versed in the racing vernacular. After her divorce, she traded in her soccer mom Blazer for a '96 Pontiac Trans Am and got involved with an all female racing team in Houston, participating in many events. She left the group and joined the Houston Area F-Body Club, so that she could participate in more domestic performance events.

She has won a number of trophies in bracket racing at various local area events, but has been less active recently due to car repairs and starting a new web site for women in racing. Carly and several of her friends decided to start an all female domestic car club. When she was trying to think of names for the club, an idea blossomed to create Raceher.com, a source for women who were interested in cars and racing. Carly plans to resume her racing activities, as well as continue to give women in racing as much exposure as she can through her website.

Junior Drag Racing

Vince Napp founded the Junior Dragster Division in 1992 and built the first half-scale Jr. Dragster. This is a wonderful class for young adults who want to get experience racing, build self esteem and spend some time in the spot light.

Jr. Drag Racing is for young racers between the ages of 8-17 years. All drag racing events are held in the eighth-mile. They use a 5 hp air-cooled engine and can run speeds up to 85 mph.

The following rules were adapted from the IHRA Rule Book. To purchase a Rule Book, contact IHRA, Post Office Box 708, Norwalk, Ohio 44857. The NHRA offers a similar series.

IHRA Junior Drag Racing

The IHRA's Phil McGee PM-1 Jr. Dragster Program allows kids the opportunity to race against their peers in cars similar to the models that the Pros drive. It is restricted to competition in half-scale cars over a 1/8 mile distance. There are five National events held yearly that crown an Eastern champion in each age group and then a Western champion in each age group. In addition to the National events, there are five divisional bracket finals, one at each of the finals. Jr. Dragsters continue to run their weekly points program at local tracks and convene at their bracket finals to determine a divisional winner.

Joining the IHRA (International Hot Rod Association) Jr. Drag Racing Program includes a rule book, jacket patch, decal, membership and license card, number, one-year subscription to *Drag Review Magazine* and $250,000 insurance policy.

Class Designations:

Beginner: Age 8-9 only, ET restricted to 12.90 seconds or slower based on either ET dial-your-own or heads-up basis. Breakout rules apply. One warning will be issued if a competitor runs quicker than 12.70. If the competitor does this a second time at the same event, they will be disqualified from the event.

Advanced: Age 10-17, modified engines meeting IHRA rules accepted. Class based on either dial-your-own ET or heads-up Pro start. ET restricted to 8.90 or slower. Breakout rules apply.

Master: Age 12-17, must meet all requirements for Advanced, plus a minimum 2 years experience; licensing by IHRA or track official after six approved runs; 3.2A-1 jacket and pants required; full face helmet, rack & pinion steering, and steel brake lines mandatory.

Due to radical combinations available for the class, additional safety requirements may be mandated if deemed necessary by the Technical Department.

Requirements & Specifications

Body: Body and cowl must be structured of aluminum or fiberglass and extend forward to firewall. Driver compartment, frame structure, roll cage and body must be designed to prevent driver's body or limbs from making contact with wheels, tires, exhaust system or track surface. Front overhang cannot exceed fifteen inches, measured from centerline of front spindle to most forward point of car. Body panels must be removable: fastened to tabs, welded to frame. Drilling of frame for mounting body prohibited.

Funny Cars: Funny Cars are acceptable, providing design has been approved by the IHRA Technical Department prior to competition. Additional safety requirements may be imposed based on design characteristics. Contact the IHRA Technical Department for specific details. Maximum front overhang 25" – minimum height (roof) 35" – maximum height (roof) 40" – and minimum roof hatch opening 15" x 10".

Burn outs: Vehicles cannot be held in place or touched by a parent or crew member during the burn out. Vehicles are not permitted to burn out past the starting line.

Dial-Ins: The driver and crew are responsible for the accuracy of their dial-in. Dial-ins must be within class and performance limits. Any dial-in below allowable limits will have to be changed to an allowable dial-in before staging.

Dial-ins and Competition Numbers must be at least four inches tall and clearly posted on both sides of the car and visible from the control tower.

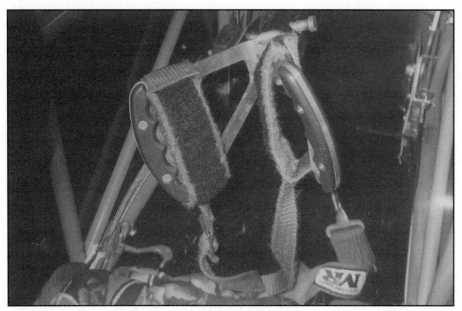

Arm restraints are required in all Jr. Dragsters

Driver

Arm Restraints: Mandatory and must be worn and adjusted in such a manner that driver's hands and/or arms cannot be extended outside of roll cage and/or frame rails. Arm restraints must be combined with the driver restraint system such that the arm restraints are released with the driver restraints. Refer to manufacturer for instructions.

Credentials: Valid IHRA Competition Certificate and IHRA Jr. Membership mandatory.

Helmet: Helmet meeting Snell 90, 95, SFI 31.1 or 31.2 Spec mandatory. Either a full face helmet, shield, or goggles mandatory. SFI Spec 31.1 = Snell SA, open-face helmet Spec 31.2 = Snell SA, full-face helmet SFI Spec 41.1 = Snell M, open-face helmet SFI spec 41.2 = Snell M, full-face helmet.

Neck Collar: Mandatory.

Protective Clothing: All drivers are required to wear a jacket meeting SFI Spec 3.2A-1, as well as full-length pants, shoes, socks, and gloves.

Restraint System: Five-point, 1 3/4" wide minimum driver restraint system mandatory. All seat belt and shoulder harness installations must be mutually compatible, originally designed to be used with each other. Only those units that release all five attachment points in one motion permitted. When arm restraints are worn with a restraint system that utilizes a "latch lever," a protective cover must be installed to prevent arm restraint from accidentally releasing the latch lever. All harness sections must be mounted to the frame, cross member or reinforced mounting, and installed to limit driver's body travel both upward and forward. Wrapping of belts around frame rail prohibited. Under no circumstances are bolts to be inserted through belt webbing for mounting.

Drivetrain

Chain/Belt Guard: All cars must be equipped with a guard to cover the width and at least the top run to the centerline of the sprocket of any chains or belts. Guards must be minimum .060 steel or .125 aluminum, and must be securely mounted; no tie wraps. Moving engine/drivetrain parts must be protected by frame rails or steel or aluminum guards to avoid unintentional contact.

Clutch: All cars must be equipped with a dry centrifugal-type engine clutch. Chain or belt drive only. Axle clutches prohibited.

Heavy metal chain guard is designed to contain the chain in the event of breakage

Flywheel: Stock cast iron flywheel or *approved* billet flywheel mandatory. Lightening or modifications prohibited. Flywheel key optional. Stock flywheels on alcohol motors must have a scattershield and blower housing. Approved billet flywheel mandatory.

Transmission: Gear-type prohibited. Torque converter belt assembly units allowed.

Brakes & Suspension: Two-wheel hydraulic drum or disc brakes, or IHRA-accepted mechanical brakes mandatory. Steel brake lines recommended-mandatory on 8.89 or quicker. No part of lines may run below bottom frame rails. Drilling of brake components prohibited. Live axle may have brakes on one wheel only if seven inch minimum go-cart, puck-type disc brake is used.

Electrical

Ignition Shutoff: A positive ignition shutoff switch, within easy reach of the driver, mandatory. A second shutoff switch on the center top portion of the deflector plate within easy reach of the crew or race official, mandatory. FC additional switch must be on the upper rear drivers side of the vehicle labeled as to function.

Highly modified five horsepower Jr. Dragster engine

Engine

Engine: All vehicles restricted to a maximum of one, rear-mounted, five horsepower based, four-cycle engine. Approved engines: Metro racing flathead, McGee racing flathead and Tecumseh flathead. Porting, polishing and relieving of block is permitted. Welding to intake port is permitted. Machining of deck surface permitted. Adding material to deck surface in any matter will be prohibited. All components must be completed isolated from the drivers compartment. This includes the fuel system.

Camshaft: Any camshaft permitted. Any valve spring permitted. No overhead cams permitted. Any size valves permitted.

Carburetor: Any means to pass fuel or air to the engine other than normally aspirated carburetor is prohibited. Auxiliary vacuum fuel pump allowed. Pressurized and/or fuel injection systems prohibited. Electric fuel pumps prohibited.

Cylinder Head: Aftermarket units permitted. No overhead valve head permitted.

Fuel: Gasoline or alcohol only. Nitrous Oxide and/or nitromethane, and/or propylene oxide prohibited in all classes. Fuel tank must be behind the driver's compartment, below the shoulder hoop of roll cage and securely mounted within frame rails. Maximum capacity of one gallon, must have screw-on or positive locking cap. All vents must be routed downward, away from driver and extend beyond the bottom of the fuel cell. No vented fuel caps permitted, except on stock tanks.

Ignition System: Coil must remain stock-type. Battery ignition systems prohibited. Maximum one spark plug.

Oil System: Oil additives for the intent of producing power prohibited.

Starter: Pull rope or remote electric starters mandatory. Any driver activated/operated starting system prohibited.

Supercharger/Turbocharger/Nitrous Oxide: Prohibited.

Throttle: All vehicles must be equipped with a positive throttle return spring which shall close throttle when released. Throttle control must be operated manually by driver's foot; electronics, pneumatics, hydraulics or any other device may in no way affect operation of the throttle. Throttle stops, other than mechanical (i.e. a positive stop under throttle pedal) prohibited. Must be mounted securely (wire ties prohibited).

Frame

Ballast: No ballast may be installed on the vehicle higher than the top of the rear tires.

Catch Cans: Mandatory. Tank and lines must be securely fastened.

Deflector Plate: A deflector plate of a minimum 1/16" aluminum must be installed between roll cage and engine extending from lower frame rail to the top and width of driver's helmet. Carbon fiber prohibited.

Catch tanks keep engine oil from spilling on the track surface

Ground Clearance: Minimum three inches on all cars.

Roll Cage: Mandatory five-point roll cage. Upper frame rails-minimum 1 1/8" diameter by .083. Diagonals-minimum 3/4" by .083. Uprights in driver's compartment must be spaced 20" or less. Must conform to standard dragster configuration as outlined elsewhere in this guide. Mild steel chassis prohibited in Master and 650 classifications. Note: .058 cm may be used in place of .083.

Sheet Metal: Driver compartment interior must be aluminum, steel or fiberglass. Magnesium prohibited.

Steering: All components must have a positive through-bolt or welded connection. All rod ends must be of aircraft quality or better, and they must have a

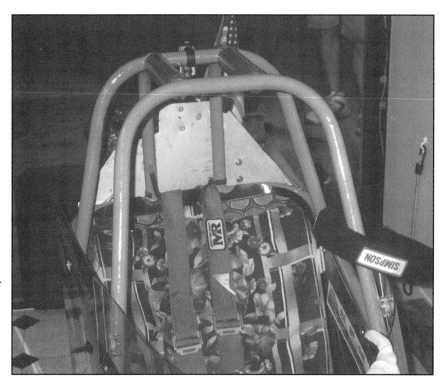

The roll cage is designed to protect the driver in the event of a roll over. Note also 5-point safety harness and neck collar.

bolt through with lock nut or drilled and cotter keyed. Steering must also have washers on bolts to keep rod ends from pulling through. Minimum spindle diameter is half inch.

Weight: Any added weight for ballast must be mounted securely using 3/8-inch through-bolts. Hose-type clamps or tie wraps prohibited.

Wheel base: Dragsters minimum 90 inches. Maximum 150 inches on long side. Maximum two-inch wheel base variations from left to right. Funny Cars 75" to 95", Roadsters 65" to 95", (two variation maximum).

Interior

Gauges: Tachometer and temperature gauges recommended.

Seat: Properly braced and supported seat constructed of aluminum or fiberglass mandatory.

Upholstery: Optional.

Restarts

After initial start-up, one chance will be given to restart the car within a reasonable time at the Starter's discretion. The crew person should keep the starter close by in case it is needed.

Push starting any vehicle is prohibited.

Staging

Once an entry reaches the front of the staging lanes for a run, it must be prepared to fire and race. In order to be a legitimate race winner, the competitor must start, self-stage the vehicle and take the green light. This rule also applies to single runs.

Once past the *ready line* or cone, no crew member may touch the car, except in the 8-9 year old class.

The AutoStart system, when available, will be in use for all classes except for the 8-9 year old class, which will be started manually. The AutoStart settings will be:

Staged Minimum: 0.6 seconds
Staged to Start: 0.14 seconds
Total time to *count-out:* 20 seconds

Deep Staging: If a car wishes to deep stage (not permitted in 660 Top Gun), they should write the word *deep* on both sides of the car so that the Starter can see it. The Starter may activate the starting system as soon as both cars are staged, so those wishing to deep stage should do so without delay.

Pull Backs in the case of over staging are permitted one time. If the driver unintentionally deep or over stages and wants to back up, they should motion with one hand to get the Starters attention. At that time the Starter may pull the car back through the stage beam in order to allow the driver to re-stage the car. This can only be done one time on a given run.

The final staging motion, using applied power, must be in a forward motion going from Pre-Stage to Stage.

Support Group

Communications: Two-way radios prohibited.
Computers/Data recorders: Prohibited.
Electronics: No electronic devices of any kind allowed.
Flag: A fluorescent or brightly colored flag, attached to Jr. Dragster anytime vehicle is towed is mandatory. Minimum of five feet in height.
Staging Devices: Mechanical, hydraulic, electric or pneumatic staging systems prohibited.

Tires & Wheels

Tires: Rear tires fifteen inch diameter x 7" wide minimum, measured at widest or tallest point. All front tires must have a manufacturer's maximum inflation rating. Tires may not be inflated above manufacturer's rating.

All tires must be pneumatic. No solid tires.

Wheels: Front wheels, five-inch diameter minimum with a minimum spindle diameter of half inch. Front spindle must be able to retain a cotter pin, or use a nylon locking-type nut. Rear wheels, eight-inch diameter minimum. No modifications allowed to any wheels.

Towing

Tow vehicles in the form of golf cart, three or four-wheel support vehicle is mandatory. Full-size tow vehicles prohibited. Driving of Jr. Racing vehicle through pits is prohibited. Tow vehicle to be operated *only* by an adult or street-licensed individual. Any time a Jr. Drag Racing vehicle is being towed, the driver must be seated in the cockpit. No passengers. The tow strap may not be attached to any point of the roll cage.

Warm-Ups

Anytime a car is started, whether in the pits or in the staging lanes, a qualified driver must be seated in the vehicle.

Teen Championship Racing (TCR)

This is IHRA's newest elimination class which was started by Beaver Springs Track Operator Bob McCardle. The following TCR rules were adapted from the IHRA Rule Book. To purchase a Rule Book write to IHRA, Post Office Box 708, Norwalk, Ohio 44857.

Teen Championship Racing was designed for teenagers who are eager to race against their peers in full-bodied street vehicles. Drivers between the ages of 13-17 and race street legal cars that have passed IHRA safety inspections. The TCR driver must also pass a vehicle orientation and basic driving test.

A parent, legal guardian or adult of 25 years of age or older, serves as a co-driver for the teen and must be in the vehicle at all times when the teen is behind the wheel. This is an inexpensive way for families to get involved in drag racing.

A photocopy of the competitor's birth certificate, a signed Parent/Guardian Minor Release and a $25 fee must accompany all license applications, with their license fee. Teen Championship Racers receive an IHRA Rule Book, a year subscription to *Drag Review* magazine and $250,000 in excess medical coverage good at IHRA member tracks at IHRA-sanctioned events.

Races are conducted over a 1/8 mile distance, with an ET dial-in formal limited to 11.00 seconds or slower.

IHRA member tracks must apply to be eligible to host this program. Some tracks may not qualify therefore, families need to check with the local track to find out if this program is available in their area.

TCR Driver:

Youth ages 13-17 (up until they have achieved a State drivers license) may be licensed to compete in TCR. All runs must be made with an approved Co-Driver.

A photocopy of every competitor's birth certificate, a signed Parent/Guardian Minor Release and a $25 fee must accompany all license applications.

TCR License:

All competitors must be licensed by an IHRA Track Official. The licensing procedure includes Vehicle Orientation, a Basic Driving Test and a minimum of six approved runs. An Official or Co-Driver must be in the vehicle at all times.

To satisfy Vehicle Orientation requirements, Licensee must demonstrate familiarity with all the vehicle's primary controls such as pedals, steering, shifter, lights, etc. Drivers must perform this orientation test for each vehicle entered in competition.

Licensee must complete a Basic Driving Test, demonstrating the ability to start the vehicle, select gears, turn, brake and stop proficiently.

The Official will make one run with the Licensee as a passenger. This will allow the Official to determine the safety and eligibility of the vehicle per Elapsed Time limits, and orient the Licensee to track fixtures, starting line, timing system, return road, time slip booth, etc.

The Licensee must make a minimum of three approved runs with the Official as Co-Driver. The Licensee must then make a minimum of three approved runs with the assigned Co-Driver, witnessed by the Official. If passed, the Official and Co-Driver sign the driver's license.

Officials will deny a license to a driver they feel cannot handle the vehicle.

Driver may only drive vehicle from the staging lanes, on the track, and on the return road as far as the time slip booth. The Co-Driver must drive the vehicle at all other times.

TCR Safety Equipment:

Seat belts are mandatory for both driver and Co-Driver.

TCR Vehicle:

Must be full-bodied car, truck, van or SUV. Convertibles, Jeeps, motorcycles and race cars are prohibited. Vehicle must pass IHRA and State safety inspection. Vehicle must be licensed. Mufflers and street tires are mandatory and electronics are prohibited.

Sponsorship Tips for Jr. Dragster Drivers

Just like adult racers, Jr. Dragster drivers greatly benefit from receiving monetary help from potential sponsors. Sponsorship for Jr. Dragsters might begin with a family member or a friend of the family who owns a company and would like to advertise their company name on the Jr. Dragster. There are many ways to try to procure sponsorship. Many tips are listed under the Sponsorship section.

The driver should start asking local companies to sponsor their racing efforts. The company does not need to be associated with racing already. It could be a dentist, doctor, restaurant, etc. Literally, it could be anyone or any company that takes an interest in helping; so keep your mind open to any possibilities for sponsorship.

It is very important to put together a portfolio listing many important items. A list of portfolio contents are listed on pages 33 - 36. There are no differences between Jr. Dragster portfolios compared to adult racer, however, you might want to add a couple more things.

List the grades you receive in school, any special activities you are involved with in school or your community, your family and family activities, tell interesting stories about yourself. Tell them how racing has made you a better person, if you are more outgoing, how it teaches you good sportsmanship and how to be comfortable in the public's eye and under pressure.

Remember that once you have a sponsor that your work has just begun. Make sure that the company is aware of everything you will try to do for them. Place your sponsor's name or logo on your race car. Be proud of their company and talk highly of them at all times. Use their products yourself, if possible. Maybe company shirts could be made up for you and your team or business cards and flyers. Invite them to your next event and, if possible, provide them with free tickets. In the pits you can advertise their company with their pamphlets, brochures or maybe some free products. If you attend any events with school or car shows, you can advertise there also.

Make sure you update your sponsor about your activities at least on a monthly basis. It can be either by telephone, in person or in writing. Let them know of any promotional activities conducted that benefit their business.

It is a nice gesture to show them how happy you are with their sponsorship by presenting them with a plaque. This plaque should include a brief inscription thanking them for their sponsorship, along with a photo of you and your race car. These plaques can be made up for around $30 at a trophy shop.

Remember that once you receive sponsorship, that you are in the public's eye and should always be on your best behavior. Always present a professional appearance. You are actually marketing yourself for their company. Make them proud of you and their choice of sponsoring you.

Some Jr. Drag Racing Drivers

Brittany Hamilton, age eleven, drives a 2000 half scale Jr. Dragster with a Blossom engine. Her best times are 8.40 @ 75 mph with a 1.792 60-foot time. She is in the 6th grade and earns all As and Bs in school. Her family stands behind her completely. Her papa, Mark Hamilton, her mama, Brenda, her mom, Sherry, her step-dad, Travis. Her family pets include Brandi, her Boxer, and Coco, her poodle.

One day Brittany's papa was racing at Moroso Motorsports Park in Palm Beach Gardens, Florida when a Jr. Dragster accidentally ran into his car trailer. When Brittany saw this Jr. Dragster for the first time, she told her papa that she would like to have one. Within the week, her papa was acquiring one for her to drive.

In a Moroso Bracket ET race, Brittany came in first place against all the other racers, which were all boys. She plans to attend a mechanics course, when she enters into high school, go to drag racing school and to make a career out of drag racing.

Brittany is currently sponsored by her "papa and mama" and Hamilton Auto Repair out of Fort Lauderdale, Florida. Her ultimate goal is to be sponsored by John Force and to race NHRA professionally either as a Funny Car or Top Fuel Driver.

Her papa races his own 1989 Ford Mustang, which runs low 10's in the 1/4 mile. Her papa and mama gave her the fantastic opportunity to own her own Jr. Dragster and Brittany would like to thank them from the bottom of her heart for helping her get started in Jr. Drag Racing. There is not a more dedicated and die-hard racer than Brittany.

Taylor Anne Puska Elson, eleven years old, races a Boss Jr. Dragster with a Briggs & Stratton engine, which runs 8.40's in the 1/8th mile. She receives As and Bs in school and is in the sixth grade.

Her family includes her dad, Rocky, her mom, Anne, five step-brothers, Austin, Andy, Dale, Wesley, Todd, her step-mom, Trina and her two dogs, Helmet Von Gross and Frysco. Taylor has been racing since the age of eight and is currently sponsored by Speed & Truck World and Rocky Elson Construction.

She finished first in Bradenton in 1998 and in 1999 and made it to the semi-finals at the Peach State Nationals in Georgia. Her goals are to attend a mechanics school and to race professionally as a top fuel driver. She also wants to thank her dad (who races) and her mom for getting her into the sport of drag racing.

Randi-Lynn Avon, age thirteen years old, races a 1998 Strickland with a Blossom engine and runs 9.00 @ 73 mph with a 1.74 60-foot time. She earns As, Bs and Cs in school and is in the eighth grade. Her family consists of her dad, Butch, her mom, Christine, her step-dad Christian Barnes, her two sisters, Andi & Tara, brother, Butchie, her dog Goodwrench, her Macaws Charlie and Harvey and her cats, Moroso and Immokalee.

Even though Randi has only been racing for four months, she made it to the semi-finals in Georgia out of 56 cars competing. Her future goals are to take a mechanics course in high school, attend a professional drag race school and race professionally, as an adult. She currently is a member of the ROTC and would like to join the Air Force. Randi's ultimate goals are to run either Top Fuel or Pro Stock Motorcycle professionally.

Her dad, Butch Avon races a 1999 Pro Stock Mountain Motor Motorcycle with a 2001 1640 cc, Big John McGath built engine which runs 7.30 @ 185 mph. in the 1/4 mile. Her brother, Butchie is also a Jr. Dragster racer.

Ricky Meloche, age fourteen, races his 2000 Half Scale Jr. Dragster with a Whaley Motor which runs 7.63 @ 85 mph with 43 horsepower. He is in the eight grade and earns all As and Bs in school. He got into racing by watching his friend Leslie drive a Jr. Dragster at his local track. He then purchased his own Jr. Dragster and has been hooked ever since. He is sponsored by the family business, Able Lawnmower in Lake Worth, Florida where he works part-time to help pay for racing.

He appreciates the help and support from his dad, Rick, his mom, Pam, his sister, Vanessa and his red nose pit bull, Angel. Ricky was victorious at the 2001 Citrus Nationals and won the Jr. Dragster class for the 14 year old group. Ricky's goals are to race professionally as a Top Fuel racer and compete as a professional football player. At the time of publication Ricky had graduated from the Jr. Dragster ranks and now drives a Pro Stock Camaro.

Cody Istock, age thirteen years, races his 2001 Motivational Tubing Jr. Dragster, which runs 9.90 @ 65 mph, 1.99 60-foot time, with 40 horsepower. He is in the eighth grade and earns all As and Bs. His family consists of his dad, Tony, his mom, Kelly, his Brother, Dylan and his dog, Chopper.

He was influenced by his father, Tony who races his Super Pro 1971 Opel Kadett, 496 ci, which runs low 9's in the quarter mile with NOS. His whole family helps with his racing expenses. Cody would like to run professionally as a Top Fuel Racer.

Butchie Avon, eleven years old, comes from a family of racers. Not only his dad races Pro Stock Motorcycle but his sister races Jr. Dragster also. He owns a 2001 Motivational Tubing Pinnacle Jr. Dragster which runs 8.39 @ 80 mph with a 1.87 60-foot time. He is in the sixth grade and earns all As, Bs and Cs and he has been driving since he was 7 years old. His fan base consists of his dad, Butch, his mom, Christine, his step-dad Christian Barnes, his sisters, Andi, Tara and Randi.

Butchie was driving dirt bikes at the age of three and running the dirt bike racing circuit at four. He has won numerous races at both Immokalee and

Moroso Motorsports Park. He placed seventh in points at both Moroso and Immokalee Track Divisions. Butchie's goals are to run the NHRA circuit as a Professional Funny Car or Top Alcohol Dragster racer.

Cory Washington, age fourteen, races his 1998 Spitzer which runs 9.60's @ 65 mph. He is in the ninth grade and earns all As and Bs in school. His family consists of his dad, Richard, his mom, Barbara and his brother, Drew. Cory's dad runs a Pro Stock chassis drag bike which runs 8's in the quarter mile @ 175 mph. His dad was his influence to get him into drag racing. He would like to run the Quick 16 races when he gets older and also run Top Fuel.

Will Keehner is an adventerous, eleven year old who competitively races a black Junior Dragster. Will is in fifth grade and has plans to take automotive courses in high school.

Will drives a 1998 Motivational Chassis Tubing Car built by his father, Bill Keehner. His Blockzilla engine is also built by his father. Will's fastest time in the 1/8th mile has been a 9.03 @ 73 mph in the Division 2 Jr. Dragster Finals.

His father, Bill is a regular competitor with his 1970 Chevy Nova. He aspires to one day professionally race a Top Alcohol Dragster. Will's family includes his dad, Bill, his mom, Bev, his sister, Joy, and his pet cat, Shelley.

Terry Cucina is 14 years old and is a student in the 9th grade. Terry's dad got him started into racing by taking Terry to go-kart races. Terry started his racing career driving a Jr. Outlaw Sprint car at the age of 9. His fellow racers gave him the nickname "TX Terry" Cucina. After racing Jr. Outlaw Sprint cars for 1 1/2 years, he switched over to Jr. Dragsters. He is now running 8.10 at just over 80 mph and holds both an IHRA Masters License and an NHRA License. His home track is the Lone Star Raceway Park in Sealy, Texas.

Terry drives a '95 Strickland Jr. Dragster updated in 2002 by his dad and a competitor's crew chief. The motor is based on a 5 horsepower Briggs & Stratton which is heavily modified. The different motors they use run from .195 to .305 over bored and from .400 to .563 over stroked with many modifications to the valve train,

ignition and most other engine components. Terry would like to race professionally in either the Top Fuel, Pro Stock or Blown Alcohol class when he is older. Their current sponsors are Thunderfoot Motorsports, Trucks and Such, Huffy Power and Metro Racing. The Cucina's are a racing family and spend all their weekends from February to November of each year on the road racing and enjoying their family sport.

Racing Classes
For All Makes of Cars

Before building your car you will need to check out the different sanctioning bodies, classes and locality of the races. Make plans before building your car to construct it within the guidelines of a certain class or sanctioning body. That way you will make sure your car is legal before you show up at the track and find out otherwise. In some cases it will be possible to run multiple classes within a single race organization or run with different groups with only minor alterations. This will increase your options and save you time and money in the long run.

For the following sanctioning bodies and classes in this chapter, the rules were adapted from each of their individual rule books. These rules were up-to-date at the time of publication and if there are any questions regarding them, you should contact the sanctioning body directly. This book in no way supersedes the respective rule books and is presented simply as an overview of each group and its classes.

NHRA – National Hot Rod Association

The National Hot Rod Association is the largest drag racing sanctioning body in the United States. This racing series consists of professional racing, sportsman racing and hobby racing. There are 24 National events held yearly with over 140 member tracks.

There are numerous competition classes in the NHRA. In the Racing Series classes, there is E.T. Handicap,

Super Pro, Pro, Sportsman, Advanced E.T., E.T. Motorcycle, Advanced E.T. Motorcycle, E.T. Snowmobile, Electric Powered Vehicles and Electric Powered Motorcycle. Also included are Super Street, Super Gas, Super Comp, Stock Eliminator, Stock Cars, Stock Trucks, Sport Compact, Super Stock Eliminator, Super Stock, GT, GT/ Truck, Modified Stock, Modified Truck, Modified, MX Class, Modified Compact, Competition Eliminator, Gas Dragster, Econo Dragster, Nostalgia Dragster, Altered & Street Roadster, Econo Altered & Funny Car, Super Modified, Pro Modified, Funny Car and Dragster. Finally, the Pro Stock Motorcycle, Pro Stock, Funny Car, Top Fuel, Jet Powered Vehicles and Exhibition Vehicles.

Double amputee, Reggie Showers frequently gives motivational speeches when not competing in the NHRA Pro Stock Motorcycle class. Photo courtesy Rich Barry

You can pick up an NHRA rule book at your local drag strip or contact the NHRA office to learn more about these classes. The rule book will give you the class requirements and specifications for all classes.

Hooters IHRA Drag Racing Series – International Hot Rod Association

The International Hot Rod Association is headquartered in Norwalk, Ohio and is the fastest growing drag racing sanctioning body in the United States. IHRA sanctions over 88 member tracks with membership of over 16,000 members. IHRA has been around for over three decades. Bill Bader, the President of IHRA, bought IHRA Motorsports in 1998. The Vice President of Sales and Marketing is Aaron Polburn.

IHRA will showcase fifteen competition classes next year and will host twelve National events. IHRA hosts the following classes.

Top Fuel - Top Fuel Dragsters represent the pinnacle of drag racing performance. Utilizing a supercharged engine producing over 6000 horsepower from 500 cubic inches of displacement, these machines can accelerate from a standing start to 100 miles per hour in less than one second, and cover the quarter mile in the 4-second zone at over 320 mph. Each quarter-mile run will cost nearly $3000 in basic wear on equipment, including almost $400 for the fifteen gallons of nitromethane fuel used for every pass. Using sophisticated computers to monitor all engine functions and complicated clutch-engagement systems, each team is typical of the $1,000,000

Top Fuel driver Clay Millican. Photo courtesy IHRA

investment needed to fund a full season of racing. The Top Fuel Eliminator field is comprised of the eight teams which recorded the quickest elapsed times during qualifying rounds. 2175 pounds minimum weight.

Pro Modified – One of the most popular divisions in the sport, Pro Modified embodies the true spirit of hot rodding, offering a wildly diverse group of race cars and a variety of 2000 horsepower engines. Combining classic body styles and modern equipment, constructors are permitted to extensively modify to enhance both appearance and performance. Competitors are offered the options of supercharging or adding nitrous oxide injection to the power plants; a displacement limit of 716 cubic inches remains on non-supercharged

Pro Modified Camaro of driver Shannon Jenkins. Photo courtesy IHRA

engines, while supercharged versions face a ceiling of 527 cid. Minimum weights include 2375 (nitrous) and 2700 (supercharged). Gasoline or methanol are the only accepted fuels pushing them to low 6-second times at over 220 mph. The Pro Modified field is composed of the 16 quickest teams from the qualifying rounds.

Nitro Harley – The Nitro Harley class is reserved for two-wheel Harley-Davidson Motorcycles. The Nitro Harleys run on a four-tenths Pro Tree and they do not have a break out rule. The engines must have the design features of Harley-Davidson engines (push rod 45 degree V Twin) and be naturally aspirated. The engine may be fuel injected (electronic or mechanical). Single engine only, limited to 175 cid, the Harleys run nitromethane of any percentage as their fuel. The use of nitrous oxide is allowed with alcohol only. The use of propoplylene oxide in any percentage is prohibited. The bikes run in the mid 6-

Nitro Harley rider, Doug Vancil. Photo courtesy IHRA

second range at well over 200 mph with a single nitromethane burning engine. Minimum weight at the conclusion of the run is 900 pounds, including driver.

The Nitro Harley Eliminator field is comprised of the eight teams which recorded the quickest elapsed times during qualifying rounds. Danger is the namesake for each and every rider. Every pass is a thrilling fright-fest. These bikes carry their front wheels almost the entire length of the quarter-mile, while the riders wrestle to keep their mounts on the straight and narrow with sheer muscle and determination. The Nitro Harley Davidson field is open to 8 quickest teams based on qualifying runs. This class has been suspended for 2003.

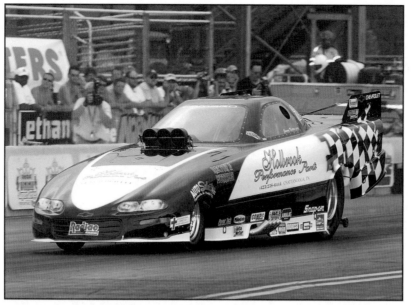

Funny Car driver Jimmy Rector. Photo courtesy IHRA

Funny Car – Among the most toughest cars to manhandle, the supercharged Funny Cars are the quickest and fastest full-bodied race cars in IHRA drag racing. Cloaked in fiberglass or carbon fiber replicas of passenger car bodies, each vehicle is powered by a supercharged, fuel-injected engine capable of 3000 horsepower, producing 5-second elapsed times at 240 mph. Funny cars are permitted to weigh no less than 2200 pounds, including the driver. Wedge engines may deduct 50 pounds. Because the engine is located in the front of the driver, the danger of fire mandates extensive safety equipment in the class. The methanol or ethanol fuels used in the class are less expensive than nitromethane, but each car represents a $100,000 minimum investment. Funny Cars rock the house with long, smoky burnouts and screaming RPMs through the gears. The Alcohol Funny Car field is open to the 16 quickest teams based on qualifying rounds.

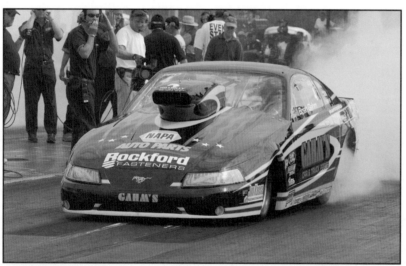

Pro Stock Mustang driver Brian Gahm. Photo courtesy IHRA

Sunoco Race Fuels Pro Stock – To the drag racing purist, Pro Stock remains the most important category in the sport. Deeply rooted within the legacy of production muscle cars, Pro Stock vehicles retain street car identibility while relying solely on gas-burning, carburetor engines to surpass 200 miles per hour. Reserved for North American built cars with North American automobile engines, wheelbase of 99" or more when allowable changes have been made. Body, drivetrain, chassis, etc., may not be altered, modified or relocated. The home of the *Mountain Motor*, IHRA Pro Stock racing often offers a field of qualifiers separated by less than a tenth of a second and consistently presents the closest professional category competition on race day. Engines are limited to no more than 816 cid, and the vehicles must weigh more than 2400 pounds. Every car runs race fuel which is put into their fuel cells in the staging lanes from the same drum. Pro Stock Eliminator field is made up of the 16 quickest teams from qualifying rounds.

Top Sportsman – As the class which spawned the Pro Modified division, Top Sportsman remains the last true *no rules* sportsman category and remains the *baddest*

Top Sportsman driver Emile Rayot from Boca Raton, Florida

sportsman class on this planet. Covering the spectrum of passenger car body styles and power plants, Top Sportsman racers are not encumbered by displacement limitations or customizing rules. In fact, the class offers some of the most radical visual and mechanical thrills in drag racing. As in Top Dragster, the drivers are allowed to use state-of-the-art electronic driving aids and the teams calculate their own performance predictions to determine handicaps during eliminations.

Big-block entries must weigh 2350 pounds, or 2450 pounds with nitrous oxide. Supercharged weight is 2600 pounds for big-block, supercharged small-block 2150 pounds, small-block 2000 pounds with or without nitrous. Top Sportsman will run on a Dial-In ET system. Maximum dial-in at divisional races is 8.00 (1/4 mile) or 5.49 (1/8 mile). Maximum dial-in at National races is 7.80. Competitors may dial quicker between rounds, but may dial no slower than .10 beyond the slowest qualified car. Top Sportsman Eliminator is composed of the 48 quickest teams from qualifying sessions.

Top Dragster – The fastest sportsman category in drag racing, Top Dragster is also renowned as one of the most innovative classes. Combining dragsters and altered vintage roadsters, it presents handicap racing with 6-second, 225 mph contestants. Dragsters powered by big block engines are permitted nitrous oxide injection, while dragster using small block engines may opt for supercharging. The altereds are allowed virtually any choice of engine modification. Teams determine their own performance predictions in order to establish handicaps during eliminations. Maximum dial-in at Divisional races is 8.00 (1/4 mile) and 5.19 (1/8 mile). Maximum dial-in at National

Top Dragster driver Matt Buck former Track Champion in Quick 32 & Super Pro and Dixie Bracket Champion. Photo courtesy of Dennis Rothacker

races is 7.70. Competitors may dial quicker between rounds, but may dial no slower than .10 beyond the slowest qualified car. The Top Dragster field is composed of the 48 quickest teams from the qualifying sessions.

Supercharged Big-block Altered 2000 pounds, Naturally aspirated Big-block Altered 1800 pounds, Supercharged Big-block Dragster 1800 pounds, NOS Big-block Dragster 1700 pounds, Naturally aspirated Big-block Dragster 1600 pounds, Supercharged Small-block Altered 1700 pounds, Supercharged Small-block Dragster 1650 pounds, NOS Small-block 1600 pounds, Naturally aspirated Small-block 1500 pounds.

Modified – For pure spectacle, sportsman division enthusiasts rate the unique entries in Modified at the top of the list, because of the predominance of manually-shifted race cars, wheelstanding starts are common. The category is composed of 64 different classifications, which include everything from 200 mph dragsters, to 110 mph four-cylinder passenger cars. Within Modified Eliminator are sub-categories of dragsters, altered vintage roadsters and passenger cars. Other classes are *Economy* dragsters, altereds and street roadsters, as well as the super modified, modified production, modified

Modified class driver Todd Logan of Braintree, MA races this A/EA '32 bantam Roadster with a 310 Chevy motor. Photo courtesy Rich Barry

stock, economy modified, modified compact and mini experimental groups. Cars within each description are classified by the ratio of vehicle weight to engine displacement. National standard elapsed times are utilized to calculate handicaps during eliminations and also determine qualifying positions of the 32 quickest teams.

Quick Rod driver Jason Lynch. Photo courtesy IHRA

Super Rod Camaro driver Damon Dabbs. Photo courtesy IHRA

Hot Rod driver Rodney Glendening, a policeman from Sugarland, TX made the Brack-et Final Team in 2001 & 2002. Photo courtesy Robert Grice, Extreme Photography

Quick Rod – The fastest of the Rod categories offers sportsman division dragsters, altered vintage roadsters and coupes, and passenger cars in races with no handicap starts. The primary objective is simple: beat an opponent to the finish line without exceeding the National Standard of 8.90 (1/4 mile) or 5.70 (1/8 mile). The methods used to achieve that goal, however, include some computerized driving aids and complex throttle manipulation. Quick Rod racing demands equal parts psychology and methodology for success. Many drivers opt for the high speed, *come from behind* strategy, which elevates the division's normal 150 mph runs to over 165 mph. Quick Rod is open to all entries with qualifying against the National Standard determining field position.

Super Rod – Combining *full-bodied* cars and vintage street roadsters. Funny cars, altereds or dragsters prohibited. Stock appearing fiberglass parts maybe used in place of stock body parts. Doors and windows must be retained. Windows need not be functional. Easily the most populated division in IHRA Drag Racing, fields of over 150 entries are not uncommon. Super Rod competitors use some of the same high-tech equipment and race strategies that Quick Rod racers employ. Like Quick Rod, vehicles are permitted virtually any engine modification. Most Super Rod machines are tremendously overpowered to use throttle manipulation to gain high top speeds. Super Rod is open to all entries with qualifying position determined by performance against the National Standard.

Hot Rod – It may appear as an entry level division with its slower 10.90 class index or 7.00 in the 1/8th mile, but Hot Rod presents some of the closest competition of any category. While each vehicle must retain a production appearance, virtually all are constructed specially for this division. Minimum weight for all 8-cylinder entries, including driver is 2600 pounds. Minimum weight for 6-cylinder entries, including driver is 2000 pounds. Minimum weight for all 4-cylinder entries, including driver is 1200 pounds.

Must be full-bodied entries. Dragsters and Funny Cars are prohibited. Hood, deck, fenders and doors may be substituted with fiberglass units. Doors must be operable on all cars with roof. Convertibles may run without windshield. Street roadsters permitted.

Super Stock – As the arena of *factory muscle car showdowns* for decades, Super Stock spotlights some of history's most powerful production vehicles. Although permitted some modifications, the cars must basically remain as *streetable* as when originally produced. The division is comprised of 98 classes in three sub-groups and for the 2003 season the addition of 17 new classes was implemented. National Standards are utilized to calculate handicaps during eliminations. Super Stock Eliminator is open to all entries; each contestant, however, must qualify for position against each classification's National Standard. Reserved for American factory-production automobiles and some foreign and domestic sports cars. All cars must be factory-production assembled, showroom available and in the hands of the general public.

Super Stock driver Monty Bogan Jr. Photo courtesy IHRA

Earl's Stock – Drag Racing's *entry-level* division offers the most economical racing machines in an extremely competitive forum. A total of 129 classifications exhibit everything from 130 mph *super cars* to 75 mph family sedans. All demand the original production equipment with which the car was marketed to the public. All entries may race in Stock Eliminator. However, teams must qualify against the National Standard for each class to determine field position. Fifty-six classes reserved for American factory-production automobiles and some foreign and domestic sports cars. All cars in stock classes must be factory-production assembled, showroom available and in the hands of the general public.

Stock driver Brenda Grubbs. Photo courtesy IHRA

Summit Sportsman SuperSeries Program – Sportsman classes are the grass-roots level of drag racing. Consists of ET classes, Motorcycle, ATV, Snowmobile and Semi-truck classes.

The program for ET racers has been divided up into Divisions. Five Divisions encompass the main areas of IHRA Racing. This could change in the future. Each of the Five Divisions will host a Team Finals event at the end of the racing season. Each IHRA member race track will send a team of racers to the Team Finals events in their respective Division. The racers on this team will

Sportsman driver Chip Horton. Photo courtesy IHRA

compete for overall Team Championship Honors as well an Individual Championship Honors and awards. The team of racers from each member track will be determined by a season long points system. The top points finishers will qualify to be part of the team.

At the Team Finals, there will be a Champion crowned in each eliminator bracket. Each entry must be an IHRA member and have an IHRA Competition License in that ET range of the vehicle utilized during Competition.

Race Regulations

These procedures and regulations are set forth in the IHRA Rule Book and are to be followed at all IHRA sanctioned events.

All drivers entering IHRA National or Divisional events must be IHRA members, have a current IHRA competition License for the class entered, and driver must display their IHRA permanent number on vehicle. Violation may deem disqualification and loss of points.

Breakout: On any run of a handicap eliminator if both cars break out, the car breaking out the least will be declared the winner. If both cars break out the same amount, the *first-to-finish* shall be declared the winner.

Co-Riders: Riders are allowed in vehicles running 14.00 or slower. Rider must comply with same safety guidelines as the driver.

Dial-Ins: No-dial in may be changed after the entry has left the head of staging, unless approved by the Race Director. Dial-ins may not be changed in the case of a re-run.

At any event with functioning scoreboards that display the *dial-in*, any racer *staging* their car has accepted that dial in, right or wrong.

Dual Infractions: In the case of dual infractions on a competitive run, the car making the worst infraction will be disqualified. If infractions are of an equal rank, the first infraction shall be disqualified.

In cases where both opponents in a race have mechanical difficulties prior to the start, every effort will be made to determine a winner and a loser of the contest. When possible, this includes the allowance of a reasonable time period for the contestants to make adjustments and repairs, then to complete the race. This rule also applies to cars making single runs.

Lane/Boundary Crossing: Any race car touching any marker line during the measured race will be disqualified.

Multiple Classes/Cars: No car will be allowed to enter/race in two classes, including ET at National Events. A contestant cannot drive in more than two classes at the same event.

Pairings/Ladders: Category pairings are based upon established IHRA *Ladder* charts; qualifying elapsed times determine positions. In Professional classes, the #1 qualifier races against the last qualifier in the field. In Sportsman classes, a modified ladder is used in which the top half of the field is matched against the lower half. Once established, ladders are not changed except as noted for required rescheduling.

Points & Point Fund Money: Points & point fund money are awarded to the driver and not the car.

Protest: Points protests must be filed with 48 hours after event conclusion.

Qualifying/Alternates: When paired for qualifying you must make the run at that time or lose that round.

Record Setting Procedure: Two passes are required within allotted time periods. One run must be under record, and one must be a backup of at least 1% of sub-record time. Whenever a record attempt is successful, the entry must report directly to the scales. In the case of ties, the driver that backs up the record first will hold the record. The competitor who holds the record at the conclusion of competition shall be considered the *New* record holder and be awarded all related points.

Re-runs: All runs will stand, except interruptions caused by electrical failure or weather. If any *single* amber bulb is burned out on the tree, the race will be re-run. Track conditions, interference from the car in the other lane, etc. will not constitute a re-run. Cars will run in the order they are paired. This includes qualifying and eliminations.

Rescheduled Events: If an event is rescheduled, the qualified entry must return to the event to retain its qualified position. If it does not return, it will be removed from the qualifying as if it was never there. In this case, the field size will be set by the returning cars, and the field will be moved up and a new ladder will be constructed. All racers, whether they return or not, will receive entry points from the original event.

Single Runs: Single runs will be avoided if at all possible. In the case where two or more cars have single passes (in one class), they will run as pairs, but each entry will advance on to the next round. The same will be true during time trials.

Sneak-Ins: Sneak-ins or stowaways will not be tolerated. Teams found to have individuals with them that did not pay as crew or spectators will lose all points accumulated up to that point in the year, their race entry and will be disqualified from the event.

Staging: All race cars will be called to the Staging Area by the announcer. Only one call is required. Five minutes after the first call, any machine not appearing in the Staging Area will be subject to disqualification. Any car left unattended in the Staging Lanes may be disqualified.

Once a car reaches the front of the staging lanes for a run, it must be prepared to fire and race. If one of the vehicles fails to start, it will be given 30 seconds to fire before being disqualified.

Note: If a car is properly equipped with a starter, battery, etc., but will momentarily not start, one chance will be given to start the car in the lanes; however, it must be repaired before the next round.

Staging must be made with the front wheels only. Rear wheel starts are prohibited.

Starting Line Access: Two crew members may accompany a Sportsman Car past the head of staging, but are not allowed past the burnout box area. Pro Modified, Pro Stock and Harley Davidson may have two crew men to assist in staging, while Top Fuel and Funny Car may have four crew men to assist in staging. Once a car is Pre-Staged in any class, all crew men must be back behind the car. Pro drivers may watch other pro runs from *Pro Viewing Area* only.

Testing: Testing is prohibited at National Event facilities the week of the event. The Sunday prior to the National Event is the last day testing is permitted.

When you become an IHRA member, you will receive 22 issues of *Drag Review* magazine, rule book,

Membership, License & Number Application Form, IHRA Driver Medical Profile and Medical FAA Type Physical Form, IHRA patch and IHRA decal. The Medical Profile Form is to be filled out and returned so that IHRA can help you at the race track in case of an emergency. Contact Sherrie Barbour, 9 1/2 E. Main Street, Norwalk, Ohio 44857, 419-663-6666, extension 230 for membership and licensing information, website: www.IHRA.com.

NMCA Super Series - National Muscle Car Association

The National Muscle Car Association (NMCA) with a combined effort with the National Street Car Association (NSCA) created the largest and most complete street legal drag racing association in the history of the sport. NMCA hosts the following classes:

Pat Musi is a fierce competitor in the Pro Street class. Photo courtesy Rod Short

Tom Heatley, Jr. of Attleboro, MA, crashed this Pro Outlaw Vega trapping at 8.39 @ 132 mph. Photo courtesy Steve Bell

Racing Classes

Pro Street: Pro Street is a heads-up class reserved for 1950 and later, 6 and 7 second, 200 mph nitrous injected and naturally aspirated American passenger cars and trucks. Vehicles in this eliminator are allowed the ultimate in performance modifications while remaining stock appearing.

Pro Outlaw: Pro Outlaw is a heads-up class for 6 and 7 second, 200 mph passenger cars and trucks. Vehicles in this eliminator are allowed the ultimate in performance modifications including nitrous, superchargers, and turbochargers.

Pro Nostalgia: Pro Nostalgia is a heads-up class dedicated to American produced passenger cars of the 60s. These high powered titans out of Detroit take us back in time to an era when horsepower was king and you could buy it at your local dealership.

Nostalgia Pro Street: Nostalgia Pro Street is a heads-up class dedicated to American produced cars remines-

Johnny Kelley with his original '65 A990 Hemi Belvedere competes in the Pro Nostalgia class. Photo courtesy Rod Short

Russ Jung's '67 Camaro – 8.20 @ 170 mph in Nostalgia Pro Street. Photo courtesy Dennis Rothacker

cent of the early 90s Pro Streeters. Vehicles in this eliminator are allowed to be tubbed and there are no limitations on tire size. Nitrous oxide and naturally aspirated V8s are permitted while V6s may utilize turbochargers.

Super Street: Super Street is a heads up class designed for all-steel, stock-bodied vehicles. Stock front frame rails and firewall are required. Entries are permitted small block or big blocks up to 650 ci with superchargers, turbochargers, or multiple stages of nitrous. All entries compete on a 10.5-inch wide sidewall designated slick.

Super Modified: Super Modified is a heads-up class reserved for 1950 and later American passenger cars and trucks. Stock front frame rails and firewall are required. There are no limitations on tire size. The only permitted power adder is nitrous.

Limited Street: Limited Street is a heads up class designed for stock appearing American produced 1950 and later cars and trucks. Vehicles in this eliminator are allowed 4-link or ladder bar suspension. Stock front frame rails and firewall are required. Entries are permitted small block or big blocks with superchargers, turbochargers, or nitrous. All entires compete on a 10.5-inch wide sidewall 'non W' designated slick or 12-inch (tread) DOT-approved tire.

Hot Street: Hot Street provides enthusiasts with street-legal racing on 10.5-inch sidewall designation slicks. With power limited to naturally aspirated small-block V8s, it is a heads-up class featuring '50-and-later American cars and trucks with full street-legal equipment.

Real Street: Real Street is a heads-up class reserved for 1950 to present American brand passenger cars and trucks. V8 entries will be naturally aspirated while V6s can use nitrous oxide. All entries must utilize DOT-approved rear tires with a maximum tread width of 11 inches.

Drag Radial Eliminator: Drag Radial Eliminator is a heads up class designated for stock appearing American produced 1950 and later cars and trucks equipped with radial tires. Cars in this eliminator are allowed nitrous oxide, blowers, and turbos but

The Scranton Brothers Racing 2000 Super Street Mustang. Photo courtesy Josh Bolger

Jim Huber runs in the Super Modified class. Photo courtesy Rod Short

Limited Street driver Mike Lebecap. Photo courtesy Rod Short

Bob "Sponge Bob" Curran competes in NMCA classes. Photo courtesy Rod Short

Hot Street competitor Rick Moroso. Photo courtesy Rod Short

Real Street driver Bruce Lagory. Photo courtesy Rod Short

Brian Merrick competes in the Nostalgia Super Stock class. Photo courtesy Rod Short

American Muscle Car drivers Kenny ('68 Cougar) and Ryan ('71 Maverick) Bush. Photo courtesy Photos to Go

American Muscle Car driver, Mark "The Preacher Man" Walter brings the Gospel message to the racing world. Photo courtesy Michael Ray

only mini tubs and minimal suspension modification. Front wheel drive conversions are not allowed. The body must retain its original apperance and profiles. Exact original OEM body shell type and dimension required. Aftermarket fiberglass replacement panels are limited to the hood, decklid, hood scoop and bumpers.

Nostalgia Super Stock: Nostalgia Super Stock is a handicap style eliminator based on class indexes. This eliminator is dedicated to passenger cars of the 60s that were produced in America with straight line performance being the primary reason for their existence.

American Muscle Car: American Muscle Car is a handicap style eliminator based on class indexes. This eliminator is reserved for various cars throughout the 50s, 60s and 70s that define the classic *American Muscle Car.* While safety is of utmost concen, some modifications may be allowed from original equipment. Classification shall be based on visual inspection and the elapsed time the car is capable of running. This is a footbrake only class; two steps, electronics, stutter boxes or other bracket racing aids are not allowed.

EFI Eliminator: EFI Eliminator is a handicap style index class for American or Import passenger cars and trucks equipped with electronic fuel injection whether factory installed or aftermarket. The class consists of eleven indexes ranging from EFI 9.0 to EFI 14.0 in .5 second intervals. These are hard indexes with no break-outs allowed. Vehicles in this eliminator are allowed modifications.

General Rules

All categories: All qualified vehicles will return on Sunday for eliminations. All vehicles must be self-starting and self-staging. Immediately following the conclusion of each run in eliminations, all vehicles must go to the scales for a weight check, fuel check, drive tire width check and/or any other inspection that the Tech Director deems necessary. Once released by the Tech Department, the driver may return to their pit area or staging lanes. In case of legitimate breakage, a vehicle may be towed back to the scales for verification after permission is granted. Permission must be granted through the Tech Department for any crew person to approach their vehicle before it has reached the scales area after the run.

Bob "The Pumpdoctor" Milar, Racing Products manager for Weldon Pump, races a 2001 Chevy Silverado in the EFI Eliminator class. Photo courtesy Photos to Go

Appeals: Anyone wishing to appeal a ruling made by the NMCA and its Directors, must do so in writing within seven days of the ruling. Be sure that the appeal is addressed to the Director responsible for the ruling.

Appearance: Drivers' crewmen, and their equipment, including the race vehicle, are required to be presentable in appearance at all NMCA events.

Burn outs: All pre-race burn outs are restricted to the designated areas, using water only. Burn outs across the starting line are allowed in Pro Street, Pro Outlaw, Nostalgia Pro Street, Super Street and Super Modified only, and are limited to one burn out across the starting line. Crossing the centerline during a burn out is not a disqualification. Fire burn outs are strictly prohibited. No person is permitted to hold or touch the cars during burn outs.

Conduct of Participants: It is the responsibility of each participant and their crew members to conduct themselves in a sportsmanlike manner throughout the course of the event. Any inappropriate conduct directed towards fellow participants, spectators or event officials deemed unsportsmanlike by the NMCA, is grounds for expulsion from the event or any other disciplinary action as prescribed by the Directors of the NMCA.

Dial-Ins: Each participant is responsible for checking the scoreboards for accuracy of both their own dial-in, as well as that of their opponent before staging. If a participant stages and races, then they have accepted both dial-ins (right or wrong), and the race will not be rerun.

Eligibility – Car: Only American makes (AMC, Buick, Cadillac, Chevrolet, Chrysler, Dodge, Ford, GMC, Lincoln, Mercury, Oldsmobile, Plymouth, Pontiac, Studebaker) and certain other makes such as Cobra and Avanti, are allowed to race in NMCA Competition. The exception is Pro Outlaw and EFI where imports are legal. An individual vehicle cannot be used for multiple qualified positions in either a single eliminator or in multiple points earning eliminators.

Night Racing: During night racing, headlights and taillights are to be used in all unlit areas of the racing facility by all street legal classes. All entries in competition, no matter what class, are required to have one working taillight.

Nitrous Oxide: Nitrous Oxide systems of several types are allowed in some of the NMCA eliminators. Nitrous oxide may not be used in conjunction with supercharger(s) or turbocharger(s). Nitrous oxide commercially available thermostatically controlled blanket-type warmer accepted. Any other external heating of bottle(s) prohibited. The use of any agents other than nitrous oxide as part of, or mixed with, this pressurized fuel system is strictly prohibited.

Pit Area Rules: Excessive speed or burn outs in the pit area, staging lanes or return road will not be tolerated and are grounds for immediate disqualification from the event. For pit control, security and emergency personnel to identify enclosed trailers in an emergency, it is recommended that car number and class designation be put on the top right hand corner of the rear of the trailer.

Staging Lane Procedures: All vehicles must be driven to the staging lanes – no towing allowed. Contestants will be called to the staging lanes in sessions for qualifying, class eliminations, and eliminations. Three calls over the PA system will be made for each eliminator in each round. It is the sole and ultimate responsibility of each contestant to answer the call to the staging lanes in order to make their run. If you are pitted in an area with poor audio from the PA, you are expected to assign a crew person to position himself or herself so they may hear the staging lane call for your category and inform you of them. If you suspect that you may have a problem making the staging lane call, notify the NMCA/NSCA Super Series Staging Director so he can be aware of your problem. Contestants not making the call to staging will either miss the qualifying run or, if in eliminations, will be scratched from competition and the round will be run without them.

Starting Line Procedures: Once a vehicle entered in competition reaches the front of the staging lanes for a run, it must be prepared to fire and race and the driver *must* have all safety specified gear for their class on, including neck restraint and gloves. Failure to adhere with these safety requirements will result in the driver being backed up until all requirements have been met and may result in a missed pass. In order to be a legitimate race winner, a contestant's vehicle must self-start and self-stage including single runs. Push starting a vehicle or push staging a vehicle is prohibited. Staging must be done under the vehicles own power with the engine running. The use of any device, mechanical or electronic, that permits the driver to position their vehicle relative to the starting line is prohibited.

The practice known as *deep staging* is allowed. The final staging motion, using applied power, must be in a forward motion going from pre-stage to stage position. The starter has the final starting line control of each race as it is being conducted. A reasonable amount of time will be permitted for drivers to stage. While a noticeable delay of staging by the second vehicle will not be tolerated, *quick staging* by the first vehicle will not necessarily force the starter to speed up the starting process. The time limit will be determined at the sole discretion of the starter. There will be no warning. The starter will simply activate the tree when it is determined that a driver is holding back.

Tear Down: Be advised that you should not enter your vehicle unless you are willing to submit to a P&G; a tear down of whatever form of inspection that the Tech Department determines is necessary to verify that your vehicle is in compliance with the category in which your vehicle is entered.

Tow Vehicles: Tow vehicles are permitted in the classes Pro Street and Pro Outlaw only. Tow vehicles are prohibited in all other classes. Vehicles that break may be towed back to the pits, by way of the scales first, but only after receiving permission from the starting line, staging or Tech Department.

Membership: All race entrants at the National Muscle Car Association events (NMCA/NSCA Super Series) must be a member of the NMCA. Membership will include a rule book, 10 issues of the NMCA/NSCA Super Series Official Newsletter/Magazine - *The Street Legal Times*, decals, a t-shirt, a lapel/hat pin, a license plate and upon request a NMCA/NSCA Super Series permanent number for your race vehicle. Contact NMCA at 496 Chambers Street, Spencerport, New York 14559, 231-873-5671, www.nmca-racing.com.

PRO Fastest Street Car Drag Racing Series

This series is one of the fastest growing Street Legal Racing Organizations that is producing the Fastest Street-Legal Racers in the World! It carries many of the biggest names in street legal racing. It features the world's top street legal drag racers competing in over 7 heads-up racing classes for over a 1.7 million dollar purse and contingency program. Over 10,000 spectators and 400 hot rods and muscle cars are expected in the PRO season opener in 2003.

This is an exhibition class including such crowd-pleasers like Jet Dragsters, Jet Funny Cars, Wheelstanders and Alcohol Funny Cars. There will be extensive television coverage and exclusive class-by-class racing coverage in the *Fastest Street Car Magazine*. This will bring much exposure to these racers to help with their sponsorship endeavors and will provide everyone with nationwide recognition of their racing accomplishments in street legal racing.

Official Rules

Denso Iridium Pro Street: Heads-up class designed for 1950 or later, 6-second, over 200 mph tube-chassis cars and trucks with blower, nitrous oxide and turbos. Pro Street is designed for both *stock-appearing* and *Outlaw-style* bodied vehicles. Vehicles in Pro Street are the fastest and quickest cars in the PRO series.

Nitto Super Street: Heads-up class designed for 1950 and later, mid 7-second, back-half cars and trucks with blowers, nitrous oxide and turbos. Super Street is designed for all-steel, glass-equipped, stock-bodied, *stock-appearing* vehicles with a 4-link or ladder bar suspension, and 31 x 10.5W tires.

Flowmaster Nostalgia Pro Street: Heads-up class designed for 1950 and later, 7-second, 180 mph, back-half and tube-chassis cars and trucks, that emulate the famous *Pro Street* cars of the early 1990's that defined the original Pro Street movement. Nostalgia Street is designed for completely stock-appearing vehicles.

Vortech Supercharger Xtreme Street: Heads-up, limited power adder class designed for real street-equipped 1950 and later, 8-second, stock-type chassis cars and trucks running on a true 10.5-inch tires with blowers and nitrous. Xtreme Street is designed for all-steel, stock-bodied, *stock appearing* vehicles with stock-type, ladder bar, or 4-link rear suspensions. Stock floor and rear frame rails required (rails may be notched).

Randy Adler's '57 Chevy in the Pro Street Class. Paul Rosner Photography, courtesy ProMedia Publishing

James Gelting competes in the Super Street Class. Paul Rosner Photography, courtesy ProMedia Publishing

Xtreme Street driver Edward McAfee. Paul Rosner Photography, courtesy ProMedia Publishing

Chris Uratchko competes in the Pro Stock class. Paul Rosner Photography, courtesy ProMedia Publishing

Cheap Street class Camaro driver Paul Smith. Paul Rosner Photography, courtesy ProMedia Publishing

Roland Crawford of Loxahatchee, FL with his Ice Blue chopped '31 Ford Coupe runs in the Open Comp class

Kevin Gass competes in the Nostalgia Super Stock class. Paul Rosner Photography, courtesy ProMedia Publishing

TCI FAST Pro Stock: Heads-up, naturally aspirated class designed for street-equipped 1950 and later, 9-second cars and trucks running on 10.5 tires. Pro Stock allows small-block engines up to 435 cubic inches, and big-block engines up to 525 cubic inches, without power adders, and limited cylinder heads, intake manifolds and induction rules.

TCI FAST Pro Stock Truck: The Pro Stock Truck is specifically for pickups. As a division of Pro Stock, Pro Stock Truck is a heads-up class reserved for American-made 1950 & newer pickup trucks. Most Pro Stock rules will be applicable in Pro Stock Truck.

MSD Ignition True Street: True Street is a racing class for mild to heavily modified high performance street vehicles that are street certified and able to drive over a 30-mile distance. All model years and engine types and power adders permitted. Vehicles must be registered, licensed and insured. There will be trophies and awards for not only the *King of True Street* (quickest average) and runner up, but also for the following: Closest averaged ET that is not quicker than the following 10.00, 11.00, 12.00, 13.00, 14.00 and 15.00. True Street is an all run class.

Car Craft Magazine Cheap Street: The ultimate *real world* class in the PRO series. Cheap Street is a heads-up, power adder class for budget-built, 1950 and later, ten-second, stock suspension cars and trucks. Cheap Street includes a $3,000 long-block claimer rule.

Superchips Open Comp: An open-comp style eliminator designed for any year, make and model vehicle and truck. Dragsters and roadsters prohibited. Open Comp features three qualified passes on Saturday, and eliminations on Sunday based on a one-tenth (1/10) breakout. Qualifying ET may not be lower than 9.10 or the entry will be disqualified. Delay boxes, air shifters or electronics of any type are prohibited on all Open Comp entries. Run on a .500 Pro Tree system.

Hamburger Oil Pan's Nostalgia Super Stock: A handicap-style eliminator in the PRO series based on class indexes. Nostalgia Super Stock is designed for 1960s Muscle Cars that defined *street car* drag racing.

DTS Nostalgia Muscle Car: A handicap-style eliminator based on indexes. Nostalgia Muscle Car is designed for cars built from the 1950s through the 1970s, and shows the PRO fans the very best in old *muscle*. Nostalgia Muscle Car's intent requires it to prohibit transbrakes and all forms of electronics.

Entry Fees: The price for PRO Fastest Street Car racers for each day is $20. The price for PRO Fastest Street Car spectators and crew for each day is $20 each or $30 for both days.

Membership: For your membership with PRO Fastest Street Car Drag Racing Series, you will receive the *PRO Fastest Street Car* magazine (one-year subscription, 12 issues a year of the official magazine), racing t-shirt, PRO rule book, license plate frame, decals, windshield banner and membership card.

Tim Clark runs this Chevelle in the Nostalgia Muscle class. Paul Rosner Photography, courtesy of ProMedia Publishing

You can contact them at PRO Fastest Street Car Drag Racing Series, ProMedia Companies, 3518 West Lake Center Drive, Suite D, Santa Ana, California 92704; or the National Mustang Racer's Association 17150 Newhope Street #301, Fountain Valley, California 92708, for event questions call the Event Hotline at (714) 444-2426. Website: www.fasteststreetcar.com

Ford Racing Classes

American Autosports Productions/Fun Ford Events

The American Autosports Productions/Fun Ford Events Drag Racing Series is the World's Largest Ford Drag Racing Series. It pays out the biggest purse and prizes and handles the greatest number of Ford drag racing events. AAP/Fun Fun Weekend Events are sponsored by Ford Motor Company's Mustang Brand Team and Built Ford Tough Divisions. AAP is the sanctioning body for the Fun Ford Weekend (FFW) Drag Racing series. Fun Ford Weekend is an organization developed 14 years ago by Ford enthusiasts specializing in the promotion of Ford drag racing and car show events. Fun Ford Weekend is dedicated to the growth and development of Ford performance and strives to provide an enjoyable and fun-filled atmosphere for racers and fans.

Fun Ford Weekend events take place at the nation's prime Ford markets with 10 to 12 events each year. The Fun Ford Weekend Series is a festival of exciting Ford power featuring Heads-Up and Open Comp drag racing classes along with Bracket racing classes. These classes compete throughout the season for cash awards, points and contingency awards.

The ever popular True Street Class highlights the series with a unique race for the street legal Ford vehicles. The two day Car Show Spectacular is the perfect venue for displaying your show quality Ford. The Manufacturers Midway and Swap Meet/Car Corral has an endless array of the latest in Ford products and services.

American Autosports Productions (Fun Ford) has ten classes to compete in. These racing categories vary from class to class depending on the modifications that have been made to your race car. Just remember, your car

John Gullet is a well known top contender in the Pro class. Photo courtesy Mac Fosmire, Photomagic Photography.

March 3, 2000 saw the untimely demise of one of the great talents of street legal drag racing. Steve Grebeck was probably the best all around competitor in the sport. He drove and won most of the time in cars of his own construction. Photo courtesy Dennis Rothacker

has to be within the rules of the class for you to participate. There are both heads up and bracket racing classes. The rules are designed to ensure a level playing field for all participants.

Mr. Gasket Pro Class: Major modifications permitted. Reserved for 1979 and later AAP approved FoMoCo two-door passenger cars. Steel production body shell or exact compositive body shell or components mandatory. Minimum weight for displacements under 580 cubic inches on nitrous equipped cars is 2200 pounds. Minimum weight for displacements under 711 cubic inches on nitrous equipped cars is 2600 pounds, 2200 pounds for supercharged or turbocharged cars with maximum displacement of 310 cubic inches. Minimum weight is 2500 for supercharged cars with 466 cubic inch maximum displacement and 2500 pounds for turbocharged cars with Windsor type small block only and 2350 pounds for naturally aspirated engines with displacements under 816 cubic inches. Any vehicle with a torque converter may deduct 200 pounds from minimum weight.

Pro will allow *Big Block* or *Mountain Motor* NHRA Legal Pro Stock '79 or later Mustang, Cougar, Thunderbird or Probe. This class will be big block non power adders against small block power adders. Maximum displacement is 816 cubic inches (naturally aspirated only) and 2350 pounds minimum weight with driver.

A Competition Factor, which may require the adjustment of weight or other restrictions to a particular competition combination, may be used at any time in the interest of safety, as well as keeping competition even. Heads up, no break out, .400 Pro Tree eliminations. Burn outs across the starting line permitted. Class designation PRO followed by permanent American Autosports Productions number. Competitive ET range mid to high 6's @ 210+ mph.

Mike Calvert of the Bullitt Boys Racing Team in Georgia competes in the Outlaw class

Procharger Street Outlaw: Major modifications permitted. Reserved for 1979 and later AAP approved FoMoCo two-door passenger cars. Minimum weight for OEM type or ladder bar rear suspension systems on nitrous cars with displacements under 650 cubic inches is 2700 pounds, 2900 pounds for nitrous cars with displacements under 650 c.i. with any block, four-link suspension.

Minimum weight for OEM type or ladder bar rear suspension systems on supercharged cars with displacements under 410 cubic inches is 2700 pounds and on any block, four-link suspension is 2800 pounds.

Minimum weight for OEM type or ladder bar rear suspension systems on turbocharged cars with displacements under 410 cubic inches is 2800 pounds and on any block, four link-suspension is 3000 pounds.

Engines under 310 cubic inches may deduct 200 pounds from minimum weight. Small block nitrous engines may deduct 300 pounds minimum weight.

A Competition Factor, which may require the adjustment of weight or other restrictions to a particular competition combination, may be used at any time in the interest of safety, as well as keeping competition even. Heads up, no break out, .400 Pro Tree eliminations. Burn outs across the starting line permitted. Class designation S/O followed by permanent American Autosports Productions number. Competitive ET range is mid to low 7's @ 190+ mph.

BF Goodrich Tires Drag Radial: Reserved for 1979 and later AAP approved FoMoCo 2-door passenger cars. Must be 1979 or later AAP approved FoMoCo 2-door passenger car body. Steel production body required. Lightweight components restricted to hood and rear deck or trunk lid. Must maintain original height, width, length and contour. Non approved alterations or customizing to gain an advantage is prohibited. Front and rear overhang must remain stock.

Drag Radial racer, Kenny Markwich. Photo courtesy Mac Fosmire, Photomagic Photography.

Minimum weight for Small block or Mod Motor under 410 cubic inches is 3100 pounds on nitrous cars. Minimum weight for Small block or Mod Motor engine under 360 cubic inches is 3100 pounds on supercharged cars. Minimum weight for Small block or Mod Motor engine under 360 cubic inches is 3200 pounds on turbocharged cars.

Vehicles with manual transmissions and more than 310 cubic inches add 100 pounds to minimum weight. Vehicles with 4.6L Modular Motors may deduct 300 pounds from minimum weight. All minimum weights include driver, measured at the conclusion of a run.

A Competition Factor which may require the adjustment of weight or other restrictions or requirements to a particular competition combination may be used at any time in the interest of safety as well as keeping competition even. Heads up, no break out, .400 Pro Tree eliminations. Burn outs across starting line prohibited. All-run field, minimum of one (1) qualifying pass mandatory. Class designation D/R followed by permanent AAP number.

Vortech Street Renegade: Significant modifications permitted. Reserved for 1979 and later AAP approved FoMoCo two-door passenger cars. Minimum weight is

John Sommerfeld won the Street Renegade class for Fun Ford in Gainesville in 1998 & 2nd place finish in Bradenton in 2000

3200 pounds for 310 cubic inch supercharged combinations. Minimum weight for supercharged combinations between 311 and 360 cubic inches is 3400 pounds. Minimum weight for nitrous oxide equipped vehicles is 3000 pounds with a maximum displacement of 360 cubic inches. All minimum weights include driver. Turbochargers, inter/after-coolers and race transmissions are prohibited. Vehicles with automatic transmissions may deduct 100 pounds from minimum weight. Wheelie bars permitted and highly recommended. Parachute is permitted.

A Competition Factor, which may require the adjustment of weight or other restrictions to a particular competition combination may be used at any time in the interest of safety, as well as keeping competition even. Heads up, no break out, .400 Pro Tree eliminations. Burn outs across the starting line prohibited. Class designation S/R followed by permanent American Autosports Productions number. Competitive ET range low 9's @ 150 mph.

Mike Freeman competes in the Street Renegade class. Photo courtesy Mac Fosmire, Photomagic Photography.

Edelbrock Street Bandit: Significant modifications but no power adders allowed. Reserved for 1979 and later AAP approved FoMoCo passenger cars. Minimum weight for displacements under 310 cubic inches is 2700 pounds. Minimum weight for displacements between 311 and 331 cubic inches is 2800 pounds. Minimum weight for displacements between 332 and 360 cubic inches is 2900 pounds. Minimum weight for displacements between 361 and 400 cubic inches is 3000 pounds. Minimum weight for displacement greater than 401 cubic inches is 3100 pounds. Manual transmission equipped vehicles and more than 310 cubic inches, add 200 pounds to minimum weight. All minimum weights include driver.

Chuck Simons races in the Street Bandit class. Photo courtesy Mac Fosmire, Photomagic Photography.

A Competition Factor, which may require the adjustment of weight or other restrictions to a particular competition combination, may be used at any time in the interest of safety, as well as keeping competition even. Heads up, no break out, .400 Pro Tree eliminations. Burn outs across the starting line prohibited. Class designation S/B followed by permanent American Autosports Productions number. Competitive E.T. range mid to low 9's @ 140mph.

Tremec Transmissions Street Warrior: (formerly known as Trophy Stock) Limited to bolt-ons only, no power adders. Reserved for 1979 and later AAP approved FoMoCo two-door passenger cars.

Jeremy Martorella competes in the Street Warrior class. Photo courtesy Mac Fosmire, Photomagic Photography.

Minimum weight is 2900 pounds for 2v modular motor vehicles. Minimum weight for 4v modular motor combinations is 3100 pounds. Minimum weight for 310 cubic inch, small block only vehicles is 3000 pounds. AOD equipped vehicles may deduct 100 pounds. Modular Motor combinations permitted in SN95 or later chassis. Vehicles with cast iron cylinder heads may deduct 50 pounds from minimum weight. All minimum weights include driver.

A Competition Factor, which may require the adjustment of weight or other restrictions to a particular competition combination may be used at any time in the interest of safety, as well as keeping competition even. Heads up, no break out, .400 Pro Tree eliminations. Burn outs across the starting line prohibited. Class designation S/W followed by permanent American Autosports Productions number. Competitive ET range is low 11's @ 120mph.

Superchips Street Stang: Reserved for 1986 and later Ford Mustangs. This is basically a showroom stock class with minor bolt-on modifications.

A Competition Factor, which may require the adjustment of weight or other restrictions to a particular competition combination maybe used at any time in the interest of safety, as well as keeping competition even. Heads up, no break out, .500 Pro Tree eliminations. Class designation S/S followed by AAP number.

Steeda/Hyland/Ford Mustang Division Modular Motor: Reserved for Ford Modular Motor powered, SN95 to present Mustangs only. Dragsters, open wheel vehicles, roadsters, trucks or non-Mustangs not permitted. Any Ford 4.6L, 5.4L Modular Motor power plant permitted. Any modifications permitted. No minimum weight requirements. Transbrake and two-step permitted. Open Comp style eliminations. Pro Tree, Handicap start, One-tenth (1/10) breakout cushion in effect with no limits set on modifications. 15.99 minimum ET required to qualify. Class designation M/M followed by permanent American Autosports Productions number. Competitive ET range is 7.50 to 15.99 seconds.

Tony Goon is a regular in the Street Warrior class. Photo courtesy Mac Fosmire, Photomagic Photography

Susan Bodnar of EastCoastStangs.com with her nitrous-assisted GT running in the Street Stang Class.

John "Mr. Mod Motor" Mihovetz is known to be the "Fastest Man in Modular Motor". He operates Accufab Performance Parts & Accessories in Ontario, CA

JDM Engineering/Ford F150 Division Tough Truck: Reserved for FoMoCo factory production pick up trucks. Non pick-up trucks or SUV's prohibited. Bracket style eliminations and no limits set on modifications. Minimum of 14.99 elapsed time required for qualification. No minimum weight requirements. Full (.500)

A real crowd pleaser is Jason Brown's red truck which runs in the 7s on a single turbo. Recently, Jason has stepped up to twin turbos

Christina Eldert is a very competitive female who runs a Turbo Technology twin turbo kit for her best ET of 8.70 @ 160 mph on stock suspension

Sportsman Tree, Handicap start, One-tenth (1/10) breakout cushion in effect. Class designation T/T followed by permanent American Autosports Productions number. Competitive ET range is low 11's to mid 13's @ 110 mph.

JBA Headers True Street: The Muscle Mustang & Fast Fords True Street Event is a race class for mildly to heavily modified late model Fords that are still street certified and drivable over a 30-mile distance. This task must be accomplished on a single tank of fuel with no outside assistance or maintenance. The fuel supply must be adequate for 30 mile road cruise, three drag strip passes and return to pits. With the street aspect of this class and a wide array of modifications allowed, this class has become very popular.

Reserved for 1979 and later FOX chassis and other AAP approved FoMoCo passenger cars. The following vehicles qualify:

1979 to present Mustang
1979 – 1986 Mercury Capri
1983 - 1992 Lincoln Mark Series, inc. LSC
1978 – 1982 Ford Fairmont & Mercury Zephyr
1980 – 1997 Ford T-Bird & Mercury Cougar
1983 – 1986 Lincoln Continental
1983 – 1986 Ford LTD & Mercury Monarch

The best average ET of three back-to-back runs will be the overall winner plus the quickest 9 second, 10 second, 11 second, 12 second, etc., will also receive awards.

All competitors must pass a track safety and credentials inspection prior to being allowed to participate. Since the True Street event will be held at both NHRA & IHRA facilities, it is the participants responsibility to be familiar with and to comply with the host track's sanctioning body Official Rules and Regulations. In all cases, the official tech inspector's decision regarding participation is final.

The thirty mile road tour is limited to vehicles that have passed the tech inspection. Police escort will be provided. All participants on road tour must obey all traffic laws. Recklessness, burn outs, speeding, etc., will not be tolerated, and may be grounds for disqualification. Police may issue citations for illegal driving or behavior. Passengers permitted during road cruise. Any support vehicles (i.e. tow vehicles, etc.) are permitted on the road tour provided they remain behind the True Street Participants at all times. Any vehicle unable to complete the road tour under it's own power, in any time frame allotted, will be disqualified from further participation. It will not be the responsibility of AAP to find or tow any participant that may suffer a breakdown during the cruise. It is advised that participants carry a cell phone in order to make arrangements for any required towing.

All vehicles will return from the road tour and assume their same position in the pit area. The cool down period will be no less than thirty minutes and will typically be more. Opening the hood for any reason is prohibited and grounds for immediate disqualification. Engine must remain turned off during cool down period.

Opening the trunk or hatch is permitted for access to nitrous bottles or intercoolers only. External cooling of the engine by any means is prohibited. Battery chargers or external electrical devices prohibited. Repairs or adjustments performed from underneath the engine compartment are prohibited. Changing tires prohibited. Tire pressure may be checked in between rounds. Tire pressure may not be added, however, it may be lowered.

In some cases due to weather or other circumstances, AAP officials may restrict the drag strip runs to only two passes. Drivers only permitted in staging lanes. Crew members are not permitted around vehicles at any time in the staging lanes or between rounds of competition. Crew members not permitted in the burn out or starting line area.

All vehicles are required to make three full passes. All vehicles must run all passes in the same running order. Stopping in the pit area or return road for any reason between rounds is prohibited.

After passes are completed, the ETs will be added up and divided by the number of rounds of competition and an average ET will be computed. The results will be posted Sunday morning. True Street participants will be eligible to enter the True Street Bracket Competition on Sunday. This is for True Street competitors only and will run on a .500 Full Tree, using a dial-in with breakout. All True Street rules will be in effect. No tire or other changes will be permitted. Competitive ET range is 8 seconds - 16 seconds.

Focus Central Focus Frenzy: Reserved for Ford factory production Focus vehicles only. Any year or type Ford Focus permitted. Any modifications and applications permitted. Line-loc, transbrake and two-step permitted. No minimum weight requirements. AAP will not be responsible for red lights due to staging, etc. All vehicles and drivers must be in compliance with class requirements as set forth by AAP. Host tracks sanctioning body driver and safety requirements mandatory. Bracket style eliminations, with a Sportsman (.500) tree, handicap

Tommy Hussey is a frequent winner in the Ford Focus class. Photo Courtesy Mac Fosmire, Photomagic Photography.

start, and breakout in effect. Class designation F/Z followed by permanent American Autosports Production number. Competitive ET range is 16 -17 secord range @ 60mph.

Fun Ford Weekend Pro Turbo Kits Bracket Classes - Reserved for Ford powered vehicles. In most cases, the Bracket Racing Classes will run a complete event on Saturday and a complete event on Sunday. Cars will be called to the lanes on both Saturday and Sunday in the morning for time trials by Class name. During time trials and eliminations, it will be the participant's responsibility to listen for the public address announcements for the Class call-ups and lane assignments. All eliminations will be on a full .500 Sportsman Tree, handicap start with a breakout in effect. Burn outs across starting line prohibited except for open wheel Fast Ford vehicles. All-run field with random pairing. All dial-ins and Class numbers must be legible and visible from the control tower. Class designation: F/F, Q/F, S/F or T/S followed by Class number. NHRA/IHRA and host track bracket racing rules and regulations in effect. All vehicles must pass a safety inspection prior to participation. All participants must be familiar with and abide by all rules, regulations and procedures defined in the sanctioning body's Official Rulebooks affiliated with the host track (NHRA or IHRA), any and all applicable SFI Specs, and AAP's windshield decal restrictions as defined in the Official FFW Rulebook.

Fast Ford: Elapsed time: 0.00 to 12.99. Any electronics, starting line aids or delay box type devices permitted. Open wheel vehicles (dragsters, roadsters, etc.) permitted. No limitations on modifications or components.

Quick Ford: Elapsed time range: 7.50 to 17.99. Reserved for *doorslammer* type vehicles only. Open wheel vehicles or roadsters not permitted. Any device that aids in achieving a pre-arranged elapsed time or elapsed time limiter is prohibited. Transbrake, two step type of device or any other type of starting line aids are prohibited. Foot brake only. The only electronics permitted are a line loc and a high RPM limiting chip. No limitations on modifications or components.

Street Ford: Elapsed time range: Any. Reserved for *doorslammer* type vehicles only. Open wheel vehicles or roadsters not permitted. All vehicles must be equipped with mufflers and DOT tires. *DOT* must be embossed on rear tires. Drag slicks and open exhaust not permitted. Mufflers required. Any device that aids in achieving a pre-arranged elapsed time or elapsed time limiter is prohibited. Transbrake, two step type of device or any other starting line aids are prohibited. Foot brake only. The only electronics permitted are a line loc and a high RPM chip. No limitations on modifications or components.

True Street: Open to True Street participants only. Time trials and eliminations will be on Sunday only. All True Street rules, regulations, requirements and restrictions will be in effect.

Proof of registration required. Rented or dealer owned cars are not permitted.

The requirements and specifications for each of these classes can be obtained from American Autosports Productions.

General Rules & Regulations

Competition: American Autosports Productions reserves the right to make adjustments to the rules at any time. This is in the interest of keeping the competition close. The most common way of keeping competition even is through weight adjustments. Additional weight will not exceed 100 pounds per event.

Competition Numbers: All showdown racers must have a permanent number and class designation clearly visible and in legible manner displayed on their windshield, side windows and rear window at all times during competition. Minimum size of letters and numbers is 4" inch high and 1" inch wide. Permanent numbers will be assigned according to last years finish based on points. Requests for specific numbers will be considered. Numbers are not transferable.

Driver: Each racer must have a valid driver's license, a valid Competition license (if required) and a current permanent number. Each driver and crew member must be fully attired when present in the staging, starting and competition areas of the race track. Shoes are mandatory. Shorts, bare torsos or bare legs and prohibited when driving in competition.

Format: All races will be heads up, no break out except for Modular Motor, Top Truck and Focus Frenzy classes. The M/M, T/T and F/Z classes will be Open Comp style eliminations and the bracket classes will be on a .500 Full Tree with a breakout in effect. All pairings with be Pro Sportsman style (i.e. in a 8-car field #1 vs #5, #2 vs #6, etc.) unless otherwise directed by the Race Director. Courtesy staging will be used.

A competitor's car must self-start and self stage. There are eight cars required to make a field. Competitors must weigh in after qualifying if they have weight requirements for their class. If they fail to stop at the scales, it will result in forfeiture of the run. If they do not improve from their previous pass, then they do not need to stop for their weigh in.

Membership: All showdown participants must be a Fun Ford Weekend member and have a permanent number affixed to their race car. Membership fee includes a permanent number, competition credentials, competition decals, rule book, an official membership card, a subscription to Tire Tracks newsletter and a 10% discount off of Fun Ford merchandise. American Autosports Productions (Fun Ford) can be reached at Post Office Box 911, Denham Springs, Louisiana 70727, 225-664-0996. Their website is located under www.funfordevents.com.

Payout Policy: Payouts will be made at the completion of the event. No payouts will be made after the conclusion of the event. All payouts will be made directly to the driver unless other arrangements are made prior to eliminations. A field of less than eight cars may receive a pro-rated purse at the American Autosports Productions discretion.

Points System: No points will be transferrable. To be awarded round points, the vehicle must stage and break the staging beams under its own power.

The point system is as follows:

20 points	Passing tech inspection
10 points	Qualifying
1 point	#1 qualifier in your category
1 point	Low ET in category
1 point	Setting ET record in category
1 point	Setting MPH record in category

Rain Out Policy: If rain interferes with competition, Fun Ford will try to reschedule for the next or best available race day at the discretion of the Event Director. Participants unable to return to a rescheduled event will be awarded points earned through the last round of competition won.

Tech Inspection: All racers need to pass a technical and safety inspection. American Autosports Productions has the right to tear down any racer's vehicle for inspection for any reason during the event.

Tire Tracks: *Tire Tracks* is the official newsletter for all registered showdown participants and is sent to racers on a regular basis. If there are any changes, additions, deletions or clarifications to be made to the rules, it will be posted in this newsletter.

National Mustang Racers Association (NMRA)

The National Mustang Racers Association (NMRA) is the official sanctioning body of the Ford Drag Racing Series. Every event held is televised by ESPN2 to give generous exposure to racers and their sponsors. They can also get exposure in the *Race Pages* magazine and national magazine event coverage.

NMRA is the World's fastest growing Ford organization with the fastest Ford racers in the world attending this Drag Racing extravaganza. The following NMRA rules and class regulations are adapted from the official NMRA Rule Book.

Billy Glidden, son of racing legend Pro Stock driver, Bob Glidden, owns the quickest and fastest nitrous small block Ford in the country. Paul Rosner Photography, courtesy ProMedia Publishing

Les Baer dominated the Pro 5.0 world for three years until retiring. He owns Les Baer Custom which manufactures custom pistols and rifles

Mike Murillo, from San Antonio, TX runs the Super Street Outlaw Division. He has attained over 50 National Event wins, 6 World Records and 6 National Championships. Paul Rosner Photography, courtesy ProMedia Publishing

Procharger Pro 5.0: Vehicles in Pro 5.0 are the ultimate in Ford sanctioned street-legal drag racing. Pro 5.0 entries are limited to single power adder small block 302, 351, big block 460, and 4.6L or 5.4L modular engine types. Up to 480 ci permitted on 302, 351, and 4.6L/5.4L engine types. Up to 525 ci permitted for nitrous 460 big block and up to 815 ci for naturally aspirated big block. Pro 5.0 permits a variety of race-proven modifications and performance enhancements on from-the-ground-up, purpose-built vehicles. Pro 5.0 is a heads-up, all-run, class for 1979 and later Foxed based vehicles. All run field will run on a Pro Tree (.400) NHRA Pro ladder. Three qualifying passes will be allowed on Saturday, with eliminations taking place on Sunday, weather permitting. Official qualifying attempt mandatory to be placed on ladder. Official qualifying attempt consists of staging car, under its own power, during an official qualifying session.

MSD Super Super Street Outlaw: Professionally built small-block and big-block, small tire 1964 and up Ford Mustangs and 1979 and up Fox-chassis Fords. Engine limited to 302, 351, 4.6, 5.4 single power adder engine types are permitted a maximum of 480 cubic inches. Turbocharged entrants are permitted a maximum of 360 cubic inches. Big block (nitrous only) entrants are permitted a maximum of 525 cubic inches. Nitrous - 2700 pounds with 302 or 351-based engine with maximum 480 cubic inches. Supercharged - 3150 pounds with 302 or 351-based engine with maximum 480 cubic inches. 4.6/5.4L modular engines may deduct 350 pounds.

Tires must be 28.6" x 10.6" maximum. Stock-type suspension or ladder bars. All races will be run on a Pro Tree (.400) NHRA Sportsman ladder. Three qualifying passes will be allowed on Saturday, with eliminations taking place on Sunday, weather permitting. Official qualifying attempt mandatory to be placed on ladder. Official qualifying attempt consists of staging car, under its own power, during an official qualifying session.

Texan attorney Chip Havemann is a familiar name and winner in Street Renegade. Paul Rosner Photography, courtesy ProMedia Publishing

Procharger EFI Renegade: Renegade is designed for small block single power adder 1979 and newer Ford Fox-bodied and Ford powered vehicles, including 1996 and newer Mustangs vehicles. Engine limited to 302W, 351W, and 4.6L/5.4L modular engine types. Any engine combination (302W, 351W, and 4.6L/5.4L modular engine types) permitted in any 1979 and newer body style. Engine swapping permitted during event. All engine types are permitted a maximum of 360 cubic inches. Nitrous - 3100 pounds, supercharged - 3400 pounds. 4.6L/5.4L Modular engines may deduct 200 pounds.

All races run on a Pro Tree (.400) NHRA Sportsman ladder. Three qualifying passes will be allowed on Saturday, with eliminations taking place on Sunday, weather permitting. Official qualifying attempt mandatory to be placed on ladder. Official qualifying attempt consists of staging car, under its own power, during an official qualifying session.

Edelbrock Hot Street: Hot Street is designed for small block naturally aspirated 1955 and newer Ford bodied and Ford powered vehicles. Hot Street entries are limited to 302, 351 and 4.6L/5.4L modular engine types. 302, 4.6, 5.4 and 351 engine types are permitted a maximum of 440 cubic inches. All Run, NHRA Sportsman Ladder, Pro Tree (.400), Heads-Up.

311 cubic inches is 2700 pounds, 360 cubic inches is 2900 pounds, 400 cubic inches is 3100, 440 cubic inches is 3200 pounds. 4.6L/5.4L Modular Engines may deduct 350 lbs. Note: 8.5 lbs/cu in penalty applies for cubic inches over weight break limit. Ex: Small block 368 cubic inch engine is 2968 pounds. Note: All weights are with driver & rounded down to the five pound increment. Ex: A calculated weight of 2968 would be required to weigh 2965 with driver at scales. 1950 – 1974 body styles – deduct 50 pounds from base weights. Standard Valve Angle Windsor Production Heads – deduct 100 lbs from base weights. Manual transmission – weight penalty of 250 pounds added to base weights.

Brian Booze competes in the Hot Street class for car owner Joe Johnston. Paul Rosner Photography, courtesy ProMedia Publishing

Michael & John Tymensky run the quickest naturally aspirated Cobra in the Hot Street class. Paul Rosner Photography, courtesy ProMedia Publishing

Three qualifying passes will be allowed on Saturday, with eliminations taking place on Sunday, weather permitting. Official qualifying attempt mandatory to be placed on ladder. Official qualifying attempt consists of staging car, under its own power, during an official qualifying session.

BF Goodrich Drag Radial: Drag Radial is designed for small block single power adder 1979 and newer Ford Fox-bodied and Ford powered vehicles using D.O.T. radial tires. Drag Radial entries are limited to 302, 351 and 4.6L/5.4L modular engine types. 302 and 351 engine types are permitted a maximum of 360 cubic inches for supercharged and turbocharged entrants, maximum of 410 cubic inches for 302/351 nitrous oxide equipped based engines. 4.6L/5.4L modular engines are permitted a maximum of 360 cubic inches. Induction entries without intercooler may deduct 200 pounds from vehicle weight. 4.6L Modular engines may deduct 150 pounds from vehicle weight.

All Run, NHRA Sportsman Ladder, Pro Tree (.400), Heads-Up. Three qualifying passes will be allowed on Saturday, with eliminations taking place on Sunday,

Dwayne "Big Daddy" Gutridge, is known as "King of the Drag Radial Class." Paul Rosner Photography, Courtesy of ProMedia Publishing

"Uncle" Robin Lawrence runs an '88 LX Coupe in the Real Street class and earned 2 runner ups in 2002, 4 wins in 2001 and two runner ups in 2000. Paul Rosner Photography, courtesy ProMedia Publishing

Gene Hindman runs in the Pure Street class. Paul Rosner Photography, courtesy ProMedia Publishing

John McGowan competes in the Pure Street class. Paul Rosner Photography, courtesy ProMedia Publishing

weather permitting. Official qualifying attempt mandatory to be placed on ladder. Official qualifying attempt consists of staging car, under its own power, during an official qualifying session.

5.0 Magazine Real Street: Real Street is designed for small block single power adder 1979 and newer Ford Fox-Chassis bodied and Ford powered vehicles including 1996 to present 4.6L Mustangs. Real Street entries are limited to 302, and 4.6L 2-valve modular engine types. 302 engine types are permitted a maximum of 311 cubic inches. 4.6L modular engines are permitted a maximum of 289 cubic inches. Nitrous or Supercharged 5.0L - 3300 pounds, nitrous oxide/Supercharged 4.6 2v is 3100 pounds.

All Run, NHRA Sportsman Ladder, Pro Tree (.400), Heads-Up.

Three qualifying passes will be allowed on Saturday, with eliminations taking place on Sunday, weather permitting. Official qualifying attempt mandatory to be placed on ladder. Official qualifying attempt consists of staging car, under its own power, during an official qualifying session.

Tremec Pure Street: Pure Street is designed for naturally aspirated small block 1979 and newer Ford Fox-Chassis bodied and Ford powered vehicles including 1996 to present 4.6L Mustangs. Pure Street entries are limited to 302, and 4.6L 2 or 4 valve modular engine types. 302 engine types are permitted a maximum of 311 cubic inches. 4.6L modular engines are permitted a maximum of 289 cubic inches. 5.0L - 3150 pounds, 4.6 2V - 2950 pounds, 4.6 4V - 3150 pounds. Carburetor applications – add 125 pounds to base weight. Deduct 50 pounds for Automatic Transmission. Ford A.O.D. Ford A.O.D.E., & 4R70W transmissions are required. Transbrake permitted.

All Run, NHRA Sportsman Ladder, Pro Tree (.400), Heads-Up.

Three qualifying passes will be allowed on Saturday, with eliminations taking place on Sunday, weather permitting. Official qualifying attempt mandatory to be placed on ladder. Official qualifying attempt consists of staging car, under its own power, during an official qualifying session.

BF Goodrich Factory Stock: Factory Stock is for naturally aspirated small block 1979 and newer Ford Fox-Chassis bodied and Ford powered vehicles including 1996 to present 4.6L Mustangs. Factory Stock entries are limited to 302, and 4.6L 2 or 4 valve modular engine types. 302 engine types are permitted a maximum of 311 cubic inches. 4.6L modular engines are permitted a maximum of 289 cubic inches. 5.0L - 3300 pounds, 4.6 2V -3000 pounds, 4.6 4V - 3375 pounds. Deduct 250 pounds for Ford OEM Stock 5.0 HO heads. Deduct 50 pounds for Automatic Transmission.

All Run, NHRA Sportsman Ladder, Pro Tree (.400), Heads-Up.

Three qualifying passes will be allowed on Saturday, with eliminations taking place on Sunday, weather permitting. Official qualifying attempt mandatory to be placed on ladder. Official qualifying attempt consists of staging car, under its own power, during an official qualifying session.

Vortech Modular Muscle: The Modular Muscle class is designed for any year, make, and model Ford vehicles & Ford trucks using 4.6L, 5.4L, & V10. Ford Modular engines only. Dragsters and roadsters prohibited. The Modular Motor class will run on an Open Comp format with a 1-tenth (1/10th) breakout.

All Run, NHRA Sportsman Ladder, Pro Tree (.500), Handicap Start.

The Modular Motor class with over 32 cars will be contested on a random (all run) basis until the field reaches 32 or less competitors. At the point in which 32 or less competitors is reached the field will be laddered accordingly.

Any modifications, vehicle weight, or power adders permitted. Any gear change must occur as a result of an internal function of the transmission or from direct action by the driver. Pneumatic, electric, hydraulic, etc. shifters prohibited. Transbrakes and two-steps permitted. Delay boxes, cross-over boxes, or any "reaction-time related" electronic bracket racing aids prohibited in this class. Throttle stops and all related throttle-stop type accessories prohibited.

Bob Cosby has the quickest stock-motored naturally aspirated Mustang in the Country in the Factory Stock class. Photo courtesy Kelly Pelrine StangCrazy.com

Joe Hutchins, Modular Motor contender, races the fastest modular motor Mustang with no power adder. Photo courtesy Bob Douglas

Lupe Davila is a frequent winner in the Modular Motor class. Paul Rosner Photography, courtesy ProMedia Publishing

The quickest qualifying ET permitted in this class is 9.100. Any qualifying pass quicker than 9.100 will be disqualified and will not be counted. Competitor will be permitted to re-qualify if additional qualifying rounds are left. There is no ET limit in eliminations. Competition will be regulated under standard NHRA *First or Worst* competition policy during qualifying and eliminations.

Three qualifying passes will be allowed on Saturday, with eliminations taking place on Sunday, weather per-

Lee Howie competes in the Wild Street class. Paul Rosner Photography, courtesy ProMedia Publishing

Terry "Beefcake" Reeves competes in the Truck class. Paul Rosner Photography, courtesy ProMedia Publishing

mitting. Official qualifying attempt mandatory to be placed on ladder. Official qualifying attempt consists of staging car, under its own power, during an official qualifying session.

Fire Control Wild Street: This is a class for real street cars, and hence they must make a 30-mile drive on public roads before doing three back-to-back passes, with no cool-down time in-between. Rules were not posted at the time of this writing. Contact the NMRA or check out their rule book.

Dynomax Truck & Lightning: The Truck & Lightning class is designed for any year, make, and model Ford trucks using Ford engines only. Dragsters, vans, and roadsters prohibited. The Truck & Lightning class will run on an Open Comp format with a 1-tenth (1/10th) breakout.

All Run, NHRA Sportsman Ladder, Pro Tree (.500), Handicap Start.

The Truck class with over 32 cars will be contested on a random (all run) basis until the field reaches 32 or less competitors. At the point in which 32 or less competitors is reached the field will be laddered accordingly.

Any modifications, vehicle weight, or power adders permitted. Any gear change must occur as a result of an internal function of the transmission or from direct action by the driver. Pneumatic, electric, hydraulic, etc. shifters prohibited. Transbrakes and two-steps permitted. Delay boxes, cross-over boxes, or any *reaction-time related* electronic bracket racing aids prohibited in this class. Throttle stops and all related throttle-stop type accessories prohibited.

The quickest qualifying ET permitted in this class is 9.100. Any qualifying pass quicker than 9.100 will be disqualified and will not be counted. Competitor will be permitted to re-qualify if additional qualifying rounds are left. There is no ET limit in eliminations. Competition will be regulated under standard NHRA *First or Worst* competition policy during qualifying and eliminations.

Three qualifying passes will be allowed on Saturday, with eliminations taking place on Sunday, weather permitting. Official qualifying attempt mandatory to be placed on ladder. Official qualifying attempt consists of staging car, under its own power, during an official qualifying session.

Toyo Tires Open Comp: The Open Comp class is designed for any year, make, and model Ford vehicles & Ford trucks using Ford engines only. Dragsters and roadsters prohibited. The Open Comp class will run on an Open Comp format with a 1-tenth (1/10th) breakout. All Run, NHRA Sportsman Ladder, Pro Tree (.500) Tree, Handicap Start.

The Open Comp class with over 32 cars will be contested on a random (all run) basis until the field reaches 32 or less competitors. At the point in which 32 or less competitors is reached the field will be laddered accordingly.

Any modifications, vehicle weight, or power adders permitted. Any gear change must occur as a result of an internal function of the transmission or from direct action by the driver. Pneumatic, electric, hydraulic, etc. shifters prohibited. Transbrakes and two-steps permitted. Delay boxes, cross-over boxes or any *reaction-time related* electronic bracket racing aids prohibited in this class. Throttle stops and all related throttle-stop type accessories prohibited.

Jon (Chris) Anderson of B & C Racing, Fort Lauderdale, FL competes in the Open Comp class. Photo courtesy Dennis Rothacker

The quickest qualifying ET permitted in this class is 9.100. Any qualifying pass quicker than 9.100 will be disqualified and will not be counted. Competitor will be permitted to re-qualify if additional qualifying rounds are left. There is no ET limit in eliminations. Competition will be regulated under standard NHRA *First or Worst* competition policy during qualifying and eliminations.

Bracket Racing - NMRA All-Ford Bracket Competition is designed for Ford Powered or Ford Bodied vehicles. NMRA Bracket Competition will feature a complete event on Sunday, and a Gambler's Competition on Saturday, time-permitting. Time trials will be permitted each day for Bracket competitors. Class designations are required on vehicle clearly as follows: Pro Ford = PF; Super Ford = SF; Street Ford = STREET, followed a class number. The track's local bracket racing regulations and safety provisions will be in effect for all competitors. All run, Full Tree (.500).

A valid state or government driver's license mandatory for vehicles running 10.00 and slower. On vehicles running 9.99 and quicker a valid NHRA/IHRA competition license for ET and speed obtained mandatory.

Pro Ford (P/F) - (electronics): All-Ford bracket class designed for *doorslammer* type vehicles and *open wheel* vehicles (dragsters, roadsters, etc.). Any E.T. range permitted. All types of NHRA/IHRA-accepted electronics are permitted, including electronics, transbrake, delay boxes, etc. Pro Ford will compete on the quarter-mile.

Super Ford (S/F) - (no electronics): All-Ford bracket class designed for *doorslammer* type vehicles only. *Open wheel* vehicles (dragsters, roadsters, etc.) are prohibited. Any ET range permitted. All types of electronics, or starting line aids, are prohibited, including electronics, two-steps, delay boxes, etc. Two-step boxes & transbrake for limiting starting line RPM are prohibited – this class designed for *Foot Brake Only*. Super Ford will compete on the quarter-mile.

Street Ford (STREET) - (no electronics): All-Ford Street Ford bracket class designed for Street Fords with D.O.T. tires and mufflers (closed exhaust). "D.O.T. must be stamped on the side of each tire". Slicks prohibited. *Open wheel* vehicles (dragsters, roadsters, etc.) are prohibited. Any ET allowed. All types of electronics, or starting line aids, are prohibited, including electronics, two-steps, delay boxes, etc. Transbrake or Two-step boxes for limiting starting line RPM are prohibited – this class designed for *Foot Brake Only*. Street Ford will compete on the quarter-mile.

Requirements and Specifications for each of these classes can be obtained from the National Mustang Racers Association.

General Rules & Regulations

Competition Requirements: You are required to carry the following stickers if racing in Super Street Outlaw, EFI/Renegade, Hot Street, Real Street, 4.6 Modular Muscle, Drag Radial, Open Comp, Truck or Factory Stock, with the exception of Pro 5.0.

Pro 5.0 category must have the approved white NMRA windshield decal installed either entirely on the top portion of the windshield or partially on the top portion of the windshield and partially on the roof line, with the entire base of the NMRA banner at the minimum touching the top of the windshield.

NMRA-Holley Ford Drag Racing Banner - Top of Windshield
Class Sponsor Decal - Lower Passenger Side of Windshield
NMRA Ford Drag Racing Series - Side Stickers

You are also required to display a permanent number which is assigned to you. This number must be displayed on the front, rear and both side windows. Numbers on the side windows must be 4-inches tall and 1-inch wide and class designation number letters on side window must be a minimum of 2-inches tall and 1-inch wide. Numbers on the windshield and rear glass must be 4-inches tall and 1-inch wide and class designation letter must be a minimum of 2-inches and 1-inch wide.

Contingency Forms: Drivers need to fill out the proper contingency forms prior to racing. However, to collect monies if you win, you will need to have that equipment on your car plus have their decals located in the proper place on your race car.

Dial-Ins: As a racer, it is your duty to verify, not only your opponent's dial-in time, but your own. If you stage that means you have accepted the dial-ins and the race will be honored. If you have a problem, please notify the starter immediately before you race.

Driver Eligibility: A racer can only compete in one vehicle and in one class. The only exceptions to this rule is if a heads-up competitor fails to qualify and wishes to enter Sunday's bracket race or with the approval of the NMRA Race Director. The NMRA has the option of permitting a vehicle change during qualifying under the following conditions: that all previous times are voided for the vehicles and drivers involved, driver must re-qualify during the normal schedule qualifying rounds for the event, and driver must remain in the class originally entered, and have the proper license to drive the replacement vehicle.

Payout Policy: Payouts will be made at the completion of each round. No payout can be mailed after the completion of the event.

Qualifying: All competitors will be given three qualifying passes on Saturday, weather permitting. In order to be counted as an official qualifying attempt, all cars must self-start and stage under their own power. After completion of qualifying, all racers must go to the scales for weigh-in and present their time slip to the Official. The Tech Official needs to initial your time slip prior to the vehicle leaving the scale to document a valid run.

The NMRA Race Director has the option to build a ladder on as little as one qualifying session if track conditions or weather require. If there are no qualifying sessions completed, the Race Director may build the ladder randomly.

In all heads-up classes, the vehicle with the quickest elapsed time will be the number 1 qualifier, the second quickest will be the number 2 qualifier and so on. In the event of identical qualifying elapsed times, the vehicle with the faster top speed recorded on the qualifying runs in question will be awarded the lower qualifying position.

Rain Out Policy: If rain interferes with competition, NMRA will either delay the race and run it later in the day or extend the eliminations into Monday, if possible. However, no gate or entry fees for anyone will be refunded under any circumstances.

Record Procedures: Owning an NMRA National Class Record is high honor awarded to the fastest and quickest drivers. Record runs can be made only under official qualifying or elimination conditions. Any record attempts with a 10-mph or greater tailwind will not be accepted. In order to set an NMRA National Class Record, a driver must run either quicker or faster than the previous record. The elapsed time and speed records may be set independently or simultaneously.

In order to actually re-set the official run, you must provide the NMRA Tech Director with the record-setting time slip directly after the run. A back up run within 1 percent is required to set an official NMRA record. Any official qualifying or elimination passes of the weekend, either before or after the record setting run, may be used as the 1 percent backup run.

Once a vehicle has set an NMRA record for either speed or elapsed time (or both) it may be inspected for compliance with the rules, including possible tear down, as the NMRA Tech Director sees fit. If two competitors tie for the same elapsed time record (to the thousandth of a second) at the event, the faster speed will be the tie breaker. If two competitors tie for the same speed record (to the hundredth of a mile per hour) at the event, the quicker elapsed time will be the tie breaker. A competitor who earns and then loses the record at the same event will not get credit or points for breaking the record.

Registration & Tech Procedures

2-day Events - Friday: All NMRA events feature inside registration. The gates open Friday at 12:00 noon for tech, registration and class tech-in. Friday admission to the track for racers and crew is free. You can pay in advance your class entry fee for the weekend's racing and your crew weekend passes at the registration.

For 2-day events, there will be no racing during the day on Friday. Some tracks, however, hold a test and tune on Friday night. NMRA will close tech at 4pm Friday afternoon.

3-day Events - Friday: All NMRA events feature inside registration. The gates open at 8am. Friday admission for the crew or spectators will be $10 per person, and $20 to race test and tune. You can pay in advance your class entry fee for the weekend's racing and your crew weekend passes at the registration. NMRA will close tech at 5pm on Friday afternoon.

Saturday & Sunday Events: All NMRA events feature inside registration. General admission is $20 for a one-day pass, $30 for a two-day pass.

After entering the track, racers need to locate a pit space, however, Pro 5.0 and Super Street Outlaw racers need to pit in the Pro Pit parking area. Then go to the NMRA Registration Booth to register. Pay the class entry fee (minus the cost of admission) and receive all necessary paperwork which includes, registration, contingency forms, tech cards and credentials. Fill out the necessary forms before proceedings to the tech area.

Race Pages: *Race Pages* magazine is the hottest Ford drag racing magazine published. When you subscribe the NMRA, you will receive a one year subscription with consists of 12 issues a year.

Race Procedures

Starting System: NMRA heads-up drag racing will be conducted using a standard NHRA starting line system. All heads-up and open comp categories will be started with a three amber Pro Tree start. All amber lights are activated simultaneously, with a four-tenths delay before green.

Runs: If you have earned a Bye run, you can choose to not make the run if you inform the Race Director prior to the race of your decision.

Safety Inspection: NMRA events are held at dragstrips sanctioned by the National Hot Rod Association (NHRA) or International Hot Rod Association (IHRA). For purposes of competing in NMRA events, the safety rules and regulations set forth by the NHRA shall be in effect and all racers competing should follow the NHRA safety rule book as a minimum to ensure legality.

NMRA uses NHRA-certified or IHRA-certified safety inspectors to conduct all safety inspections. All vehicles must first pass safety inspection before they will be "teched in" for NMRA heads-up classes. The NMRA will not be held responsible for failed safety inspections and no refunds of entry fees shall be made to racers failing to comply.

Safety Rules: If any racer exceeds his elapsed time or MPH for which he is safety certified, he will be found in violation and depending on the severity, will be disqualified as a driver or the vehicle will be prevented from further runs until the problem is fixed.

Tech Inspection: All racers need to pass the NMRA technical inspection. Also, NMRA has the right to tear down any racer's vehicle for inspection for any reason during the event.

Membership to NMRA: If you become a member of NMRA, you will receive a permanent number, windshield banner, decals, rule book, membership card, season poster, t-shirt, license plate frame and a one-year subscription to Race Pages magazine. For more information, contact them at 3518 West Lake Center Drive, Suite D, Santa Ana, California 92704, 714-444-2426. Their website is www.nmraracing.com.

Chevy Racing Classes

Super Chevy Shows

The Super Chevy Show Tour is the largest bracket racing series in the country. The average race car field at a Super Chevy Show is over 400. The year 2003 marks the 23rd Anniversary season for Super Chevy and it currently promotes twenty-one events yearly. This is the largest group of Chevrolet enthusiasts and includes sponsors and vendors.

The show consists of drag racing, car show, swap meet, car corral and the Performance and Restoration Marketplace. Each event is editorialized in Super Chevy Magazine and many are televised on ESPN2. At each event, ESPN2 will produce two one-half hour television shows, one on drag racing and the other on the car show. This provides comprehensive national television coverage of the Super Chevy Show.

Nitro Coupe Class: The highlight of the show is an eight-car field of nostalgic Chevrolet-bodied coupes with supercharged monster motors running on nitromethane-enhanced fuel. These cars run with elapsed times of low sixes and speeds well over 235 mph and are considered the fastest *Doorslammer* drag cars in the world. In addition to this show, the twice-daily, professional show features jet cars and wheelstanders.

All engines must be Chevrolet-type engines, 526 cid maximum, supercharged only, Alan Johnson design and Fontana Chevrolet, Hemi-head design engines approved, maximum two valves per cylinder, one spark plug per cylinder, one magneto. Dry sump system must have tank mounted inside frame rails. Turbocharger prohibited. Engine must be equipped with an SFI Spec 7.1 lower engine ballistic/restraint device, and blower belt guard and restraint. A positive method (flange, lip, etc) must be attached to the intake manifold or engine block to retain both the front and rear manifold to block gasket(s) in the event engine crankcase/valley become over pressurized. The flange/lip must extend past the surface of the gasket and be contoured to closely fit the block and manifold surfaces to prevent the gasket from extruding. Weight for supercharged is 2600 pounds, including driver.

Roger Gustin - Roger Gustin, NHRA Hall of Fame member, owner of Gustin Racing jet funny car team and AutoStar Productions, producers of the Super Chevy Shows, the World's largest touring drag race and car show series. Photo courtesy of AutoStar Productions

All cars will be required to pass tech inspections, per the sanction of the host track. Track tech is final. Any car/team violating the thirty percent (30%) nitro rule or maximum twenty percent (20%) OD will not be paid for the appearance and will be banned from AutoStar events for the remainder of the season, first offense; banned for two years after second offense.

Each driver receives 5 points per appearance for each car entered, 10 points per round win during eliminations and 5 points for speed or ET record. Must back up within one percent (1%), qualifying or eliminations (not test runs). No transfer of points.

All drivers must appear at the autograph session. All nitro coupe teams understand that nitro coupe is an AutoStar Productions, Inc. class, not an NHRA class per se, and cannot race at a non-Autostart Event at an NHRA-member track.

There are two qualifying runs on Saturday and Sunday. Eliminations are at noon, 3:00 and 4:00 p.m. and televised on ESPN2. If Saturday qualifying is rained out, drivers will draw for first round position Sunday.

All nitro coupes are booked through Nichols & Associates, points are to establish the championship of the Super Chevy Show only. A seven thousand dollar ($7000) points fund will be paid at the end of the season ($5000 to winner; $2000 to runner-up).

Nitro coupe drivers must hold an NHRA or IHRA license for Pro-Mod competition. A driver may qualify a nitro coupe for another driver/team.

The main attraction at the Super Chevy Show is the Gustin jet cars. Roger Gustin was the first driver to be licensed to race a jet car. He began a one-man crusade to convince the National Hot Rod Association (NHRA) to sanction the jets to run back in 1974. Roger was inducted into the NHRA Hall of Fame in 1981.

Dan Nickelson races a '94 Chevy Beretta GT, with 526 cubic inch blown Pontiac Nickelson Racing Engine. Photo courtesy of AutoStar Productions

Roger Gustin gave up driving after thirty-five years, however, the Gustin Racing Team would continue to campaign the top jet-powered Chevrolet race car in the nation with winning driver Jerry Gannon. The year 2002 marked 45 years in the fast lane for Roger Gustin and his team. The Gustin Team has won more races and set more records than any other team in jet racing history. Regrettably, team driver Jerry Gannon lost his life in early 2002 as a result of injuries sustained in a jet car accident at Atlanta Dragway.

Drag Racing Information:

Bracket One - This class allows slicks and electronics and follows the safety tech rules for either IHRA or NHRA, depending on which track they are racing on.

Bracket Two - This class allows slicks, but no electronics, and follows the safety tech rules for either IHRA or NHRA, depending on which track they are racing on.

DOT Street Tire - This class only allows Chevy-bodied race vehicles (no GM). The safety rules are for either IHRA or NHRA, depending on which track they are racing on.

Bracket 1 Nova. Photo courtesy AutoStar Productions.

Bracket 2 Camaro. Photo courtesy AutoStar Productions

Bracket 2 racer Bob Mendenhall raced his '72 Super Sport until a 150 mph crash in 2002 when his transmission exploded at the finish line. he no longer races, but still participates in other aspects of drag racing

Theresa Anton, the winner of a Wally in 2001, races her '69 SS Camaro in the Bracket 2 class with crew chief, Bob Serena. Photo courtesy Joe Herrmann

GM Street Class - This class is open to all late-model GM models (including Chevrolet, Pontiac, Buick, Oldsmobile, Cadillac and Saturn) with a 4 or 6 cylinder engine – stock or modified and front wheel drive. V-8s and rear wheel drive cars are not including in this new class. The safety rules are for either IHRA or NHRA, depending on which track they are racing on.

DOT Street class El Camino. Photo courtesy AutoStar Productions

After receiving your drag race ticket, fully complete the tech card and proceed to tech area for inspection. Please print legibly; all winner and magazine information is derived from what you write. A run card will be issued after successfully passing tech. Return to your pit area and wait for your class to be called to staging area for timed runs (except Friday) Test and Tune may be *open call*.

Make sure your class designation and car number are clearly written on the windshield, side glass on both sides of vehicle and rear window for easy identification. (Number issued by host track in tech).

It is important to listen to the public address system and/or AM/FM radio simul-broadcast at all times to be sure of hearing your class call.

To minimize waiting time in the staging area, all timed runs are to run in sessions according to class; you will not be allowed to enter the staging lanes unless your class has been called. When your class is called, proceed immediately to the numbered lanes assigned to your class. Be sure to take your run card.

Upon completion of your timed run, return to your assigned pit area and wait for your next call to the staging area.

Bracket eliminations begin Sunday at 9:30 am at most Super Chevy locations; Sunday morning time trials are not guaranteed due to car counts, weather and curfews. At Pomona, Maple Grove and Norwalk, eliminations begin Saturday at 1:00 pm.

At your convenience, present your bright yellow or green drag racing admittance ticket (NOT run card) at the Car Show Central registration tent during show hours to receive a participant dash plaque and Super Chevy Show decals. It is a good idea to safeguard your ticket; you must have it on your person to exit and re-enter the facility.

ET breaks and electronic issues are determined by the host tracks and may vary by event location; contact host track for specific guidelines as definitions vary by sanctioning body (NHRA or IHRA), divisions and tracks. The following general guidelines are anticipated for the season: All brackets – no computers or data recorders. Bracket One – electronics allowed. Bracket Two, DOT Street Tire and GM Street – no electronics.

Mufflers and DOT street tires required for DOT Street Tire and GM Street classes (slicks okay in Bracket One and Bracket Two). At Pomona Raceway Fairplex, mufflers are required on all bracket cars.

NHRA/IHRA and host track tech and safety rules apply. Host track staging and tree rules will also apply. It is your responsibility to check your dial-in; incorrect dial-in will not be cause for re-runs.

Bracket One and Bracket Two will run 1/8 mile at Memphis, Bristol, Atlanta, Montgomery, and Rockingham events; DOT Street Tire, GM Street, and professional/feature show cars will run 1/4 mile. At all other events – all classes run 1/4 mile.

An optional Friday test and tune (weather permitting) is offered at all Super Chevy Show locations except Pomona, Indy, Maple Grove and Norwalk. Entry fee is $25 and you must be entered in the weekend Super Chevy bracket race to enter. Staging lanes are open from noon - 5 pm unless otherwise posted.

An optional Saturday bonus race (weather permitting) will be offered at all Super Chevy Show locations except Pomona, Maple Grove and Norwalk. You must be entered in the weekend Super Chevy bracket race to enter. Entry fee and purse may vary by location; inquire at gate or tower. At most locations, the race will begin after two complete rounds of time trials. See event-specific Saturday bonus race flyers available at the gate for specific entry fees, purses and additional rules.

At Norwalk Raceway Park event, a test and tune will be available on Thursday, from noon to 5 pm at no additional charge. An optional Friday Bonus Race will be available on Friday afternoon after two time trials at Maple Grove and Norwalk Raceway Park. See Bonus Race flyer available at Maple Grove and Norwalk gates for additional information.

At Maple Grove and Norwalk, there will be a *Last Chance Race* on Sunday at noon for racers eliminated during the first round Saturday afternoon, and second round Sunday morning. Newly-arriving racers may pay Sunday gate admittance of $20 plus Last Chance Race entry fee to participate – no time run. See Last Chance Race flyers available at gate at Maple Grove and Norwalk for specific entry fees and purses.

Scheduled times for eliminations will be announced; however, listening to the public address system and/or AM/FM radio broadcast at all times is necessary because of possible changes. Every attempt should be made to follow the racing format schedule published in event advertising and brochures regarding time trials and race elimination times. Deviations in published or traditional times due to curfews, noise restraint and car count should be arranged well in advance of your scheduled event with AutoStar President Roger Gustin.

Jr. Dragsters may participate at the AutoStar events at the discretion of the host track.

Car Show: The show features the largest single-make show series in the world. Over 400 show cars are in attendance at each event. On Saturday, Editor's Choice Awards are presented in twenty categories.

Swap Meet/Car Corral: The car corral is the place to buy and sell vehicles from classics to show cars. The swap meet is where you can look for hard to find parts. Participant set up begins at 10 am on Friday.

Youth America Program: This Super Chevy Show program is held for young people ages 18 and younger each Sunday morning. The program teaches young adults to take pride in their abilities and set positive goals to accomplish: to be successful in life, do well in school and to make positive choices. They want young people to learn what they can do to better themselves with their families and their communities.

This program is designed to help young adults learn about the world in a positive and uplifting manner and to teach morals and values that will be beneficial for the rest of their lives.

If you would like additional information regarding Super Chevy Shows, please contact them at: Post Office Box 310, Etna, OH 43018, 1-800-692-6230 or 740-964-2350 Monday through Friday, 9 am – 5 pm Eastern or by fax anytime at 740-964-2340. If you become a member of the Super Chevy Show Association you receive a bi-monthly newsletter, event discounts and collectibles.

Mopar Racing Classes

Mopar Nationals

The Mopar Nationals are held once a year in the beginning of August at National Trail Raceway in Columbus, Ohio. The Nationals attract over 50,000 people, with 3000 cars competing, and over 1700 vendors in their three-day event. They continue to lead all Mopar Car Shows in the advancement of the judging of collector cars.

Max-Wedges, Hemis, small blocks, big blocks, turbo-fours and V-10 Mopars; all will compete in side-by-side racing action. The top horsepower delivered to the rear wheels and *Modified* Mopar will be awarded the Mopar National's Top Gun award. The Nostalgic Shoot Out where Max Wedge and Hemi compete, keeps the audience on their feet. Competition includes wheelstanders, pro mods, super stocks and concept cars.

Classes: There are two main categories, one that competes for money and the other for trophies. Within the money class, there are six ET brackets along with the three shoot out classes. Within the trophy competition, there will be one bracket. Vehicles entered in the trophy class or the Mopar Performance Street bracket class are limited to street tires (DOT approved) and mufflers. Vehicles competing in the race classes are allowed to bring trailers.

Quick 16: This class will be divided into 8 doorslammers and 8 open wheel cars (if the qualifying numbers are met). Each class will run off against one another until the finals.

Super Pro: (7.50-11.99). Allows electronics.

Pro: (10.00-13.99). No electronics.

Street: (14.00-Up) Street tires only (DOT Approved) and mufflers.

ET Challenge: Run what you brung!

Mopar Action: Follow the NHRA tech guidelines

Neon Challenge: Dodge/Plymouth/Chrysler Neon Body & Engines, Bolt on aftermarket parts open, i.e. blocks, heads, intakes and other

Ken & LaDonna Prevette, of Lexington, NC own this 1970 Plymouth and Ken runs in the Pro class

Len Prevette's 1974 440 Barracuda also is a contender in the Pro class

common speed equipment. Must run four-cylinder engine, fuel injection or carburetion allowed. Full-bodied: Fenders, doors, glass, etc. Lightweight replicas of body panels permitted. Operational Headlights, taillights, turn signals and horn. Stock appearing for body use. Fully functional muffler systems in use during all runs. Slicks or DOT street tires up to 12" wide. NHRA/IHRA safety specs and license to ETs run. Interior must retain reasonable stock/factory apperaance, stock floorboard and firewall required, two buckets required. Back seat optional. Stock dash, carpet on floorboards. Stock appearing wheel wells. No SS/A style fender openings. Single plate nitrous system allowed. No stacked systems. Dual shot okay. Open to streetable cars. No Pro-Stock, funny or altered drag cars. All cars subject to P & G or head removal. Race Format: Qualified field. Heads up Pro Tree.

Neon Bracket: Follow the NHRA tech guidelines. Run on a Sportsman tree.

Nostalgia Shoot Out: Slicks or DOT street tires up to 12" wide.

FWD Shootout: Heads up class. Slicks or DOT street tires up to 12" wide.

Trophy Class: Street tires only (DOT approved) and mufflers.

Rules

General Shoot Out: Dodge/Plymouth/Chrysler Body & Engines. Bolt-on aftermarket parts open, i.e. blocks, heads, intakes and other common speed equipment. Fuel injection, single four barrels allowed. Full bodied: fenders, doors, glass, etc., Lightweight replicas of body panels permitted. No Lexan. Operational head lights, taillights, turn signals and horn. Stock appearing for body use. Fully functional muffler systems in use during all runs. Slicks or DOT street tires up to 12" wide. NHRA/IHRA safety specs and license to ETs run.

Interior must retain reasonable stock/factory appearance, stock floor board and firewall required, two buckets re:, back seat optional. Stock dash, carpet on floorboards. Stock appeared rear wheel wells. No SS/A style quarters, inner tubs allowed. No electronics, transbrake or throttle control okay. Single plate nitrous system allowed. No stacked systems. Dual shot okay. Open to streetable cars, No Pro Stock, funny or altered drag cars. All cars subject to P & G or head removal. Race format: Qualified field, heads up Pro Tree.

Drag Racing: All cars that entered into the Drag Racing Program must be NHRA tech inspected. Tech is available on Thursday before the race, from 12 noon to 6 pm. Tech is open on Friday and Saturday from 9 am to 5 pm. There is no tech inspection on Sunday. Tech is located at the finish line of the quarter mile on the east side of the track. Your confirmation package contains the necessary paperwork for tech inspection. Please have it filled out ahead of time. If you fail tech inspection, refunds will only be paid on days left on ticket(s). All NHRA rules apply.

Rules: All racing classes abide by the NHRA sanctioning rule book. Vehicles must pass NHRA rules for the ET the vehicle runs. Helmets are required for cars running faster than 13.99. All race type entries can compete in one of the classes. Once a car is entered into a selected class, it must remain in that class, unless it is one of the classes that require qualifying. If the vehicle fails to qualify in that class, it can be entered into one of the other bracket classes.

Once a vehicle has been eliminated in a class, they cannot enter another class. Only one driver is allowed per car, unless two entries have been purchased under one car. The classes are available along with the tentative pay outs. Note: Some classes have contingency money in addition to the listed payouts. Payouts may be reduced based on the number of entries per class. The Quick 16 class will be divided into 8 *doorslammers* and 8 open wheel cars (if the qualifying numbers are met). Each class will run off against one another until the finals. The Neon and FWD Shoot Outs are heads up classes at this time. There is an overlap on the Super Pro and Pro classes based on if the vehicle is running electronics. No electronics are allowed in Pro, Super Pro allows electronics.

Souvenirs: The Mopar Nationals sell a limited number of t-shirts, die-cast cars, squirt guns, license plate brackets, dash plaques, magnets and decals.

Trailer Parking: Trailer parking is allowed for those vehicles that have entered the Bracket/Shoot Out Style classes and have paid the $25 permit fee. Vehicles racing in the street bracket or the trophy class are not allowed on-grounds trailer parking. Leave the trailer at the motel or in the general parking area. There is also trailer parking at the Gate H lot in the northeast corner of the track. Open race car parking is clearly marked on the map and must be adhered too.

Car Show: The Mopar Nationals car show is very popular as there are over 230 cars entered into 39 Judging categories as well as the OE Certification class. The OE Certification class (original equipment) is Gold/Silver/Bronze certified based on Mopar Nats' Gold Standards.

Young Guns: This is a new class where young Mopar enthusiasts (ages 16-24) compete against one another. This class is not separated by year/body style, but rather by original and modified. Depending on the number of entries, first, second, third and fourth places will be awarded. Must show proof of vehicle ownership and registration at the time of entry. On the application circle either the original or modified class and then write YOUNG GUNS, if you want to enter as such.

Original: Vehicle is in same configuration as delivered from factory, original color paint, engine designation and options.

Clone: Vehicle is stock in appearance or close. Non-original engine, or non-original color, or non-original interior, etc. Vehicle is basically a clone or color changes have occurred. Vehicles that have slight modifications would not enter this class, but rather the modified.

Modified: Vehicle is basically stock appearing, except for mag wheels, chrome parts, paint or aftermarket gauges, parts, etc.

Pro Street: Vehicle is heavily modifed. Custom paint, custom interior/dash, or tubbed, high rise manifold, blower, etc.

Street: 1962-1973 vehicles only that have the same aftermarket parts that were offered at the time that the car was built. ET mags, Sun tach, glass packs, etc. This is a class for the vehicles that are modified in a way that was popular for the time period of their car. In 1969, a lot of people would use the same wheels that Sox & Martin were running, or some other racer. The modified parts must be respective of that era. Custom wheels of today, gauges, exhaust, do not qualify.

All car show winners are posted at the Judging Tent & Mopar Nationals Registration Tent on Saturday afternoon. Winners are instructed to pick up their plaque at this time. Along with a plaque, winners are given a 3 x 5 card with vehicle information and show location. Keep this card on hand for the Sunday Award ceremony. After the award ceremony, the winners are asked to proceed to the Road Show trailer. Pictures are taken and these photographs appear in most of the major magazines that cover the Nationals.

To receive an Official Mopar Nats Internet Newsletter free, contact: www.moparnats.org. *Rapid Transit News* features the latest information on the Mopar restoration tips, how to articles, new product release, New Mopar Performance parts and accessories.

The Mopar Nationals Office is located at Post Office Box 2303, Dearborn, Michigan 48123, 313-278-2248, www.moparnats.org.

Keith Downing competes in the Mopar Shootout S.W. Pro class

John Schurr competes in the Sportsman class

Angelo Phillips runs in the Street class

Blaine Anderson races his white truck in the Dakota R/T class

Mopar Shootout Southwest

This is an *All Chrysler Powered Program* held once a year at Southwestern International Raceway in Tucson, Arizona. It is presented by Earnhardt Dodge and is a drag race, car show and swap meet event.

The event is scheduled for Saturday and Sunday with tech time trials from 9 am to 2 pm. Saturday at 2 pm begins the Gambler - Quick 8 door & Quick 8 Open class and Sunday at 2 pm eliminations begin. The Gambler and Quick 8 classes are handicapped races and they follow the NHRA safety rules.

Bracket races are run which consist of Pro, Sportsman, Street and Dakota R/T. All bracket races will adhere to the NHRA safety guidelines and rules.

Pro class allows electronics.

Sportsman class allows no electronics.

Street class allows no electronics. This class allows no slicks to be driven and mufflers to be used.

The Combo Race consists of Super Stock and Stock classes which follow the NHRA safety rules.

There is overnight track camping with security provided. After the race is completed, a Saturday Night get together is held at the track in the pits. Barbecue hamburgers, beans, potato salad and chips are served.

To find out more information about this once a year Mopar race, please contact Dennis Maurer at 480-968-5056 or email at dmaurer10@juno.com.

Chrysler Classic Events

Chrysler Classic Events features the following yearly events; Winter Chrysler Classic, Columbus Chrysler Classic, Tri-State Chrysler Classic, Kansas City Chrysler Classic, Milan Chrysler Classic and the Norwalk Chrysler Classic. They feature point classes, heads up street legal classes and specialty classes. For more information contact Classic Events at www.chryslerclassic.com.

Moparfest

This event is the largest of all Mopar/AMC events in New Hamburg, Ontario, Canada. There are over 1,000 collector and special interest Mopars in this year's event and over 12,000 people in attendance.

This event is held annually for two purposes: to raise funds for Children and Youth Programs and to give Mopar enthusiasts from across Canada and the United States, an opportunity to show their Mopars, meet and exchange information, buy and sell cars, parts and paraphernalia.

Through the Old Chrysler Corporation Auto Club (O.C.C. Inc.), in conjunction with Moparfest, money is raised which is used to make the wishes of disadvantaged children come true. They fund projects ranging from sending a plane load of 80 children to Disney World, to supplying a computer to a homebound child providing a window on the world that they would not ordinarily have.

It is open to all Mopar/AMC/Jeep show vehicles 1985 and older. Custom Truck/Van Class available, and Special Interest Vehicles (Newer cars and trucks). Photos and details about the vehicle must be included with Special Interest Vehicle registration requests. Vendors begin set-up at 8 am. Show grounds are open to participants 9:30 am to 4 pm.

A Grand Prize car is given away each year to the pre-registered show participants.

Team Sheriff Racing

Deputy Scott Graham and Deputy Bill Chaffin developed this program which assists the STAR DARE Program to boost public relations in the Los Angeles County Sheriff's Department.

The program's mission is to create a positive image of law enforcement with youth who otherwise may only encounter deputies in a negative way; to create a deterrent for the use of drugs and gang involvement; and for the importance of education.

It presents a positive police image and allows up close contact with the race crews, vehicles and deputies. It promotes a competitive spirit to allow more productive citizens. It provides positive influences for the young adults and channels negative energy into positive energy. Their website is www.teamsheriff.com.

Funny Car driven by Deputy Joe Lomonaco, 500 cubic inches, blown alcohol Keith Black motor, runs 6.30 at over 200 mph. Deputy Lomonaco is a member of the Team Sheriff Racing Organization through the Los Angeles County Sheriff's Office. Photo courtesy Cody Coleman

Project R.A.D.I.C.A.L.

Deputy Dean Mirra of the Broward County Sheriff's Office with his Project Radical race car. Photo courtesy of Dennis Rothacker

In June 1992, the Broward Sheriff's Office implemented a program entitled *Project Radical*, which stands for *Racing Against Drugs in Communities and Lives*. This program is being utilized in many educational programs in Florida to help educate young people to the problems of illegal drug and alcohol use. It helps to educate everyone to the terrors of alcohol and drug impaired driving and to promote a better understanding between police and the communities. It shows that drag racing is against street racing and that anyone can race at the track legally and have fun.

Project Radical's message is to get kids to stay in school and away from drugs and alcohol. It teaches about peer pressure and provides alternative activities, such as drag racing. Using a race car enables the racer to get the attention of the students to teach them about certain dangers associated with the alcohol and drugs.

The project coordinator/driver is Dean Mirra and Matt Buck is the crew chief. The car is a 1971 Z28 Chevy Camaro, 496 cubic inch, 2 speed Powerglide transmission with a Dana rear. The Z28 runs speeds of 9.20 @ 150 mph in the quarter mile with 675/700 horsepower.

Exhibition Classes

Miami Zoo Crew

The *Miami Zoo Crew* is an exclusive trick bike organization that performs bike stunts for major events. They perform nationally and also have a website, www.miamizoocrew.com. They are a group of highly talented young men that love to entertain the crowds with their motorcycles.

Leo performing a "Nac-Nac" wheelie

They perform many stunts for the crowds including High Chair Wheelies, Tank Wheelies, the Flamingo, Twelve o'clock Wheelie, Rolling Endo, Skitching, SuperCow and many, many others.

Their bikes and outfits are designed with different animal prints: the Cheetah, the Cow, the White Tiger, the Zebra and the Snake. Most of their helmets and pants carry the animal prints, as well.

Members of the Zoo Crew, left to right: Junior, Chris, Tony (not pictured), Leo & Cosmo

These men are all extremely well-trained and in great physical shape and muscular build. They do not recommend for anyone to try these skills on their own, as all their tricks and stunts are extremely dangerous. These men are considered to be *thrill-seekers* or *dare-devils*. They are definite crowd pleasers and extremely exciting to watch.

CannonBall Express - Jet Powered Dragster/Locomotive
Engineer/Driver - K. C. Jones

This Jet Locomotive is a unique jet powered dragster. It actually looks like a locomotive with a cow catcher in the front with bells and whistles blowing as it makes its way down the track. Smoke puffs out of the stack and it throws 30 feet of flames out of the back. It is an incredible show stopper and is especially entertaining to the young ones in the crowd.

The driver, K.C. Jones, began racing at the age of 12. He has crewed and toured with many elite racers, including Dennis Geisler's *Instant T* which is an AA/Fuel Altered, Pete Everett's *Pete's Li'l Demon* which is a Funny Car, Fred Goeske's *Fearless* which is AA/Fuel Funny Car and John Force's *Mountain Dew* Fuel Funny Car. In 1988 and 1989, he toured and drove for John Faitori's *Simple Pleasure* jet dragster.

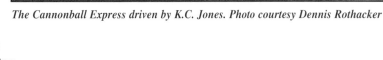

The Cannonball Express driven by K.C. Jones. Photo courtesy Dennis Rothacker

It was 1983 when K.C. built, owned, licensed and drove the first *Cannonball Express* jet locomotive. During his rookie year as a driver, K.C. won the 1985 Jet World Finals. In 1995 K.C. built and toured in his newly modified *Cannonball Express,* which is licensed and certified by NHRA & IHRA.

From 1995 until the present time, K.C. has been touring throughout the United States, Canada and Mexico. He has participated in over 150 races and special events at over 75 different facilities, including drag strips, circle tracks, air shows and many charity events. He has been down the track more than 600 times and claimed the win of the Jet World Finals from 1985-1999. K.C. is very much involved in the *Racers for Christ* program also.

His Jet Powered Dragster/Locomotive's specs are a Westinghouse J34-34 engine from a U.S. Navy *Banshee*, wheelbase of 217' and height of 42', weighing in at 2300 pounds without the driver. It carries two 16' Deist ring-slots parachutes. It produces 6500 pounds of thrust with the afterburner, which is the equivalent to 13,000 horsepower, and uses over 26 gallons of diesel fuel for one run. This engine consumes over 12,000 cubic feet of air per second (same as emptying a 3-bedroom house of all its air in one second). His average speed is 275 mph with an elapsed time of 6 seconds in the quarter mile.

Team Cannonball always welcomes everyone to come join them in the pits. Parents can allow their children to ring the bell, get a free autographed picture and meet Mr. K. C. Jones, the fastest locomotive jet car driver.

Cannonball Express Enterprises is located at 15436 Lemac Street, Van Nuys, California 91406, with a website of www.KCJonesRacing.com.

The Chicago Rush is operated by Dan Sullivan. Photo courtesy of Dennis Rothacker

Chicago Rush
Driver/Owner - Dan Sullivan
Crew: Dave Duax, Pro Custom Works, Odyssey Jet Services

The *Chicago Rush* jet powered dragster is powered by a Pratt & Whitney J60 engine which was designed in 1960. The dragster weighs 1300 pounds, with a Sullivan Racing Chassis, Body-Tin by Tom Gorney Race Cars, Jet Starter - Scott Collins of Pro Custom Works, with over 6000 horsepower in his afterburner.

The driver, Dan Sullivan has quite a collection of race cars that he has driven throughout his 35 years of drag racing. His first race car being a B Stocker 1962 Ford. He switched over to a 1934 Ford 3 window Coupe which ran 9.90s. In 1996, Dan started racing a UDRA Pro Stock, the *Old Chicago* Barracuda.

In 1978, Lee Austin offered Dan the opportunity to drive his Jet Dragster. Then, in the early 1980s he switched over to the *Chicago Rush* Funny Car until 1983, when Chuck Scheer took over.

Dan sat on the sidelines for ten years conducting himself as crew and car owner only. Then Dan decided to have the Jet Shop in Texas build the *Chicago Rush* Jet Dragster for him. He now races approximately 20 times a year with his best run being 5.20 @ 308 mph. And believe-it-or-not, this man is a 54-year old grandfather to boot. Go Grandpa!

Shockwave Jet Truck. Photo courtesy of Dennis Rothacker

Shockwave Jet Truck
Driver - Kent Shockley
Crew Chief: Tony Hoium

Kent was born in California and moved to Kansas in 1979. He has worked around jet powered vehicles since the age of 18 with his famous father, Les Shockley. He worked as the crew chief for his dad since that time, as his school schedule would permit.

Kent worked after school in his father's shop performing jet maintenance, fabrication of vehicles and helped with the building, tuning and repairing of custom jet powered race cars. During these years, he helped his dad set hundreds of track records and had the pleasure of watching his dad become the three-time National Jet Car Champion of the World. In 1996, Les Shockley turned over the driving honors of the *Shockwave* to his son.

Kent was already a 20 year veteran of motorsports at the age of 38. In June 1984, Kent became the first person to be licensed to drive a multi-engine jet powered vehicle. The *Shockwave Jet Truck* runs speeds over 300 mph and holds the world record for trucks at 376 mph. The *Shockwave* has the power to accelerate to almost 3 Gs vertical, which is as fast as the space shuttle. It is powered by 3 Pratt & Whitney J34-48s engines with 36,000 horsepower which uses up to 120 gallons of fuel each run.

If you ever get the chance to see this talented family in action, stop by the pits as Kent always has time to sign autographs and talk about this jet truck to the racing fans.

Super Shockwave Jet Truck
Driver: Scott *Superman* Shockley
Crew Chief: Jay Olson

Scott was born on August 7, 1963 in Pasadena, California. He grew up in California and is the son of Les Shockley, whose career is described above. Scott, at the age of 12, was already fascinated with his dad's jet powered vehicles.

When Scott turned 20, he designed his own drag bike with which he entered and won his first National Event. He drove IMCA modified cars and it was natural that Scott would follow in his famous dad's footsteps.

Les Shockley turned over the driving chores of the *Super ShockWave* to Scott in 2001. Scott loves the interaction with the race fans in the pits and shares stories about this powerful jet truck. He finds it an honor to be the new driver of this super Jet Truck.

Super Shockwave Jet Truck. Photo courtesy Dennis Rothacker

The *Super ShockWave* twin engine jet truck consists of 2-Pratt & Whitney J-34-48's, with 25,000 horsepower, 5000 pounds of thrust and uses 80 gallons of diesel on each run down the track. The jet truck is a special fiberglass 1957 Chevy.

For additional information contact the Super Shockwave Jet Shows, 10110 SE Highway 26, Galena, Kansas 66739, (620) 856-5127

Wheelstander School Bus

Driver/Owner: Ken Nelson

Ken Nelson driving the famous "Cool Bus"

This one of a kind, crowd-pleasing, exhibition vehicle is a 1/3 scale school bus. This wheel-standing School Bus (also known as the *Cool Bus*) is twenty feet long, six feet wide and six feet high and it is the *longest wheelstander in the world.*

The school bus was designed by the driver and owner, Ken Nelson. It is built of aluminum and fiberglass and painted in school regulation yellow and black, but it is not like any school bus you have ever seen. While making his run down the track, the lights and flashers operate just like a regular school bus.

The driver sits in the middle compartment of the vehicle encased with a full roll cage, safety harness and emergency shut-off switch. He actually views the track through the floor of his vehicle because he performs a wheelstand the whole 1/4 mile of the track.

The school bus chassis is constructed of steel tubing and is powered by a rear mounted alcohol fueled, blown and injected big block Chevrolet engine, which produces around 1000 horsepower. The power is transferred to the rear wheels with a GM 400 Turbo transmission.

It took Ken approximately two years to complete this exhibition vehicle. He and his wife, Anita, travel to all parts of the country to show their fabulous machine at many different drag strips.

Ken has over thirty years driving experience with most years spent driving wheelstanders. Ken is an outstanding chassis builder and has built his last five wheelstanders and many other exhibition vehicles and street rods. These include *The Starshot, The Back-up Pickup* and the *North Coast Flyer*, a 2/3 scale version of a Kenworth semi-tractor.

Ken is an active member in the *Racers for Christ* program and speaks for *Race Against Drugs* to encourage youth to stay in school and say no to drugs. If you ever get the opportunity to see this *Cool Bus* check it out – you will never forget it!

North American Drag Strips

United States

Alabama

Alabama International Dragway (IHRA) – Steele, Alabama
Post Office Box 426
Steele, Alabama 35987
256-538-7223
Elev. 519'

Atmore Dragway (IHRA) – Atmore, Alabama
1/8th mile track
Post Office Box 770
Flomaton, Alabama 36441
334-368-8363
ARDragway@aol.com
karen@atmoredragway.com
Elev. 380'

Baileyton Good Time Drag Strip – Baileyton, Alabama
1/8th mile track
Post Office Box 64
Baileyton, Alabama 35019
256-796-2892
Elev. 780'

Bama Dragway (NHRA) – Jasper (Sumiton), Alabama
1/8th mile track
1401 – 13th Avenue
Pleasant Grove, Alabama 35127
205-648-8890
www.bamadragway.com
Elev. 330'

Chilton County Motorsports Park – Maplesville, Alabama
1/4 mile & 1/8th mile track
7904 Highway 191
Maplesville, Alabama 36750
205-755-8169
Elev. 100'

Dallas County Dragway – Selma, Alabama
1/8th mile track
3182 County Road 63
Selma, Alabama 36702
334-874-6197
Elev. 200'

Dothan Dragway & Raceland – Cottonwood, Alabama
1/8th mile
2165 Mona Lisa Drive
Montgomery, Alabama 36111
334-691-4431
Elev. 100'

Holiday Raceway (IHRA) – Woodstock, Alabama
1/8th mile track
20062 Highway 11
Woodstock, Alabama 35188
205-938-0417
www.holidayraceway.com
hraceway@aol.com
Elev. 600'

Huntsville Dragway (NHRA & Jr.) – Huntsville, Alabama
1/8th mile track
913 West 16th Avenue
Birmingham, Alabama 35204
256-859-0807
www.huntsvilledragway.com
george@georgehowardracing.com
Elev. 660'

Lassiter Mountain Dragway (IHRA) – Birmingham, Alabama
1/8th mile track
3936 Raceway Park Road
Mt. Olive, Alabama 35117
205-841-8696
Elev. 500'

Mobile Dragway (NHRA) – Irvington, Alabama
1/8th mile track
Post Office Box 1076
Theodore, Alabama 36590
334-957-3054
www.mobiledragway.com
mobiledragway.com
Elev. 50

Montgomery Motorsports Park (NHRA & Jr.) – Montgomery, Alabama
2600 Northbelt Drive
Montgomery, Alabama 36104
334-260-9660
www.mmpdragracing.com
anthony@mmpdragracing.com
Elev. 171'

Moulton Dragway – Moulton, Alabama
1/8th mile track
2961-C Wimberly Drive SW
Decatur, Alabama 35603
Elev. 600'

North Alabama Dragway (IHRA) – Tuscumbia, Alabama
1/8th mile track
Post Office Box 108
Moulton, Alabama 35650
256-383-5025
www.northalabamaspeedway.com
twin1brit@aol.com
Elev. 550'

Phenix Dragstrip – Phenix City, Alabama
1/8th mile track
332 Woodland Drive
Phenix City, Alabama 36869
334-291-0494
Elev. 400'

Sand Mountain Dragway – Section, Alabama
1/8 mile track
Post Office Box 472
Fyffe, Alabama 35971
256-228-3320
phillip@sandmountaindragway.com
Elev. 1200'

Winston County Dragstrip – Lynn, Alabama
1/8th mile track
6.5 mile SE of YS 278 on SR 5
Lynn, Alabama
Elev. 750'

Alaska

Alaska Raceway Park (IHRA & Jr.) – Palmer (Butte), Alaska
Post Office Box 2746
Palmer, Alaska 99645
907-746-7223
michelle@akracewaypark.com
www.akracewaypark.com
Elev. 100'

Fairbanks Racing Lions – Fairbanks, Alaska
Post Office Box 75333
Fairbanks, Alaska 99707
907-457-8602
www.racinglions.com
racinglions@mosquitonet.com
Elev. 472'

Arizona

Firebird International Raceway (NHRA) – Chandler, Arizona
20000 Maricopa Road
Chandler, Arizona 85226
602-268-0200
www.firebirdraceway.com
info@firebirdraceway.com
Elev. 1100'

Southwestern International Raceway (NHRA & Jr.) – Tucson, Arizona
11300 South Houghton Road
Tucson, Arizona 85747
520-762-9700
www.sirace.com
office@sirace.com
Elev. 3075'

Speedworld Motorplex (NHRA) – Wittmann, Arizona
19421 West Jomax Road
Wittmann, Arizona 85361
623-388-2424
www.speedworldmotorplex.com
joe@speedworldmotorplex.com
Elev. 1280'

Arkansas
Centerville Dragway – Centerville, Arkansas
Post Office Box 160
Centerville, Arkansas 72829
501-576-4001
www.centervilledragway.com
cvdrag@arkwest.com
Elev. 300'

George Ray's Wildcat Dragstrip – Paragould, Arkansas
1/8th mile track
485 Highway 135 South
Paragould, Arkansas 72450
870-236-8247
Elev. 160'

Newport Raceway – Newport (Diaz), Arkansas
1/8th mile track
3803 East Highland
Jonesboro, Arkansas 72401
870-523-1055
Elev. 250'

Prescott Raceway – Prescott, Arkansas
1/8th mile track
472-D Catherine Park Road
Hot Springs, Arkansas 71913
501-262-9498
cindyd@cei.net
Elev. 300'

California
Carlsbad Raceway – Carlsbad, California
649 Daisy
Escondido, California 92027
760-480-9574
Elev. 200'

Drag City (NHRA)
1/4 mile track
Post Office Box 197
Banning, California 92220
909-874-5198
Elevation 2100'
Opens April 2003
www.drag-city.com

Famoso Raceway (NHRA & Jr.) - Bakersfield, California
33559 Famoso Road
McFarland, California 93250
661-399-2210
www.famosoraceway.com
webmaster@famosoraceway.com
Elev. 625'

Holtville Raceway – Holtville, California
2975 East Norrish Road
Holtville, California 92250
760-356-4641
Elev. 100'

Infineon Raceway (NHRA) Sonoma, CA
Highways 37 & 121
Sonoma, California 95476
800-870-RACE
www.InfineonRaceway.com
trackinfo@infineonraceway.com
Elev. 17

Interstate 5 Raceway Park – Orland, California
27654 Camino Vista
Shingletown, California 96088
530-474-3955
Elev. 100'

Inyokern Dragstrip (NHRA & Jr.) – Inyokern, California
Post Office Box 182
Ridgecrest, California 93556
760-375-8832
www.Inyokerndragstrip.com
5clarkes@iwvsp.com
Elev. 2432'

Los Angeles County Raceway (NHRA & Jr.) - Palmdale, California
6850 East Avenue T.
Littlerock, California 93543
661-533-2224
www.lacr.net
admin@lacr.net
Elev. 2640'

Pomona Raceway (NHRA & Jr.) – Pomona, California
2780 Fairplex Drive
Pomona, California 91768
909-593-7010
Elev. 1000'

Redding Dragstrip (NHRA & Jr.)
6750 Old Oregon Trail
Redding, California 96049
530-347-4237
www.Reddingdragstrip.com
duckyrds@c-zone.net
Elev. 490'

Rialto Raceway (NHRA & Jr.)
Rialto, California
714-695-0523

Sacramento Raceway Park (NHRA & Jr.) - Sacramento, California
5305 Excelsior Road
Sacramento, California 95827
916-363-2653
www.sacramentoraceway.com
jennifer@sacramentoraceway.com
Elev. 50'

Samoa Dragstrip (NHRA & Jr.) - Eureka, CA
Post Office Box 212
Miranda, California 95553
707-443-5203
www.samoadragstrip.com
webmaster@samoadragstrip.com
Elev. 10'

Sears Point Raceway (NHRA) - Sonoma, CA
Highway 37 & 121
Sonoma, California 95476
707-938-8448
www.searspoint.com
trackinfo@searspoint.com
Elev. Sea level

Team Possibilities Jr. Raceway (NHRA Jr. Drag Racing Only)
Qualcomm Stadium
9449 Friars Road
San Diego, California 92108
619-641-3100
www.teampossibilities.com
drsonny@teampossibilities.com

Colorado
Bandimere Speedway (NHRA & Jr.) – Denver (Morrison), Colorado
3051 South Rooney Road
Morrison, Colorado 80465
303-697-6001
www.bandimere.com
johnjr@bandimere.com
Elev. 5814'

Julesburg Dragstrip (NHRA & Jr.) - Julesburg, Colorado
Post Office Box 377
Yuma, Colorado 80759
970-848-2388
www.julesburgdragstrip.com
Elev. 3520'

Pueblo Motorsports Park (NHRA & Jr.) - Pueblo, Colorado
524 North Santa Fe Avenue
Pueblo, Colorado 81003
719-543-7747
www.pueblomotorsportspark.com
webmaster@pueblomotorsportspark.com
Elev. 4900'

TSM Raceway (Jr. Drag Racing Only)
Mt. View Race Park
Mead, Colorado
888-627-5437

Western Colorado Dragway (NHRA & Jr.) - Grand Junction, Colorado
Post Office Box 760
Clifton, Colorado 81520
970-243-9022
www.westerncoloradodragway.com
Elev. 4993'

Delaware

US 13 Dragway (NHRA & Jr.) - Delmar,
Delaware
Route 2, Box 181
Laurel, Delaware 19956
302-846-3968
www.delawareracing.com
info@delawareracing.com
Elev. 15'

Florida

Bradenton Motorsports Park (IHRA) –
Bradenton, Florida
21000 State Road 64 East
Bradenton, Florida 34202
941-748-1320
www.bradentonmotorsports.com
BMPFla@aol.com
Elev. 50'

Emerald Coast Dragway (IHRA) – Holt,
Florida
1/8th mile track
7134 Garner Landing Road
Holt, Florida 32564
850-537-7223
www.emeraldcoastdragway.com
Elev. 180'

Gainesville Raceway (NHRA & Jr.) –
Gainesville, Florida
11211 North County Road 225
Gainesville, Florida 32609
352-377-0046
www.gainesvilleraceway.com
raceway@gainesvilleraceway.com
Elev. 165'

Immokalee Regional Raceway (IHRA) –
Immokalee, Florida
1/8th mile track
Post Office Box 2023
Immokalee, Florida 34142
800-826-1947
www.immrace.com
www.immokaleeraceway.com
Elev. 50'

JAX Raceways (NHRA & Jr.) – Jacksonville,
Florida
(1/8th mile track)
186 Pecan Park Road
Jacksonville, Florida 32218
904-757-5425
www.jaxraceways.com
mary@jaxraceways.com
Elev. 40'

Lakeland Dragstrip – Lakeland (Polk City),
Florida
1/8th mile track
8100 US 33 North
Lakeland, Florida 33809
863-984-1145
www.lakelanddragstrip.com
Elev. 50'

Moroso Motorsports Park (NHRA & Jr.) –
Palm Beach Gardens, Florida
17047 Beeline Highway
Palm Beach Gardens, Florida 33410
(561) 622-1400
www.morosomotorsportspark.com
mail@morosomotorsportspark.com
Elev. 6'

Orlando Speed World Dragway (NHRA & Jr.)
– Orlando, Florida
19442 East Colonial Drive
Orlando, Florida 32820
407-568-2717
www.speedworlddragway.com
oswd1320@aol.com
Elev. 66'

Powerhouse Dragway (IHRA) – Chason, FL
1/8th mile track
4408 Cato Road
Panama City, Florida 32404
850-762-8885
Elev. 27'

Sunshine Dragway (IHRA) – Pinellas Park, FL
1/8th mile track
1980 Saddle Hill Road North
Dunedin, Florida 34698
727-573-9700
Elev. 30'

Georgia

Atlanta Dragway (NHRA & Jr.) – Commerce,
Georgia
500 East Ridgeway Road
Commerce, Georgia 30529
706-355-2301
www.atlantadragway.com
info@atlantadragway.com
Elev. 1100'

Brainerd Optimist Dragstrip (Jr.) - Ringgold, GA
1/8th mile track
745 Scruggs Road
Ringgold, Georgia 30736
706-891-9831
www.brainerdracing.com
slongley54@aol.com
Elev. 700'

Head Hunters Putt Putt Dragway – Eatonton, GA
1/8th mile track
Post Office Box 3272
Eatonton, Georgia 31024
706-485-2302
Elev. 250'

Hinesville Raceway Park (IHRA)
1/8th mile track
Route 7, Box 224-P
Hinesville, Georgia 31313
912-408-7223
www.hinesvilleracewaypark.com
larrymillsaps@hinesvilleracewaypark.com
Elev. 98.2'

Macon National Dragway – Jeffersonville,
Georgia
1/8th mile track
1041 Honey Creek Road
Conyers, Georgia 30013
912-962-0232
www.maconnationaldragway.com
Elev. 300'

Paradise Drag Strip – Calhoun, Georgia
1/8 mile track
500 Chatsworth Highway NE
Calhoun, Georgia 30701
706-629-6161
Elev. 600'

Savannah Dragway (NHRA & Jr.) – Savannah,
Georgia
1/8th mile track
4704 Ogeechee Road
Savannah, Georgia 31405
912-234-1965
www.savannahdragway.com
Elev. 56'

Silver Dollar Dragway (NHRA & Jr.) –
Reynolds, Georgia
1/4 mile and 1/8th mile track
Post Office Box 512
Reynolds, Georgia 31076
912-847-4414
www.silverdollardragway.com
Elev. 445'

Southeastern International Dragway (NHRA &
Jr.) – Dallas, Georgia
1/8th mile track
700 Lake Road
Hiram, Georgia 30141
770-445-2183
www.sedragway.com
Elev. 1100'

Southern Dragway (IHRA & Jr.) – Douglas,
Georgia
1/8th mile track
1560 Ronnie Walker Road
Nicholls, Georgia 31554
912-384-7733
www.southerndragway.com
scott@southerndragway.com
Elev. 100'

Troup County Dragway - LaGrange, Georgia
1/8th mile track

US 19 Dragway (NHRA & Jr.) – Albany,
Georgia
1/8th mile track
1304 Williamsburg Road
Albany, Georgia 31705
912-431-0077
www.us19dragway.com
john@us19dragway.com
Elev. 376'

Hawaii

Hawaii Raceway Park (NHRA & Jr.) – Ewa
Beach (Oahu), Hawaii
92-1323 Hauone Street
Kapolei, Hawaii 96707
808-485-8767
www.hrpdragracing.com
paulg@slider.net
Elev. 1500'

Hilo Dragstrip (NHRA) – Hilo, Hawaii
Post Office Box 5265
Hilo, Hawaii 96720
808-959-8059
Elev. 25'

Kauai Raceway Park (NHRA) – Mana
(Kauai), Hawaii
Post Office Box 3207
Lihue, Hawaii 96766
808-639-2754
Elev. 50'

Maui Raceway Park (NHRA) – Puunene
(Maui), Hawaii
Post Office Box 6020
Kahului, Maui, Hawaii 96732
808-891-2083
Elev. 150'

Idaho

Firebird Raceway (NHRA & Jr.) – Boise,
Idaho
Post Office Box 1398
Eagle, Idaho 83616
208-938-8986
www.firebirdonline.com
race@firebirdonline.com
Elev. 2700'

Snake River Speedway - Blackfoot, Idaho
Post Office Box 455
Shelley, Idaho 83274
208-529-4707
www.snakeriverspeedway.com
speedway@dcdi.net
Elev. 4500'

Illinois

Byron Dragway (IHRA & Jr.) – Byron, Illinois
1924 23rd Avenue
Rockford, Illinois 61104
815-234-8405
www.byrondragway.com
Elev. 756'

Coles County Dragway USA (NHRA & Jr.) –
Charleston, Illinois
1/8th mile track
4205 East Oaks Road
Irbana, Illinois 61802
217-345-7777
www.colescountydragway.com
wingleracing64@msn.com
Elev. 800'

Cordova Dragway Park (IHRA) – Cordova, Il
Post Office Box 442
19425 Route 84 North
Cordova, Illinois 61242
309-654-2110
www.cordovadrag.com
info@cordovadrag.com
Elev. 632'

Gateway International Raceway (NHRA & Jr.)
– East St. Louis, Illinois
700 Raceway Boulevard
Madison, Illinois 62060
618-482-2400
www.gatewayracing.com
Elev. 407'

I-57 Drag Strip – Benton, Illinois
1/8th mile track
6112 Hill City Road
Benton, Illinois 62812
618-439-6039
Elev. 500'

Mason County Raceway (IHRA) – Havana, Il
1/8th mile track
13627 – 4th Street
Pekin, Illinois 61554
309-543-6124
www.masoncountyraceway.com
masonco@bwsys.net
Elev. 440'

Route 66 Raceway (NHRA & Jr.) - Joliet, Il
500 Speedway Boulevard
Joliet, Illinois 60433
815-722-5500
www.route66raceway.com
Elev. 550'

Indiana

Brown County Dragway – Nashville (Bean
Blossom), Indiana
1/8th mile track
4396 West Branstetter Road
Nashville, Indiana 47448
812-988-1505
Elev. 600'

Bunker Hill Dragstrip (NHRA & Jr.) –
Kokomo, Indiana
1/8th mile track
8672 South 150 West
Bunker Hill, Indiana 46914
765-689-8248
www.bunkerhillrace.com
Elev. 750'

E.T. Raceway (NHRA) - Bloomfield, Indiana
1/8th mile track
Post Office Box 9
Bloomfield, Indiana 47424
812-384-4959
www.etraceway.com
tim@etraceway.com
Elev. 500

Freedom Drags – Freedom (New Hope),
Indiana
1/8th mile track
Not operating yet
Elev. 500'

Greater Evansville Raceway (IHRA) –
Chandler, Indiana
1/8th mile track
6301 Maxwell Avenue
Evansville, Indiana 47715
812-925-3685
Elev. 500'

Indianapolis Raceway Park (NHRA & Jr.) -
Clermont, Indiana
Post Office Box 34300
Indianapolis, Indiana 46234
317-291-4090
www.irponline.com
Elev. 850'

Muncie Dragway (IHRA) – Muncie, Indiana
Post Office Box 397
Yorktown, Indiana 47320
765-789-8470
munciedragway@yorktown.net
www.munciedrag.com
Elev. 900'

Osceola Dragway (IHRA) – Osceola, Indiana
56328 Ash Road
Osceola, Indiana 46561
219-674-8400
www.osceoladragway.com
info@osceoladragway.com
Elev. 757'

U.S. 41 International Dragway – Morocco
(Enos), Indiana
31421 South Ridgeland Avenue
Peotone, Indiana 60468
219-285-2200
www.dragnbreath.com/us41dragway/index.html
Elev. 650'

Wabash Valley Dragway (NHRA & Jr.) – Terre
Haute, Indiana
Formerly known as Terre Haute Action
Dragstrip
1/8th mile track
Post Office Box 78
Owensburg, Indiana 47453
812-238-1760
www.wabashvalleydragway.com
webmaster@wabashvalleydragway.com
Elev. 500'

Iowa

Cedar Falls Raceway (IHRA) – Cedar Falls, IA
1924 23rd Avenue
Rockford, Iowa 61104
815-398-1060
www.cedarfallsraceway.com
cfriowa@aol.com
Elev. 850'

Eddyville Raceway Park (IHRA) – Eddyville, Iowa
1/8th mile track
3260 Merino Avenue
Oskaloosa, Iowa 52577
641-969-5596
www.eddyvilleraceway.com
information@eddyvilleraceway.com
Elev. 720'

Humboldt County Dragway – Dakota City, IA
1/8th mile track
1987 – 220th Street
Fort Dodge, Iowa 50501
515-332-2510
Elev. 1000'

Tri-State Raceway (NHRA & Jr.) – Earlville, IA
2217 – 270th Avenue
Earlville, Iowa 52041
319-923-3724
www.tristateraceway.com
mail@tristateraceway.com
Elev. 850'

Kansas
Heartland Park Topeka (NHRA & Jr.) - Topeka, Kansas
425 East 61st Street
Topeka, Kansas 66619
785-862-4781
www.hpt.com
pierce@hpt.com
Elev. 1000'

Mid-America Dragway (NHRA & Jr.) - Arkansas City, Kansas
Post Office Box 40
Geuda Springs, Kansas 67051
316-447-3355
www.midamericadragway.com
midamerd@kanokla.net
Elev. 1379'

Midwest Raceway – Manhattan, Kansas
1/8th mile track
1895 East 175th Road
Lecompton, Kansas 66050
785-776-7223
Elev. 1000'

S.R.C.A. Dragstrip (NHRA & Jr.) - Great Bend, Kansas
Post Office Box 1362
Great Bend, Kansas 67530
316-792-5079
www.srcadragstrip.com
steve@myvine.com
Elev. 1900'

Wichita International Raceway (NHRA & Jr.) - Wichita, Kansas
7020 Glenda
Valley Center, Kansas 67147
316-755-3474
Elev. 1280'

Kentucky
Beech Bend Raceway (NHRA & Jr.) – Bowling Green Kentucky
798 Beech Bend Road
Bowling Green, Kentucky 42101
270-781-7634
www.beechbend.com
beechbendpark@msn.com
Elev. 480'

Bluegrass Raceway Park (NHRA & Jr.) - Owingsville, Kentucky
Post office Box 444
Morehead, Kentucky 40351
606-674-3987
www.bluegrassracewaypark.com
info@bluegrassraceway.com
Elev. 701"

Lake Cumberland Dragway (IHRA) – Jamestown, Kentucky
1/8th mile track
Post Office Box 277
Russell Springs, Kentucky 42642
270-343-6101
Elev. 800'

London Motorplex (NHRA & Jr.) - London, Kentucky
3835 White Oak Road
London, Kentucky 40741
606-878-8883
Elev. 1194'

Mountain Parkway Motorplex (IHRA) – Clay City, Kentucky
1/8th mile track
502 Richmond Road
Berea, Kentucky 40403
606-663-2344
Elev. 710'

Ohio Valley Dragway (NHRA & Jr.) - Louisville, Kentucky
1/8th mile track
8900 Kathryn Station Road
West Point, Kentucky 40177
502-922-4152
www.ohiovalleydragway.com
ohiovall@ohiovalleydragway.com
Elev. 450'

Thorn Hill Dragway – Kenton, Kentucky
1/4 mile & 1/8th mile tracks
443 Bagby Road
Crittenden, Kentucky 41030
859-356-7702
Elev. 600'

U.S. 60 Raceway – Hardinsburg, Kentucky
1/8th mile track
325 North Myers Road
Brooks, Kentucky 40109
270-756-6744
Elev. 486'

Windy Hollow Raceway Park (NHRA & Jr.) - Owensboro, Kentucky
1/8th mile track
4705 Windy Hollow Road
Owensboro, Kentucky 42301
270-785-4300
www.windyhollowraceway.com
Elev. 600'

Louisiana
Louisiana Raceway (IHRA) – Eunice, LA
204 Madewood Drive
Destrehan, Louisiana 70047
318-546-6031
Elev. 50'

No Problem Raceway Park (NHRA & Jr.) - Belle Rose, Louisiana
6470 Highway 996
Belle Rose, Louisiana 70341
985-369-3692
www.noproblemraceway.com
thetrack@noproblemraceway.com
Elev. Sea level

Red River Raceway (IHRA) – Shreveport (Gilliam), Louisiana
Post Office Box 7
Gilliam, Louisiana 71029
318-296-4500
www.redriverraceway.net
darldrag@aol.com
Elev. 172'

State Capitol Dragway (NHRA & Jr.) - Baton Rouge (Erwinville), Louisiana
Post Office Box 159
Erwinville, Louisiana 70729
225-627-4574
www.statecapitoldragway.com
info@statecapitoldragway.com
Elev. 36'

Twin City Dragway (NHRA & Jr.) - Monroe, Louisiana
433 Downing Pines Road
West Monroe, Louisiana 71292
318-324-8700
Elev. 95'

Maine
Oxford Plains Dragway (IHRA) - Oxford, ME
1/8th mile track
Post Office Box 208
Oxford, Maine 04270
207-539-8865
www.oxfordplainsdragway.com
info@oxfordplainsdragway.com
Elev. 100'

Winterport Dragway (IHRA) - Winterport, ME
1/8th mile track
73 Bolton Road
Dover-Foxcroft, Maine 04426
207-223-3998
Elev. 171'

Maryland

75-80 Dragway (NHRA & Jr.) - Monrovia, Maryland
11508-C Fingerboard Road
Monrovia, Maryland 21770
301-865-5102
www.7580dragway.com
info@7580dragway.com
Elev. 500'

Capitol Raceway (NHRA & Jr.) - Crofton, Maryland
Post Office Box 3698
Crofton, Maryland 21114
410-721-9664
www.capitolraceway.com
capitolracing@usa.net
Elev. 250'

Cecil County Dragway (NHRA & Jr.) – Rising Sun, Maryland
807 Chance Court
Street, Maryland 21154
410-287-5486
www.cecilcountydragway.com
owner@cecilcountydragway.com
Elev. 320'

Maryland International Raceway (IHRA) – Budds Creek, Maryland
27861 Budds Creek Road
Mechanicsville, Maryland 20659
301-884-9833
www.mirdrag.com
info@mirdrag.com
Elev. 80'

Mason-Dixon Dragway (NHRA & Jr.) - Hagerstown, Maryland
21344 National Pike
Boonsboro, Maryland 21713
301-791-5193
www.masondixondragway.com
Elev. 535'

Michigan

LaPeer International Dragway (Jr.) - LaPeer, Michigan
788 Mellish Drive
LaPeer, Michigan 48446
810-667-8988
www.lapeerdragway.com
lid@usol.com
Elev. 600'

Mid-Michigan Motorplex (IHRA)
2589 North Wyman Road
Stanton, Michigan 48888
517-762-5043
www.midmichmotorplex.com
info@midmichmotorplex.com
Elev. 650'

Milan Dragway (IHRA & Jr.) - Milan, Michigan
Post Office Box 3186
Centerline, Michigan 48015
734-439-7368
www.milandragway.com
info@milandragway.com
Elev. 600'

Northern Michigan Dragway (IHRA) - Kaleva, Michigan
1/8th mile track
Post Office Box 19
Kaleva, Michigan 49645
231-362-2894
www.ublydragway.com
trackmanagers@hotmail.com
Elev. 650'

Ubly Dragway - Ubly, Michigan
Post Office Box 275
Ubly, Michigan 48475
517-658-2331
www.ublydragway.com
track@ublydragway.com
Elev. 600'

US 131 Dragway (NHRA) - Martin, Michigan
Post Office Box 130
Otsego, Michigan 49078
616-672-7800
www.131dragway.com
Elev. 650'

West Michigan Sand Dragway – Hart (Mears), Michigan
100 yard Sand Dragstrip
8266 West Lake Holiday Drive
Mears, Michigan 49436
231-873-3345
www.sanddragway.com
Elev. 660'

Minnesota

Colonel's Brainerd International Raceway (NHRA & Jr.) - Brainerd, Minnesota
4343 Highway 371 North
Brainerd, Minnesota 56401
218-824-7220
www.brainerdrace.com
info@nufrog.com
Elev. 1700'

Grove Creek Dragway (NHRA) - Grove City, Minnesota
1/8th mile track
15050 Lawndale Lane
Dayton, Minnesota 55327
320-857-2152
www.grovecreek.com
raurace@aol.com
Elev. 1050'

Interstate Dragways (NHRA & Jr.) – Moorhead (Glyndon), Minnesota
RR 2, Box 15
Glyndon, Minnesota 56547
218-236-9461
www.interstatedragways.com
schifner@loretel.net
Elev. 900'

Mississippi

Battlefield Raceway – Philadelphia, MS
1/8th mile track
11840 Highway 15 North
Philadelphia, Mississippi 39350
601-656-2194
Elev. 350'

Blue Mountain Dragway – Ripley (Blue Mountain), Mississippi
600 foot Dragstrip
2678 Highway 22 South
Michie, Tennessee 38357
Elev. 400'

Byhalia Raceway – Byhalia, Mississippi
1/8th mile track
Post Office Box 732
Fulton, Mississippi 38843
Elev. 400'

Fulton Dragway – Fulton, Mississippi
1/8th mile track
Post Office Box 732
Fulton, Mississippi 38843
Elev. 400'

Greenville Raceway Park – Greenville, MS
1231 John Street
Leland, Mississippi 38703
662-335-6318
Elev. 300'

Gulfport Dragway - Gulfport, Mississippi
Post Office Box 885
Long Beach, Mississippi 39560
228-822-2225
www.gulfportdragway.com
cdr39560@aol.com
Elev. 21'

Hub City Dragway (IHRA) – Hattiesburg, Mississippi
1/8 mile track
101 Greenwood Place
Hattiesburg, Mississippi 39402
601-307-3724
www.hubdrag.com
hubdrag@aol.com
Elev. 280'

Junkyard #1 Dragway – Canton, Mississippi
1/8th mile track
619 Lottville Road
Canton, Mississippi 39046
601-855-0704
Elev. 300'

Northeast Mississippi Motorsports – Aberdeen, Mississippi
1/8th mile track
Post Office Box 326
Aberdeen, Mississippi 39730
662-369-6888
Elev. 250'

Tuscola Motorsports (IHRA) – Lena, Mississippi
624 Highway 487 South
Lena, MS 39094
601-298-9990
Elev. 382'

Missouri
Auto Tire & Parts Race Park - Benton, Missouri
1/8th mile track
370 Deer Creek Road
Cape Girardeau, Missouri 63701
573-335-7463
www.autotireandpartsracepark.com
therulesguy@yahoo.com
Elev. 500'

Kansas City International Raceway (NHRA & Jr.) - Kansas City, Missouri
8201 South Noland Road
Kansas City, Missouri 64138
816-358-6700
www.kcir.net
jma1020982@aol.com
Elev. 800'

Mid-America Raceways (NHRA & Jr.) - Wentzville, Missouri
1112 Highway T
Foristell, Missouri 63348
636-673-2434
www.midamericaraceway.com
vehige@earthlink.net
Elev. 550'

Mo-Kan Dragway - Asbury, Missouri
219 Mosher Avenue
Asbury, Missouri 64832
417-642-5615
www.mokandragway.com
Elev. 100'

Ozark International Raceway - Rogersville, Missouri
1/8th mile track
779 North 20th
Ozark, Missouri 65721
www.ozarkdragstrip.com
phil@ozarkdragstrip.com
Elev. 1350'

Sikeston Drag Strip – Sikeston, Missouri
1/8th mile track
389 Sandywood
Sikeston, Missouri 63801
573-471-9099
Elev. 220'

Thundervalley Raceway
1/8th mile track
3 miles each of Bethany, Missouri
660-748-4902
jbmiller@grm.net

Montana
Lewiston Raceway (NHRA & Jr.) - Lewistown, Montana
Post Office Box 887
Great Falls, Montana 59403
406-453-7555
Elev. 4150'

Lost Creek Raceway Park (NHRA & Jr.) – Anaconda, Montana
1/8th mile track
Post Office Box 655
Anaconda, Montana 59711
406-949-3724
www.lostcreek-raceway.com
lc1320@montana.com
Elev. 5200'

Nebraska
Kearney Raceway Park (NHRA & Jr.) - Kearney, Nebraska
Post Office Box 266
Minden, Nebraska 68959
308-832-0302
www.krpi.com
ja65817@navix.net
Elev. 2180'

Nebraska Motorplex (NHRA & Jr.) - Scribner, Nebraska
6645 Y Street
Lincoln, Nebraska 68505
402-466-1759
Elev. 1200'

Nevada
Fiftys Fever – Winnemucca, Nevada
330' Paved Dragstrip
Post Office Box 818
Winnemucca, Nevada 89446
775-623-3168
Elev. 4300'

Las Vegas Motor Speedway (NHRA & Jr.) - Las Vegas, Nevada
7000 Las Vegas Boulevard North
Las Vegas, Nevada 89115
702-644-4444
www.lvms.com
web@lvms.com
Elev. 2100'

Top Gun Raceway (NHRA & Jr.) - Fallon, Nevada
Post Office Box 2590
Fallon, Nevada 89407
800-325-7448
www.topgunraceway.com
racing@topgunraceway.com
Elev. 4000'

New Hampshire
New England Dragway (IHRA) – Epping, New Hampshire
Route 27 & Epping Road
Post Office Box 1320
Epping, New Hampshire 03042
603-679-8001
www.newenglanddragway.com
info@newenglanddragway.com
Elev. 90'

New Jersey
Atco Raceway (NHRA & Jr.) – Atco, New Jersey
1000 Jackson Road
Atco, New Jersey 08004
856-768-0900
www.atcorace.com
Elev. 93'

Island Dragway (NHRA & Jr.) - Great Meadows, New Jersey
Post Office Box 184
Great Meadows, New Jersey 07838
908-637-6060
www.islanddragway.com
id1320@nac.net
Elev. 520'

Old Bridge Township Raceway Park (NHRA & Jr.) - Englishtown, New Jersey
230 Pension Road
Englishtown, New Jersey 07726
732-446-7800
www.etownraceway.com
official@etownraceway.com
Elev. 86'

New Mexico
Albuquerque National Dragway – Albuquerque, New Mexico
1309 Eubank NE
Albuquerque, New Mexico 87112
Elev. 5400'

Arroyo Seco Motorplex - Las Cruces (Akela), New Mexico
Post Office Box 199
Fairacres, New Mexico 88033
www.arroyo-seco.com
mark@arroyo-seco.com
Elev. 4405'

Carlsbad Dragway – Carlsbad, New Mexico
702 North Canal
Carlsbad, New Mexico 88220
Elev. 3200'

Hobbs Motorsports Park - Hobbs, New Mexico
322 West Blanco
Hobbs, New Mexico 88240
505-393-6926
Elev. 3600'

Roswell Dragway (IHRA) – Roswell, New Mexico
412 Northwood Drive
Roswell, New Mexico 88201
505-624-2167
www.roswelldragway.com
themoon@trailnet.com
Elev. 3600'

New York
Esta Safety Park Dragstrip (NHRA & Jr.) - Cicero, New York
Post Office Box 1189
Cicero, New York 13039
315-622-4348
www.estadrags.com
estadrag@aol.com
Elev. 400'

Glad Rag Raceway – Saratoga Springs, New York
300 foot Sand Dragstrip
29 Holmes Road
Porter Corners, New York 12859
518-893-2788

Lancaster Motorsports Park (IHRA) – Buffalo, New York
1/8th mile
Post Office Box 338
Clarence, New York 14031
716-759-6818
www.lancasterracing.com
lmp@lancasterracing.com
Elev. 600'

Lebanon Valley Dragway (NHRA & Jr.) - West Lebanon, New York
Post Office Box 880
New Lebanon, New York 12125
518-794-7130
www.dragway.com
lvd@dragway.com
Elev. 603'

Long Island Motorsports Park (NHRA & Jr.) – West Hampton, New York
Old Country Road
West Hampton, New York 11977
631-288-1555
www.limotorsportspark.com
info@motorsportspark.com
Elev. 25'

New York International Raceway Park (IHRA) – Leicester, New York
Post Office Box 296
2011 New Road
Leicester, New York 14481
716-382-3030
www.nyirp.com
Elev. 918'

Spencer Speedway (NHRA & Jr.) - Williamson, New York
1/10 mile Dragstrip
288 Jefferson Avenue
Fairport, New York 14450
315-589-3018
Elev. 500'

North Carolina
Brewer's Speedway – Rocky Mount, North Carolina
1/8th mile track
6728 Reedy Branch Road
Rocky Mount, North Carolina 27803
252-446-2631
Elev. 100'

Canton Motorsports & Expo Park – Canton, North Carolina
1/8th mile track
1969 Ashville Highway
Canton, North Carolina 28716
828-235-8725
Elev. 2200'

Coastal Plains Raceway Park (NHRA & Jr.) - Jacksonville, North Carolina
1/4 & 1/8th mile track
111 Marine Boulevard
Jacksonville, North Carolina 28540
910-347-2200
www.coastalplainsraceway.com
Elev. 50'

Dunn-Benson Dragstrip (IHRA) – Dunn, North Carolina
1/8th mile track
Post Office Box 1750
Buies Creek, North Carolina 27506
919-894-1662
Elev. 100'

Farmers Union Community Speedway – Hallsboro, North Carolina
1/8th mile track
16055 Twisted Hickory Road
Bladenboro, North Carolina 28320
Elev. 50'

Farmington Dragway (IHRA) – Winston-Salem, North Carolina
1/8th mile track
4441 Bridle Path Lane
Winston-Salem, North Carolina 27103
336-998-3443
www.farmingtondragway.com
farmdrag@bellsouth.net
Elev. 1120'

Fayetteville Motor Sports Park (IHRA) – Fayetteville, North Carolina
1/8th mile track
Post Office Box 53926
Fayetteville, North Carolina 28305
910-484-3677
Elev. 51'

Harrells Raceway – Harrells, North Carolina
1/8th mile track
632 North Norwood Street
Wallace, North Carolina 28466
910-532-2363
www.harrellsraceway.com
pkfk@duplin.net
Elev. 20'

Kingston Drag Strip (IHRA) – Kingston, North Carolina
1/8th mile track
2869 Hull Road
Kingston, North Carolina 28504
252-527-4337
info@kdsmotorsports.com
Elev. 125'

Mooresville Dragway (IHRA) – Mooresville, North Carolina
1/8th mile track
8415 Highway 152 West
Mooresville, North Carolina 28115
704-663-4685
dragway@mooresvilledragway.com
wedrag2@aol.com
Elev. 875'

New Bern Motorsports Park - New Bern (Bridgeton), North Carolina
1/8th mile track
Post Office Box 14076
New Bern, North Carolina 28562
252-637-7701
www.newbernmotorsports.com
info@newbernmotorsports.com
Elev. 50'

Northeast Dragway (IHRA) – Winfall, North Carolina
1/8th mile track
1099 Lake Road
Hertford, North Carolina 27944
252-264-2066
Elev. 50'

Piedmont Dragway (IHRA) – Greensboro, North Carolina
1/8th mile track
6750 Holt Store Road
Greensboro, North Carolina 27283
336-449-7411
www.piedmontdragway.com
piedmontdragway@mindspring.com
Elev. 1000'

Rockingham Dragway (IHRA) – Rockingham, North Carolina
2153 Highway U.S. 1 North
Post Office Box 70
Marston, North Carolina 28363
910-582-3400
www.rockinghamdragway.com
steveearwood@carolina.net
Elev. 350'

Roxboro Motorsports (IHRA) – Roxboro,
North Carolina
1/8th mile track
Post Office Box 888
Roxboro, North Carolina 27573
336-364-3724
www.roxboromotorsports.com
info@roxboromotorsports.com
Elev. 700'

Shadyside Dragway - Boiling Springs, North
Carolina
1/8th mile track
2149 Honey Haven Road
Shelby, North Carolina 28150
704-434-7313
www.shadysidedragway.com
shadyside@shadysidedragway.com
Elev. 848'

Thunder Valley Raceway – Red Springs, North
Carolina
2240 Airbase Road
Laurinburg, North Carolina 28352
910-843-2934
Elev. 100'

Wayne County Speedway & Dragstrip –
Pikeville, North Carolina
1/8th mile track
3451 Nahunta Road
Pikeville, North Carolina 27863
www.wcsracing.com
Elev. 166'

Wilkesboro Raceway Park (IHRA) – North
Wilkesboro, North Carolina
1/8th mile track
774 Dragway Road
Wilkesboro, North Carolina 28697
336-973-7223
www.wilkesbororacewaypark.com
ddunn@wilkesbororacewaypark.com
Elev. 1100'

North Dakota
Aero Drag Racing - Harvey, North Dakota
1/8th mile track
Post Office Box 341
Harvey, North Dakota 58341
701-324-4481
www.aerodragracing.ontheinter.net
aerodrag@ndak.net
Elev. 1605'

Dakota Flat Track (IHRA) – Minot, North
Dakota
1/8th mile track
Post Office Box 879
5820 Highway 2 East
Minot, North Dakota 58701
701-857-7620
www.dakotaflattrack.com
terri@minot.com
Elev. 1550'

Ohio
Dragway 42 (IHRA & Jr.) – West Salem, Ohio
Post Office Box 816
West Salem, Ohio 44287
419-886-4284
www.dragway42.com
toby@dragway42.com
Elev. 700'

Edgewater Sports Park (NHRA & Jr.) –
Cincinnati (Cleves), Ohio
4819 East Miami River Road
Cleves, Ohio 45002
513-353-4666
www.edgewaterrace.com
tg@edgewaterrace.com
Elev. 492'

Friendship Park Raceway (IHRA) -
Smithfield, Ohio
1/8th mile track
Post Office Box 530
Smithfield, Ohio 43948
740-733-8058
www.friendshipparkraceway.com
friendshipdrag@hotmail.com
Elev. 1125'

K.D. Dragway - South Webster, Ohio
1/8th mile track
11902 SR 140
South Webster, Ohio 45682
740-778-2453
www.kddragway.com
kddragway@surfbest.net
Elev. 600'

Kil-Kare Raceway (NHRA & Jr.) - Xenia,
Ohio
1166 Dayton-Xenia Road
Xenia, Ohio 45385
937-426-2765
www.kilkareraceway.com
news@kilkareraceway.com
Elev. 880'

Magnolia Dragstrip – Canton (Magnolia),
Ohio
1/8th mile track
1033 Hartwood Road NW
Magnolia, Ohio 44643
330-866-1500
www.magnoliadragstrip.com
nprovost@sssnet.com
Elev. 962'

Marion County International Raceway (IHRA)
– La Rue, Ohio
2303 Richwood-LaRue Road
LaRue, Ohio 43332
740-499-3666
shelbyg@mcir.net
www.mcir.com
Elev. 900'

National Trail Raceway (NHRA & Jr.) –
Newark, Ohio
2650 National Road, S.W.
Hebron, Ohio 43025
740-928-5706
www.nationaltrailraceway.com
inquiry@nationaltrailraceway.com
Elev. 912'

Norwalk Raceway Park (IHRA) – Norwalk, OH
1300 State Road 18
Norwalk, Ohio 44857
419-668-5555
www.norwalkraceway.com
comments@norwalkraceway.com
Elev. 852'

Pacemakers Raceway Park (NHRA & Jr.) –
Mount Vernon, Ohio
1/8th mile track
8926 Columbus Road
Mount Vernon, Ohio 433050
740-397-2720
Elev. 950'

Quaker City Raceway (IHRA) – Salem, Ohio
10359 West South Range Road
Salem, Ohio 44460
330-332-5335
quaker@raex.com
www.quakercityraceway.com
Elev. 1300'

Thompson Drag Raceway (IHRA) –
Thompson, Ohio
8233 Sidley Road
Thompson, Ohio 44086
440-298-1350
promotions@thompsondragraceway.com
www.thompsondragraceway.com
Elev. 1400'

Tri-State Dragway (IHRA) – Hamilton, Ohio
2362 Hamilton-Cleves Road
Hamilton, Ohio 45013
513-863-0562
www.tristatedragway.com
owners@tristatedragway.com
Elev. 600'

Oklahoma
Ardmore Raceway – Ardmore (Springer), OK
1000 foot Dragstrip
Post Office Box 141
Springer, Oklahoma 73458
Elev. 975'

Texhoma Motorplex (NHRA & Jr.) - Walters,
Oklahoma
1/8th mile track
Route 2, Box 56
Walters, Oklahoma 73572
580-875-6040
www.texhomamotorplex.com
info@texhomamotorplex.com
Elev. 1014'

Thunder Valley Raceway Park (NHRA & Jr.) –
Norman (Noble), Oklahoma
Post Office Box 617
Noble, Oklahoma 73068
405-872-3420
www.okthunder.com
Elev. 1054'

Tulsa International Raceway (IHRA) - Tulsa,
Oklahoma
3101 North Garnett Road
Tulsq, Oklahoma 74116
918-437-3278
www.tulsainternationalraceway.com
tulsadrags@hotmail.com
Elev. 700'

Oregon
Coos Bay International Speedway (NHRA &
Jr.) – Coos Bay, Oregon
1/8th mile track
Post Office Box 1559
Coos Bay, Oregon 97420
541-269-2474
www.coosbayspeedway.com
Elev. 8'

Lakeview Dragstrip (NHRA & Jr.) –
Lakeview, Oregon
1/8th mile track
Post Office Box 1083
Lakeview, Oregon 97630
541-947-4458
Elev. 4720'

Madras Dragway (NHRA & Jr.) – Madras,
Oregon
1/8th mile track
Post Office Box 7939
Bend, Oregon 97708
541-389-7518
Elev. 2400'

Southern Oregon Dragway (NHRA & Jr.) -
Medford, Oregon
2201 South Pacific Highway
Medford, Oregon 97501
541-826-3477
www.sodragway.com
dlewis8451@aol.com
Elev. 1400'

Woodburn Dragstrip (NHRA & Jr.) -
Woodburn, Oregon
7730 State Highway 219
Woodburn, Oregon 97071
503-982-4461
www.woodburndragstrip.com
race@woodburndragstrip.com
Elev. 182'

Pennsylvania
Beaver Springs Dragway (IHRA) – Beaver
Springs, Pennsylvania
500 Summit Drive
Lewistown, Pennsylvania 17044
570-658-9601
beaverbob@beaversprings.com
www.beaversprings.com
Elev. 642'

Lowville Drag Raceway (Jr.) – Wattsburg
(Lowville), Pennsylvania
1/4 mile & 1/8th mile tracks
9060 Jones Road
Wattsburg, Pennsylvania 16442
814-739-2735
Elev. 1320'

Maple Grove Raceway (NHRA & Jr.) –
Mohnton, Pennsylvania
Rd 3, Box 3420
Mohnton, Pennsylvania 19540
610-856-7812
www.maplegroveraceway.com
maple@maplegroveraceway.com
Elev. 544'

Numidia Raceway (NHRA & Jr.) – Catawissa
(Numidia), Pennsylvania
48 Mill Street
New Buffalo, Pennsylvania 17069
570-799-0480
www.numidiaraceway.com
nr@numidiaraceway.com
Elev. 972'

Pittsburgh Raceway Park (NHRA & Jr.) - New
Alexandria, Pennsylvania
109 Ray Street
Apolla, Pennsylvania 15613
724-668-7600
www.keystoneraceway.com
Elev. 1210'

South Mountain Dragway (NHRA & Jr.) -
Boiling Springs, Pennsylvania
1/8th mile track
19 Bentz Mill Road
East Berlin, Pennsylvania 17316
717-258-6287
Elev. 537'

South Carolina
Carolina Dragway (IHRA) – Jackson, South
Carolina
Post Office Box 260
Elko, South Carolina 29826
803-471-2285
www.carolinadragway.com
info@carolinadragway.com
Elev. 350'

Cooper River Dragway (IHRA) – Moncks
Corner, South Carolina
1/8th mile track
Post Office Box 2021
Goose Creek, South Carolina 29445
843-761-2566
www.crdragway.com
info@crdragway.com
Elev. 20'

Darlington International Dragway (IHRA) –
Hartsville, South Carolina
2056 East Bobo Newsome Highway
Hartsville, South Carolina 29550
843-332-0123
www.darlingtondragway.com
larry@darlingtondragway.com
Elev. 131'

Dorchester Dragway (IHRA) – Dorchester,
South Carolina
1/8th mile track
Post Office Box 166
Dorchester, South Carolina 29437
843-563-5412
Elev. 100'

Greer Dragway (IHRA) – Greer, South
Carolina
1477 Highway 357
Lyman, South Carolina 29365
864-879-4634
Greerdrag@aol.com
Elev. 700'

Jefferson Pageland Dragway (IHRA) –
Jefferson, South Carolina
1/8th mile track
1824 Dean Lane
Heath Springs, South Carolina 29058
843-658-3556
Elev. 300'

Midlands Raceway Park (IHRA) – Lugoff,
South Carolina
1/8th mile track
Post Office Box 746
Lugoff, South Carolina 29078
803-438-4399
Elev. 250'

Midway Dragstrip (IHRA) – Greeleyville,
South Carolina
1/4 mile & 1/8th mile tracks
Highway 52 & 521
Greeleyville, South Carolina 29056
843-426-4419
info@midwaydragstrip.com

Orangeburg Dragstrip (IHRA) – Orangeburg,
South Carolina
1/8th mile track
204 Acacia Lane
Orangeburg, South Carolina 29115
803-534-3428
Elev. 250'

Ware Shoals Dragway (IHRA) – Ware Shoals, SC
1/8th mile track
17052 Highway 25
Ware Shoals, South Carolina 29692
864-861-2467
wm9929@aol.com
Elev. 726'

South Dakota
Hot Springs Airport – Hot Springs, SD
1/8th mile track
HC 56, Box 45-A
Oral, South Dakota 57766
605-424-2590
Elev. 3400'

Thunder Valley Dragway (NHRA & Jr.) -
Marion, South Dakota
1/4 mile & 1/8th mile track
27121 – 469th Avenue
Tea, South Dakota 57064
605-297-3777
Elev. 1500'

Tennessee
Bristol Dragway (NHRA & Jr.) – Bristol, TN
Post Office Box 3966
Bristol, Tennessee 37625
423-764-3724
www.bristoldragway.com
mark@bristoldragway.com
Elev. 1478.15'

Cherokee Raceway Park (IHRA) –
Rogersville, Tennessee
1/8th mile track
Post Office Box 102
Surgoinsville, Tennessee 37873
423-272-2555
www.cherokeeracewaypark.com
info@cherokeeracewaypark.com
Elev. 1400'

English Mountain Dragway (IHRA) –
Newport, Tennessee
1/8th mile track
3275 Newport Highway, Building 5A
Sevierville (Newport), Tennessee 37876
423-625-8375
engmtndw@bellsouth.net
www.englishmoutaindragway.com
Elev. 1086'

Four-Eleven (411) Dragway – Knoxville, TN
1/8th mile track
409 Fletcher Street
Maryville, Tennessee 37804
865-984-5249
Elev. 1000'

Gateway Motor Drags – Clarksville, Tennessee
1/8th mile track
152 East Regent Drive
Clarksville, Tennessee 37043
931-642-3897
Elev. 500'

Great River Road Raceway – Dyersburg, TN
1/8th mile track
Post Office Box 1425
Dyersburg, Tennessee 38025
901-286-4414
Elev. 450'

I-40 Dragway (IHRA) – Crossville, Tennessee
1/8th mile track
142 Hollow Drive
Crossville, Tennessee 38555
931-484-0049
i40drag@multipro.com
Elev. 1700'

Jackson Dragway (Jr.) - Jackson, Tennessee
1/8th mile track
Post Office Box 1911
Jackson, Tennessee 38302
901-427-5536
www.outlawten5.com/Jackson/jackson.html
Elev. 400'

Knoxville Dragway (IHRA) – Knoxville, TN
1/8th mile track
7729 Andersonville Pike
Knoxville, Tennessee 37938
423-992-5000
www.knoxvilledragway.com
mosheat@knoxvilledragway.com
Elev. 860'

Memphis Motorsports Park (NHRA & Jr.) -
Memphis, Tennessee
5500 Taylor Forge Drive
Millington, Tennessee 38053
901-358-7223
www.memphismotorsports.com
mmp@gpalb.com
Elev. 345'

Middle Tennessee Dragway (IHRA) –
Cookeville, Tennessee
1/8th mile track
14496 Nashville Highway
Buffalo Valley, Tennessee 38548
931-858-2912
Elev. 1000'

Music City Raceway (NHRA & Jr.) –
Nashville (Union Hill), Tennessee
1/8th mile track
3302 Ivy Point Road
Goodlettsville, Tennessee 37072
615-876-0981
www.musiccityraceway.com
musiccityraceway@comcast.net
Elev. 620'

Northwest Tennessee Motorsports (NHRA &
Jr.) – Dresden, Tennessee
1/8th mile track
Post Office Box 691
Huntingdon, Tennessee 38344
731-648-9567
Elev. 320'

U.S. 43 Raceway Park (IHRA) –
Lawrenceburg, Tennessee
1/8th mile track
Dooley Drive
Ethridge, Tennessee 38468
931-829-2072
us43raceway@cs.com
www.us43raceway.com
Elev. 550'

Texas
Abilene Regional Airport (IHRA) – Abilene,
Texas
1/8th mile track
6201 Nevada
Odessa, Texas 79762
915-362-2241
Elev. 1750'

Alamo Dragway (NHRA) – San Antonio,
Texas
15030 Watson Road
San Antonio, Texas 78073
210-628-1371
www.alamodragway.com
bobcastracecar@aol.com
Elev. 368'

Amarillo Dragway (NHRA) - Amarillo, Texas
12955 Burlington Road
Amarillo, Texas 79118
806-622-2010
www.amarillodragway.com
racer@arn.net
Elev. 3640'

Ben Bruce Memorial Airpark Raceway
(IHRA) - Evandale, Texas
1/4 mile track

Cedar Creek Dragway – Seven Points (Aley),
Texas
1/8th mile track
RR 5, Box 615
Kemp, Texas 75143
903-498-8643
Elev. 500'

Central Texas Raceway Park (IHRA) -
Georgetown, Texas
Post Office Box 1063
Round Rock, Texas 78680
512-388-2704
www.centexraceway.com
info@centexraceway.com
Elev. 680'

Hallsville Raceway (NHRA) – Longview
(Hallsville), Texas
Post Office Box 88
Rusk, Texas 75785
903-668-2858
www.hallsvilleraceway.com
webmaster@hallsvilleraceway.com
Elev. 300'

Houston Raceway Park (NHRA) – Baytown, Texas
Post Office Box 1345
2525 Cove Road
Baytown, Texas 77522
281-383-RACE
www.houstonraceway.com
feedback@houstonraceway.com
Elev. 5'

I-35 North Texas Dragway Park (IHRA) – Denton, Texas
1/8th mile track
3916 East McKinney
Denton, Texas 76208
940-382-2709
www.northtexasdragway.com
Elev. 600'

Idalou Motorsports (NHRA) – Lubbock (Idalou), Texas
4603 - Itasca Street
Lubbock, Texas 79416
806-762-0627
www.raceidalou.com
db428@raceidalou.com
Elev. 3300'

International Racetrack (NHRA) – Edinburg, Texas
1/4 mile & 1/8th mile tracks
15920 Expressway North 281
Edinburg, Texas 78539
Elev. 65'

Lone Star Raceway Park (IHRA) – Sealy, TX
1/8th mile track
120 Old Columbus Road
Sealy (Denton), Texas 77474
979-885-0731
www.lonestarraceway.com
deebrabham@aol.com
Elev. 250'

Navasota Raceway (IHRA) – Navasota, Texas
1/8th mile track
27226 State Highway 6 South
Navasota, Texas 77868
936-825-3202
Elev. 200'

Paris Dragstrip (NHRA) - Paris (Reno), Texas
1/8th mile track
4725 Lamar Avenue
Paris, Texas 75462
903-982-5358
www.parisdragstrip.com
Elev. 554'

Pine Valley Raceway Park (IHRA) – Lufkin, Texas
Route 4, Box 8190
Lufkin, Texas 75904
936-699-3227
www.pinevalleyracewaypark.com
Elev. 300'

Red Line Raceway (IHRA) – Caddo Mills, Texas
1/8th mile track
4904 Samuel Boulevard
5326 FM 1565
Caddo Mills, Texas 75135
903-527-3877
www.redlineraceway.com
harry@redlineraceway.com
Elev. 500'

River City Raceway Park (IHRA) – San Antonio, Texas
3641 South Santa Clara Road
Marion, Texas 78124
830-914-4646
rcr@rivercityracewayinc.com
www.rivercityracewayinc.com
Elev. 450'

Temple Academy Dragway (IHRA) – Temple (Academy), Texas
1/8th mile track
Route 1, Box 191
Holland, Texas 76534
254-982-4512
www.templeacademy.com
promoter@templeacademy.com
Elev. 700'

Texas Motorplex (NHRA) – Ennis, Texas
State Road 287
Post Office Box 1439
Ennis, Texas 75120
972-878-2641
www.texasmotorplex.com
jbaffrey@texasmotorplex.com
Elev. 500'

Texas Raceway (NHRA) - Fort Worth (Kennedale), Texas
1/8th mile track
Post Office Box 262
Kennedale, Texas 76060
817-483-0356
www.texasraceway.com
txraceway1@aol.com
Elev. 500'

Thunder Alley Dragway (IHRA) - El Paso, Texas
Post Office Box 960457
El Paso, Texas 79996
915-849-0888
www.thunderalley.com
info@thunderalley.com
Elev. 4200'

Wall Dragway - San Angelo (Wall), Texas
1121 Glenna
San Angelo, Texas 76901
915-949-6149
www.walldragway.com
wdragway@wcc.net
Elev. 1850'

West Texas Raceway Park (IHRA) – Odessa (Penwell), Texas
1/4 & 1/8th mile tracks
2713 Cumberland
Odessa, Texas 79762
915-362-4242
Elev. 3010'

Utah
High Country Raceway – St. George, Utah
1447 Montezuma Circle
St. George, Utah 84790
435-628-3016
Elev. 3100'

Rocky Mountain Raceways (NHRA & Jr.) - Salt Lake City, Utah
6555 West 2100 South
West Valley City, Utah 84128
801-252-9557
www.rmrracing.com
syoung1860@aol.com
Elev. 4225'

Wendover Raceway – Wendover, Utah
Post Office Box 805
Wendover, Utah 84043
435-665-2563
Elev. 4100'

Virginia
Colonial Beach Dragway – Colonial Beach, Virginia
1/8th mile track
506 Shaw Road
Building 317
Sterling, Virginia 20166
804-224-7455
Elev. 50'

Eastside Speedway - Waynesboro, Virginia
1/8th mile track
8340 Lock Lane
Warrenton, Virginia 20186
540-942-1219
www.eastsidespeedway.com
christy@cfw.com
Elev. 780'

Elk Creek Dragway (IHRA) – Elk Creek, VA
1/8th mile track
Post Office Box 760
Hillsville, Virginia 24343
540-728-0057
www.elkcreekdragway.com
Elev. 3700'

Natural Bridge Speedway (IHRA) - Natural Bridge, Virginia
1/8th mile track
Post Office Box 483
Greenville, Virginia 24440
540-291-2856
www.nbspeedway.com
nbs-ds@excite.com
Elev. 2000'

New London Dragway – Lynchburg, Virginia
1/8th mile track
8340 Lock Lane
Warrenton, Virginia 20186
804-525-3650
Elev. 1100'

Old Dominion Speedway - Manassas, Virginia
1/8th mile track
10611 Dumfries Road
Manassas, Virginia 20110
703-361-7223
www.olddominionspeedway.com
feedback@olddominionspeedway.com
Elev. 50'

Richmond Dragway (IHRA) – Richmond, VA
10108 Georgie Drive
Mechanicsville, Virginia 23116
804-737-1193
chris@richmonddragway.com
www.richmonddragway.com
Elev. 107'

Sumerduck Dragway (IHRA & Jr.) – Culpeper,
Virginia
1/8th mile track
130 Garr Avenue
Culpeper, Virginia 22701
540-439-8080
www.sumerduckdragway.com
Elev. 360'

Virginia Motorsports Park (IHRA) –
Petersburg, Virginia
Post Office Box 600
Dinwiddie, Virginia 23841
804-862-3174
bpierce@virginiamotorsportspk.com
www.virginiamotorsportspk.com
Elev. 188'

Washington
Bonana Raceway
(revitalized old airstrip)
1/8th mile track
Walla Walla, Washington

Bremerton Raceway (NHRA & Jr.) -
Bremerton, Washington
Post Office Box 396
Bremerton, Washington 98337
360-674-2280
www.bremertonraceway.com
bremertonraceway@bigplanet.com
Elev. 500'

Pacific Raceways (NHRA & Jr.) - Kent, WA
(Formerly known as Seattle International
Raceway)
31001 – 144th Avenue S.E.
Kent, Washington 98042
253-631-1550
www.pacificraceways.com
info@pacificraceways.com
Elev. 150'

Renegade Raceway (NHRA & Jr.) - Yakima,
Washington
1395 North Track Road
Wapato, Washington 98951
509-877-4621
www.renegaderaceway.com
Elev. 920'

Spokane Raceway Park (AHRA) – Spokane,
Washington
North 101 Hayford Road
Spokane, Washington 99224
509-244-2372
www.spokaneracewaypark.com
srp@spokaneracewaypark.com
Elev. 2200'

West Virginia
Kanawha Valley Dragway Park (IHRA) –
Winfield, West Virginia
1/8th mile track
Post Office Box 704
Dunbar, West Virginia 25064
304-675-6760
kanrace@hotmail.com
www.kanrace.com
Elev. 560'

Mountaineer Dragway (IHRA) – Beckley,
West Virginia
1/8th mile track
Post Office Box 1477
Oceana, West Virginia 24870
304-682-4754
Elev. 3240'

Wisconsin
Great Lakes Dragaway (IHRA) – Union
Grove, Wisconsin
Post Office Box 7
Union Grove, Wisconsin 53182
414-878-3783
gld@execpc.com
www.greatlakesdragaway.com
Elev. 715'

Rock Falls Raceway (NHRA & Jr.) - Eau
Claire (Caryville), Wisconsin
Post Office Box 326
Elk Mound, Wisconsin 54739
715-879-5089
www.rockfallsraceway.com
therock@rockfallsraceway.com
Elev. 980'

Wisconsin International Raceway (IHRA) –
Kaukauna, Wisconsin
W 1460 County Road KK
Kaukauna, Wisconsin 54130
920-766-5577
www.racingonline.com/wir
gypsy1@athenet.net
Elev. 750'

Wyoming
Douglas International Raceway (NHRA & Jr.)
- Douglas, Wyoming
Post Office Box 2471
Casper, Wyoming 82602
307-234-0685
Elev. 4860'

Canada

Alberta
Budweiser Motorsports Park (NHRA & Jr.) -
Edmonton, Alberta
7003 Girard Road
Edmonton, Alberta T6B 2C4
877-331-RACE
www.budpark.com   info@budpark.com
Elev. 2372'

Medicine Hat Dragstrip (NHRA & Jr.) -
Medicine Hat, Alberta
Box 1599-C-166
Medicine Hat, Alberta T1A 7Y5
403-548-7061
Elev. 2400'

Race City Motorsport Park (NHRA & Jr.) –
Calgary, Alberta
11550 – 68 Street SE
Calgary, Alberta T2Z 3E8
403-272-RACE
www.racecity.com
thetrack@racecity.com
Elev. 3380'

Tailwind Raceway – Fort Macleod, Alberta
Box 247
Fort Macleod, Alberta T0L OZO
Elev. 3150'

British Columbia
Mission Raceway Park (NHRA & Jr.) –
Mission, British Columbia
Post Office Box 3421
Mission, British Columbia V2V 4J5
604-826-6315
www.missionraceway.com
info@missionraceway.com
Elev. 24'

NL'Akapxm Eagle Motorplex (NHRA & Jr.) –
Cache Creek, British Columbia
(Pronounced Na-La-Cap-Um)
Post Office Box 440
Ashcroft, British Columbia VOK 1AO
250-457-9344
www.eaglemotorplex.com
info@eaglemotoplex.com
Elev. 1680'

North Central Motorsports Park (NHRA & Jr.)
- Prince George, British Columbia
9285 Raceway Road
Prince George, British Columbia V2K 5K2
250-967-4130
Elev. 2275'

Saratoga Speedway – Courtenay, British
Columbia
1/16 mile Dragstrip
3950 York Road
Campbell River
Courtenay, British Columbia V9H 1B2
www.saratogaspeedway.bc.ca
race@saratogospeedway.bc.ca
Elev. 20'

Thunder Mountain Raceway (Jr.) – Kelowna,
British Columbia
1/8th mile track
Post Office Box 61
Kelowna, British Columbia V1Y 7N3
250-769-4562
www.thundermountainraceway.com
mr.jym@shaw.ca
Elev. 4200'

Western Speedway – Victoria, British
Columbia
500 foot Dragstrip
3703 Duke Road
Victoria, British Columbia V9E 4B6
250-478-6329
www.westernspeedway.bc.ca
trakside99@shaw.ca

Manitoba
Viking International Raceway (NHRA & Jr.) –
Gimli, Manitoba
15 Gusnowsky Road
St. Andrews, Manitoba R1A 3C9
204-338-8200
Elev. 800'

New Brunswick
Miramichi Dragway Park (IHRA) –
Miramichi, New Brunswick
902 North Napan Road
Napan, New Brunswick E1N 5E2
506-773-4871
www.miramichidragway.com
mirdrag@nb.sympatico.ca
Elev. 200'

Newfoundland
Clarenville Dragway – Clarenville,
Newfoundland
Post Office Box 922
Mt. Pearl, Newfoundland A1N 3C8
709-749-7572
Elev. Sea Level

Ontario
Earlton – Temiskaming Dragway (NHRA) –
Earlton, Ontario
Box 531
Cobalt, Ontario POJ 1CO
705-679-5113
Elev. 798

Grand Bend Motorplex (IHRA) – Great Bend,
Ontario
Post Office Box 668
Grand Bend, Ontario NOM 1T0
519-238-7223
Motorplx@hay.net
www.grandbendmotorplex.com
Elev. 800'

Saint Thomas Dragway (NHRA & Jr.) - St.
Thomas, Ontario
Post Office Box 1320
Sparta, Ontario NOL 2HO
519-775-2263
www.stthomasdragway.com
sttdrags@skynet.ca
Elev. 660'

Shannonville Motorsports Park – Belleville,
Ontario
Post Office Box 259
Shannonville, Ontario KOK 3AO
613-969-1906
www.shannonville.com
Elev. 200'

Toronto Motorsports Park (IHRA) - Cayuga,
Ontario
(Formerly known as Cayuga International
Dragway & Raceway)
1040 Kohler Road
Cayuga, Ontario NOA 1EO
905-772-0303
www.torontomotorsportspark.com
info@torontomotorsportspark.com
Elev. 600'

Prince Edwards Island
Raceway Park
Charlottetown, Prince Edwards Island

Quebec
Autodrome St-Eustache (ANCA) - St-Eustache
(Laval), Quebec
1/8th mile track
1016 Boul. Arthur-Sauve
St-Eustache, Quebec J7R 4K3
450-472-6222
www.autodrome-st-eustache.com
info@autodrome-st-eustache.com
Elev. 285'

Autodrome St-Felicien – St-Felicien, Quebec
1/8th mile track
2365 Boul. du Jardin
St-Felicien, Quebec G8K 2N8
418-679-5690
Elev. 200'

Circuit Ste-Croix – Ste-Croix, Quebec
1/8th mile track
C.O. Box 8447
Val-Belair, Quebec G3K 1Y9
418-843-6223
Elev. 100'

Luskville Dragway (NHRA & Jr.) – Aylmer,
Quebec
77 Lotta Street
Nepean, Quebec K2G 2B6
613-224-1162
www.luskvilledragway.com
arnie.malcolm@sympatico.ca
Elev. 200'

Napierville Dragway (IHRA & Jr.) –
Napierville, Quebec
233, Charles Street
C.P. Box 549
Napierville, Quebec JOJ 1LO
450-245-7656
www.napiervilledragway.com
info@napiervilledragway.com
Elev. 100'

Piste D'Acceleration Pont Rouge – Pont
Rouge, Quebec
1016. Boul. Arthur-Suave Street
St-Eustache, Quebec J7R 4K3
450-720-0256
Elev. 200'

Sanair Acceleration (NDRA & Jr.) - St. Pie,
Quebec
(NDRA - National Drag Racing Association)
77 Lotta Street
Nepean, Ontario K2G 2E6
450-772-6400
www.sanairracing.com
ndra@total.net
Elev. 165'

Saskatchewan
Saskatchewan International Raceway (NHRA)
– Saskatoon, Saskatchewan
Ox 7859
Saskatoon, Saskatchewan S7K 4R5
306-955-3724
www.saskracing.com
Elev. 1600'

Mexico
Baja Raceway (NHRA & Jr.)
Mexicali, B.C.
(0115265) 52-48-21

Puerto Rico
Carolina Raceway Park (IHRA) – San Juan,
Puerto Rico
Post Office Box 7830
Carolina, Puerto Rico 00986
787-768-3424
Elev. 20'

Puerto Rico International Speedway (NIIRA)
– Salinas, Puerto Rico
Post Office Box 9148
Caguas, Puerto Rico 00726
787-747-0319
www.salinasspeedway-pr.com
Elev. 100'

United Kingdom

North Weald-Londons Drag Strip
17 Southhampton Road
London
NW54JS
02074850473
www.dragstrip.co.uk
info@dragstrip.co.uk

Santa Pod Raceway (FIA)
Airfield Road
Podington
Wellingborough
Northants
NN297XA
England
08700782828
www.santapod.com
info@santapod.com

Shakespeare County Raceway (FIA)
Airfield House
Long Marston
Stratford-upon-Avon
Warks
CV378LL
01789414119
www.shakespearecountyraceway.com
info@shakespearecountyraceway.com

York Dragway
01422843651
www.yorkdragway.intrica.co.uk
yorkdragway@btinternet.com

Addresses

Accufab, Inc.
www.accufabracing.com
1514-B East Francis
Ontario, California 91761
(909) 930-1751

American Autosports (Fun Ford Events)
Productions
www.FunFordEvents.com
Post Office Box 911
Denham Springs, Louisiana 70727
225-664-0996

Autostar Productions
Super Chevy Show Association
www.superchevyshow.com
Post Office Box 310
Etna, Ohio 43018
(800) 692-6230

DRAW (Drag Racing Association of Women)
www.drawfasthelp.org
4 Hance Drive
Charleston, Illinois 61920
(217) 345-6537

Frank Hawleys Drag Racing School
www.frankhawley.com
Post Office Box 484
LaVerne, California 91750
(888) 901-7223

Hoosier Racing Tire Corporation
www.hoosiertire.com
65465 U.S. 31
Lakeville, Indiana 46536
(574) 784-3152
(941) 915-2100

Hubbard Downing, Inc.
HANSdevice
www.hansdevice.com
240 Mountain View Court
Unit 4060
Ellijay, Georgia 30540
(770) 457-1046

IHRA - International Hot Rod Association
www.IHRA.com
9 1/2 East Main Street
Norwalk, Ohio 44857
419-663-6666

JUNG Performance
3557 North West 9th Terrace
Oakland Park, Fl.orida
(954) 561-5225

Lupus Foundation of America
www.Lupus.org
75 Northeast 6th Street
Suite 218A
Delray Beach, Florida
800-339-0586

Mopar Nationals
www.MoparNats.com
Post Office Box 2303
Dearborn, Michigan 48123
313-278-2248

Mothers
www.mothers.com
5456 Industrial Drive
Huntington, Beach, California 92649-1519
(800) 221-8257

Mustang Specialties
1401 South Dixie Highway
Pompano Beach, Florida
954-942-5202

NHRA – National Hot Rod Racers Association
www.NHRA.com
Post Office Box 5555
Glendora, California 91740
(818) 914-4761

NMCA - National Muscle Car Association
www.NMCA.com
Post Office Box 598
Hermitage, Tennessee 37076
615-242-NSCA

NMRA - National Mustang Racers Association
www.NMRARacing.com
17150 Newhope Street #301
Fountain Valley, California 92708
(714) 444-2426

PRO Fastest Street Car Drag Racing Series
www.fasteststreetcar.com
ProMedia Companies
3518 West Lake Center Drive
Suite D
Santa Ana, California 92704
(714) 444-2426

Racers for Christ
Post Office Box 1208
Gilbert, Arizona 85299
(480) 507-5323

RECARO No. America
www.recaro.com
3275 Lapeer Road West
Auburn Hills, Michigan 48326

Super Street Racing
10930 South West 188 Street
Miami, Florida 33157
(305) 235-8180

Team Simpson Racing
www.simpsonracing.com
328 FM 306
New Braunfels, Texas 78130
(800) 654-7223

Track Guys Performance Driving Events
Chief Instructor - Jeff Lacina
2109 SE Maish Avenue
Des Moines, IA 50320

Vortech Engineering
www.vortechsuperchargers.com
1650 Pacific Avenue
Channel Islands, California 93033-9901
805-247-0226

Racing Websites

CarCraft.com - Online information about Car Craft magazine
ChassisEngineering.com – chassis shop and racing components
CompetitionPlus.com – drag racing internet magazine
Corral.net – late model mustang site
CSPracing.com – Mopar website
DoorSlammers.com – sportsman drag racing
DragList.com – drag racing list and news
DragNews.com – online magazine
DragRacer.com – e-mail for race fans
DragRaceresults.com - latest news and results in Sportsman racing
DragRacingOnline.com - full service NHRA drag racing
DragRacingUnderground.com - hardcore drag racing forum
DRCRaceCarProducts.com - Quality race parts and service
DriversRoom.com – drag & circle track racing
FastestStreetCar.com – Pro Drag Racing series
FordMuscle.com – web magazine for tech and forums
FordSpeed.com – speed shop
FordvsChevy.com – Ford & GM racers site
FunFordEvents.com – Fun Ford racing events
GR8ride.com – all auto guides
Hardcore50.com – Mustang racers forum
HeadsUpPreview.com – street car racing site
HeadsUpRacer.com – Drag racing news
HorsepowerHeaven.com – information source
HotRod.com - Online information about Hot Rod Magazine
HotRodder.com - An online community for rodders and racers
InsayneStangs.com - Hawaii racing site
JobsinMotorsports.com – Racing jobs and promoters
LaffyAsphalt.com – drag cartoons
LS1tech.com – GM website
MiamiZooCrew.com – Motorcycle trick bike organization
MoparChat.com - Home for Mopar enthusiasts
MoparNats.com – Mopar drag racing site
MuscleMustangFastFords.com – Ford magazine
MustangWeekly.com – Premier Mustang site
MustangWorld.com – late model mustang website
MustangWorks.com – on line magazine for Fords
NHRA.com – National Hot Rod Association
NMRARacing.com – National Mustang Racers Association
NorthernThunder.com – drag racing site
NSCARacing.com – National Street Car Association
Ocalastreetrace.homestead.com – street racers site for Florida
PreStage.com – racing site
ProjectRadical@aol.com – Sheriff's Office race team
ProModifieds.com - the world's fastest doorslammers
ProMustangs.com – Mustang racing site
RacePages.com – internet drag racing website
RaceRock.com – Florida supercharged restaurant
Ready2Race.com – listing for related websites
SN95.com – modern stang website
SpeedworldDragway.com – Streetnational events held in Florida
StagingLight.com – Michael Beard's resource & drag racing guide
StangCrazy.com - Mustang racers website
Stanggear.com – racewear
StangNet.com – mustang website
StreetMachine.com – UK magazine

SuperFord.com – Ford racing magazine
SuperStallions.com – Internet mustang club
SuperChevyShow.com - Chevy racing events
TeamFordRacing.com – Ford website
TeamSheriff.com – Los Angeles County Sheriff's Office Racing
TheFordMall.com – NMRA racing coverage
Trackguys.com – driving school
TurboFast.com – racing fuel information
UK1320.com – United Kingdom drag racing site
V6Power.net – dedicated to the 3.8L V6 mustang
VortechSuperchargers.com – supercharger site
WorldFordChallenge.com – World Ford racing event

Women in Racing Websites
AngelleRacing.com – Angelle Savoie Racing News
DistantThunder.com – newsletters for female racers
DrivingDivas.co.uk – female racing site
FastJane.com – female drag racing clothing
Girliegirlracing.com - female racing apparel
GirlRacer.co.uk – United Kingdom female racing site
Girlracing.org - female racing website
GirlsCanToo.com - Nicolle Douglas's racing site
GirlSpeed.org – female racing imports
GoCindy.com – Cindy Crawford's personal website
LeadFootLucy.com – female racing site
MustangWorks.com/GirlsCanToo – female ford enthusiasts
MxGirls.com – female motorbike site
RaceHer.com – RaceHer is an e-zine and website devoted to providing information and support for females in auto racing. The site features profiles of women involved in several venues of motor sports as well as photographs, message forums, articles and merchandise. It provides features on autocross and drag racing. For more information contact Carly@Raceher.com
RacerChicks.com – The premier website promoting female racers while providing informative and entertaining content for all ages and both genders. The site features female racers from across the world and a racerchicks 101 tutorial to help up and coming racers with their goals. At the same time racerchicks.com is a place for female car enthusiasts to gather and learn. Contact nika@racerchicks.com
Shedevilracers.com - website for female and their rides
SportBikeGirl.com - female motorcycle site
Team-star.com - female racing website
ThunderfootMotorsports.com – female dragster team
ThunderValleyRacing.com – Thunder Valley Racing is an automobile racing promotions, marketing and management company created to develop female race car drivers. It celebrates, supports and promotes women in racing at all levels of the sport.
WAAI.com – Women's Automotive Association International is a voice and net for female racers.
WomanMotorist.com - Woman Motorist is the oldest and largest regularly published consumer automotive magazine for women worldwide with 2.5 million readers. The online publication is available free-of-charge and contains over 26,000 articles covering car reviews, car prices, new and used car buying tips, locating dealerships, safety, maintenance, travel, industry news, products & accessories, automotive law, racing, RVs & motorcycles.

Glossary

Aftermarket – Replacement parts that are not manufactured by OEM (Original Equipment Manufacturer).

Bellhousing – Encases the clutch and the flywheel.

Bleach Box – Where you do your burn out prior to staging.

Blower – A supercharger.

Blown – An engine equipped with a supercharger.

Break out – The racer has run quicker than his dial in.

Burnout – Warming and heating your tires in water to clean them and knock off debris before a race.

Catch Can – A container which catches liquid overflow to prevent spilling on the track.

Christmas Tree – The electronic lighting device used by the drivers to stage and start that is located between the lanes on the starting line.

Chromoly – A strong lightweight tubing, short for Chromium Molydenum steel.

Chute – Slang for a parachute that is used for high-speed breaking.

Competition License – If you are running 9.99 or quicker you will need a valid competition license. You will have to pass a physical examination and driving test.

Deep Stage – After staging, the car rolls a few inches further, which causes the pre-stage light to go out. This allows the driver to be closer to the starting line, however, he could also easily red light.

Dive – Dipping of the car's nose when the brakes are applied.

Doorslammer – Any impressive, very fast race car that has the qualities and regular working parts of a regular factory automobile.

Driveshaft Loop – A loop that surrounds the driveshaft to protect you in case your driveshaft breaks.

Drop the Hammer – Engage the clutch.

Elapsed Time (E.T.) – The time it takes from start to finish on a drag strip.

Grudge Match – A race between two drivers, sometimes with money involved.

Hang out the Laundry – Slang for pulling the parachute.

Heads up – A race where both cars leave the starting line at the same time and the car that reaches the finish line first wins.

Knock Sensor – A sensor that is mounted on the engine and designed to detect vibrations caused by detonation.

Lexan – A lightweight, durable, and fire-resistant material used to replace glass.

Loose – Oversteer.

NHRA – National Hot Rod Racers Association.

Nitrous Oxide – A blend of oxygen and nitrogen that increases the power output of an engine by extreme amounts.

NMCA – National Muscle Car Association

NMRA – National Mustang Racers Association.

Nomex – A fabric used to manufacture fire resistant, protective race clothing.

On the juice – A car equipped with a nitrous oxide system.

P & G – Pump and Gauge. The gauge measures the volume of a cylinder within 2 cubic inches. It is used to determine the displacement of an engine without having to disassemble it.

Pits – A meeting place at the races where you prepare your race car.

Power Adder – Nitrous oxide, a supercharger, or a turbocharger.

Pre-Stage – The driver has lit up the top bulb on the Christmas Tree and is approximately seven inches behind the starting line.

Pro Tree – Christmas Tree start when all three amber lights come on simultaneously, followed by the green light.

Purge System – An extra solenoid that forces all the air out of the NOS system.

Reaction Time – The time it takes the driver to react to the starting light on the Christmas Tree.

Redline – It is when the markings on your tachometer turn from black to red, indicating that you are taking the car to its maximum rpm. This will put a lot of strain on your motor.

Roll bar/cage – A frame work made out of strong metal tubing that encases the driver and protects him from being crushed in the event of a crash.

RPM – Revolutions per minute is measuring engine speed.

Sanctioning – Privately owned dragstrips.

Sandbagging – Dialing in a time slower than your car should actually run.

Shot – Engage the NOS.

Shoulder Harness – A five-point seat belt with a quick release for emergencies.

Sixty Foot Time – The time it takes to drive the first 60 feet of the racetrack.

Skinnies – These are skinny tires (15 x 3.5's) that go on the front of your race car that help lighten the front end.

Slicks – Tires with no grooves that are strictly for racing use.

Squat – The dipping of the car's rear end during a hard launch.

Stage – When the front wheels of the car are on the starting line.

Subframe Connectors – They connect the front and rear subframes together, making the chassis stiffer.

Synthetic Oil – Chemically created oil, not derived from natural petroleum. Special more expensive oil made from ultra-refined petroleum or non-petroleum products.

Systemic Lupus Erythematosus – Lupus is a chronic, autoimmune disease which causes inflammation of various parts of the body, especially the skin, joints, blood, and kidneys.

Tachometer – It is a gauge on the dash that measures your rpms or engine speed.

Tracks – Slang for where a street race takes place.

Transshield – A blanket or shield that will guard you against a transmission explosion.

Traps – Timing lights at the end of the 1/4 mile dragstrip.

VHT – Liquid traction compound which is poured on the ground where you do a burn out.

Wheelies – Traction which lifts the front end of a vehicle off the ground.

Wrenches – Mechanics.

Information on Lupus

I would like to share with everyone some information on Systemic Lupus Erythematosus. Lupus is a chronic autoimmune disease which causes inflammation of various parts of the body.

For most people, lupus is a mild disease affecting only a few organs. For others, it may cause serious and even life-threatening problems. More than 16,000 Americans develop lupus each year. It is estimated that 500,000 to 1.5 million Americans have been diagnosed with Lupus. Lupus is more common in women between the ages of 15 and 44. The cause(s) of Lupus is still unknown. Lupus is often called a *women's disease* despite the fact that many men are affected. Lupus is not contagious.

The many signs of Lupus are:

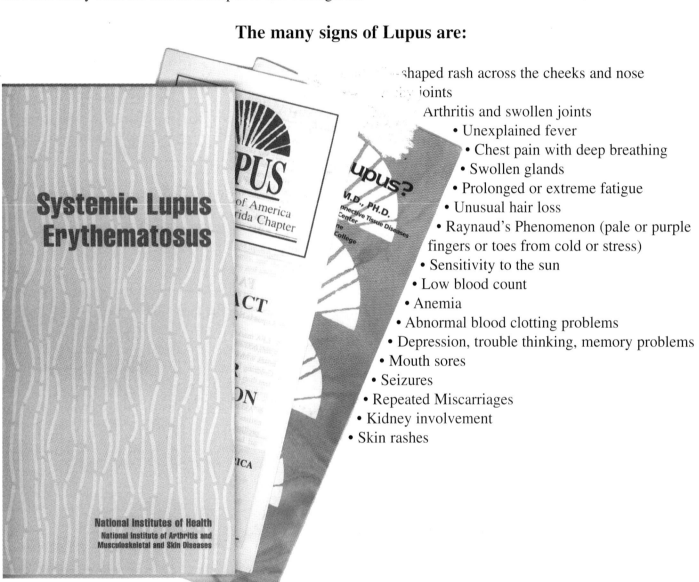

shaped rash across the cheeks and nose
joints
Arthritis and swollen joints
- Unexplained fever
- Chest pain with deep breathing
- Swollen glands
- Prolonged or extreme fatigue
- Unusual hair loss
- Raynaud's Phenomenon (pale or purple fingers or toes from cold or stress)
- Sensitivity to the sun
- Low blood count
- Anemia
- Abnormal blood clotting problems
- Depression, trouble thinking, memory problems
- Mouth sores
- Seizures
- Repeated Miscarriages
- Kidney involvement
- Skin rashes

Diagnosis: To find out if you have lupus, contact a rheumatologist and tell them your medical history. They will do extensive laboratory testing of blood and urine. The following are eleven criteria used for diagnosis and if you have at least four of them, you might possibly have Lupus.

Malar Rash: Rash over the cheeks.

Discoid Rash: Red raised patches.

Photosensitivity: Reactions to sunlight, resulting in the development of or increase in skin rash.

Oral Ulcers: Ulcers in the nose or mouth, usually painless.

Arthritis: Non-erosive arthritis involving two or more peripheral joints (arthritis in which the bones around the joints do not become destroyed).

Serositis: Pleuritis or pericarditis (inflammation of the lining of the heart or lung).

Renal Disorder: Excessive protein in the urine (greater than 0.5 gm/day or 3+ on test sticks) and/or cellular casts (abnormal elements in the urine, derived from red and/or white cells, and/or kidney tubule cells).

Neurologic: Seizures (convulsions) and/or psychosis in the absence of drugs or metabolic disturbances which are known to cause such effects.

Hematologic Disorder: Hemolytic anemia or leukopenia (white blood count below 4,000 cells per cubic millimeter) or lymphopenia (less than 1,500 lymphocytes per cubic millimeter) or thrombocytopenia (less then 100,000 platelets per cubic millimeter). The leukopenia and lymphopenia must be detected on two or more occasions. The thrombocytopenia must be detected in the absence of drugs known to induce it.

Antinuclear Antibody: Positive test for antinuclear antibodies (ANA) in the absence of drugs known to induce it.

Immunologic Disorder: Positive anti-double stranded DNA test, positive anti-Sm test, positive antiphospholipid antibody such as anticardiolipin, or false positive syphilis test.

For more information, contact the Lupus Foundation of America, 1300 Piccard Drive, Suite 200, Rockville, Maryland 20850, 800-558-0121, www.lupus.org.